9

Sport and History Series

Sports and Games

Wolfgang Decker

Translated by Allen Guttmann

# of Ancient Egypt

Yale University Press New Haven and London

Published with assistance from the foundation established in memory of Philip Hamilton McMillan of the Class of 1894, Yale College.

Originally published in German as Sport und Spiel im Alten Ägypten by Wolfgang Decker. Copyright © C. H. Beck'sche Verlagsbuchhandlung (Oscar Beck), München, 1987.

Set in Joanna type by The Composing Room of Michigan, Inc. Printed in the United States of America by Vail-Ballou Press, Binghamton, New York.

Library of Congress Cataloging-in-Publication Data

Decker, Wolfgang.
   [Sport und Spiel im Alten Ägypten. English]
   Sports and games of ancient Egypt / Wolfgang Decker ; translated
  by Allen Guttmann.
     p. cm. — (Sport and history series)
   Translation of: Sport und Spiel im Alten Ägypten.
   Includes bibliographical references and index.
   ISBN 0-300-04463-1
   1. Sports—Egypt—History. 2. Games—Egypt—History. 3. Egypt—
History—To 640 A.D. I. Title. II. Series.
GV573.D4213 1990
796'.0962—dc20   90-36482

10   9   8   7   6   5   4   3   2   1

To my sons

Andreae Memoriaeque Constantini

Filiis Carissimis

Artis Gymnicae Peritissimis

Contents

Preface

Ancient Egypt stands out among the early civilizations because of its rich visual and literary remains, among them evidences of sport as a cultural phenomenon. In Egypt, for the first time in history, sport played a significant social and political role. The study of sport in the Egypt of the pharaohs was for a long time overshadowed by research into the sport of ancient Greece. The results, however, of recent work in the fields of Egyptology and sport history have now made it possible to approach Egyptian sport from an interdisciplinary perspective and, at last, to give it its due.

As a system, Egyptian sports were oriented principally toward the participants and toward the various sports disciplines. For this reason, a chapter on contests per se and a short account of previous research are in order. It is important for readers to consider the Introduction carefully because it affords them a general view of the topic before they are confronted with details that might seem strange to those accustomed to today's sports.

In order to make the presentation as broad as possible within the relatively narrow confines of the present study, specific topics that might interest the modern reader, such as questions about the educational purpose, the technicalities, or the training methods of Egyptian sport, are discussed at the moment they appear in the narration rather than in separate chapters. The index allows easy access to these topics.

If I am successful in making readers conscious of the fact that ancient Egypt is an important new area of sport history, the book will have achieved its purpose. Beyond this, I consider that my task is to demonstrate the function of sport in Egyptian society.

The presentation of materials undertaken in this book anticipates the eventual publication of extensive research in the form of a handbook for the study of Egyptian sports. Although it may seem paradoxical, the results presented here are to some degree a précis of this book which has yet to be written. They may also be considered as the quintessence of that which will eventually be presented in greater detail to specialists in the field.

In order to avoid burdening the text with chronological data, Egyptian kings are identified by their dynasties when first mentioned and again in the index. The exact years of their reigns—to the degree that we can be sure about them—can be found in the appendix. In the interest of stylistic simplicity, "Egyptian" and "Egypt" often appear where "ancient Egyptian" and "ancient Egypt" would be more correct. I hope that no one will be bothered by this. In translations from Egyptian texts, square brackets indicate lacunae in the original and my conjectural insertions. Parentheses contain my clarifying comments. Those who wish to study the topic further are invited to consult the bibliography and the notes.

Despite difficult conditions, Anne Rickmann prepared the typescript of the German edition of this book with her customary reliability. Photographs have been made available to me from my colleagues Hartwig Altenmüller (Hamburg), Jean-Philippe Lauer (Paris), and Steffen Wenig (Berlin and Vienna), for which I wish now to express my warmest thanks. Erich Winter (Trier) made it possible for me to consult at length the Schott-Photographs and also very kindly fulfilled my requests for photographs. To him also, my thanks. My special thanks to Dieter Kurth (Hamburg), for his critical reading of the entire manuscript.

For permission to reproduce photographs and for their preparation I am grateful also to the following colleagues: J. S. Karig, Ägyptisches Museum (Berlin); O. Keel, (Fribourg, Switzerland); R. Drenkhahn, Kestner-Museum (Hannover); S. Bedier and M. Saleh, Egyptian Museum (Cairo); D. Johannes (Cairo); M. J. Raven, Rijksmuseum van oudheden (Leiden); E. Graefe (Münster); J. F. Romano, Brooklyn Museum (New York); L. Kunsch, Metropolitan Museum of Art (New York); B. Abbo and J. L. de Cenival, Musée du Louvre (Paris); R. Hachmann and M. Zorn, University of Saarbrücken. M. Luther and S. Schönmetzler of the Deutsche Sporthochschule Köln provided valuable technical assistance with these illustrations.

And I wish to stress my gratitude for the harmonious cooperation of Adelheid Schlott-Schwab and Hans von Steuben of Beck's Archäologische Bibliothek and to Ingrid Kinzel-Amuser of C. H. Beck Verlag.

I should like to express my gratitude to Edward Tripp and to Yale University Press for bringing my discussion of ancient Egyptian sports to the attention of English-speaking readers. I am also grateful to Michael B. Poliakoff for his help and his appreciation of my work. I take it as a compliment that Allen Guttmann volunteered to undertake the work of translation. I wish to thank him warmly for his sensitive and often empathetic transformation of German sentences into English ones. I have the impression that his translation of my thoughts into a foreign language could scarcely be bettered. He and I are both indebted to Fred Kameny for numerous stylistic suggestions and to Michael Poliakoff for a careful vetting of the entire translation.

It should be noted that the English translation of this book is based upon the unrevised German edition of 1987. Although no publications since then in the field of Egyptian sport history have subjected my work to scholarly debate or occasioned any revision of my thesis, I have encouraged the translator to make minor alterations to the text where these seemed advisable in a book intended for English-speaking readers.

1   Introduction

Sport in the Egypt of the pharaohs: the subject unites in an unusual way two topics, each of which, for various reasons, can claim a certain current relevance, even though at first glance their combination might seem surprising. The increasing political, social, and medical significance of sport in recent decades has entitled it to closer scholarly attention. Within the larger, emerging field of sport studies, one of the subfields has also experienced a remarkable renaissance: sport history, which investigates the historical dimensions of sport as a cultural phenomenon. Seen in this light, it is not surprising that there is now a lively interest in the study of sport in the Nile Valley in the days of the pharaohs. Additional impetus for such a study has come from the larger development of history as a discipline that increasingly recognizes the legitimacy of cultures distant in space and time and feels a responsibility to conduct research into these cultures. At the same time, there has been a growing popular interest in the civilization of ancient Egypt. One sees this not only in the large printing of books devoted to the cultural history of pharaonic Egypt but also in the steadily rising number of study-trips to the land of the pharaohs. This fascination with the ancient culture of the Nile has been most impressively manifested in the great Egyptian exhibitions of recent years. The exhibition of selected art and artifacts from the tomb of Tutankhamon, which had some striking sport-historical facets, attracted millions of visitors.

One reason for these signs of interest is surely the progress of Egyptology itself, which, in turn, has profited from popular interest. Egyptology, too, which had its beginnings with J. F. Champollion's deciphering of the

Rosetta Stone, has now, after a century of preoccupation with more important themes, shown increasing interest in the topic of sport history.

If the charge of anachronism is to be avoided, an explanation is necessary
before the term *sport* can be applied to the activities of ancient Egypt. *Sport* is
a modern word first used in English around 1440. It derives from middle
French *de(s)porter*, a word that has its roots in late Latin *deportare*—"to amuse
oneself." It is not attested in German before 1828. Ancient Egyptian does
have words that refer, in part, to the phenomena discussed in this book—
swtwt and *sd3j-ḥr*. There may even be a general term whose meaning approaches that of the broad-reaching English word. Just as eighteenth- and
early nineteenth-century British usage of the word *sport* included hunting,
the chosen leisure activity of the nobility, so hunting was also included the
Egyptian word *sḥmḥ-ỉb*: "to amuse oneself" or, more literally, "to have the
heart forget." But unlike the Greek *Gymnastike* (physical training) and *Agon*
(contests) or the Latin *ludus* (game), the Egyptian word, known only to
Egyptologists, is not suitable as a designation for sport. It seems best,
therefore, to follow conventional international practice in sport history
and to use the word *sport* to refer to physical exercises and activities for
which the cultures in question can provide no generally understood term.
I am quite aware that the modern term has been used in a variety of ways
and must be redefined when applied to different times and cultures. Since
sport itself has been subject to historical change, the concept of sport can
be used for a particular sport culture and its typical elements even when
that culture lacks features of modern sports and includes elements no
longer common. We may not like it, but "Roman sports" include gladiatorial combats; just as the tournament is considered a symbol of medieval
sport, hunting is part of the ancient Egyptian concept of sport. Other sports
falling under this rubric are described at the end of this introduction. In
short, since it is not a simple matter to give an exact definition of a phenomenon that has undergone many modifications in the course of its long
history, I have resisted choosing among brief and therefore superficial
formulations.

To describe sports in the age of the pharaohs—a period of nearly three
thousand years—means to discuss an aspect of ancient Egyptian life that is
sometimes congruent with our own and sometimes divergent from it.
Egyptian civilization emerges at the beginning of the third millennium B.C.,
when an organized state was created in the Nile Valley. Hieroglyphic writing, invented at about the same time, was used to serve this state, which
survived—with interruptions—until it finally lost its sovereignty as a result
of the conquest of Egypt by the Greeks under Alexander the Great (332
B.C.) This scarcely imaginable length of time becomes a bit more understandable when we compare it with a period taken from sport history. The

modern Olympic Games, undoubtedly the most important international event of the contemporary sports world, have lasted less than a century, faint longevity compared to the majestic life-span of ancient Egyptian sports. The long-lived Olympic Games of antiquity endured nearly twelve hundred years (from the listing of the first victor in 776 B.C. to the banning of the games as a pagan cult towards the end of the fourth century A.D.), but this lengthy record does not begin to approach the unbroken sport tradition of pharaonic culture.

Within this period sport in the Nile Valley came under the influence of the lively sport culture of the Greco-Roman epoch, about which we are well informed thanks to the preservation of papyrus manuscripts; but I shall not discuss this development. I shall limit myself instead to the thirty-one dynasties of ancient Egypt. The work that has been done on this period seems disproportionately meager when compared to the research into the sports of classical antiquity, to the available sources for Egyptian sport history, and to the significance of ancient Egypt within the larger historical framework of sport as a worldwide cultural phenomenon. The reason for this neglect is that the discipline of Egyptology was born in the early nineteenth century, at a time when valuable work by the Humanists had prepared a fertile field for the eager study of Greek sports by phil-hellenic European Neo-Humanists. In archeological research as well, Egypt trailed the Greek cultural centers of antiquity. Archeological expeditions to Egypt were in no way comparable to such grand projects as the German excavation of Olympia, which, begun under the direction of Ernst Curtius in 1875 and still under way, nourished interest in the history of Greek sport. The founding of the modern Olympic movement by Pierre de Coubertin at the turn of the century and the development of its worldwide ideals also favored the scholarly treatment of the Greek experience at the expense of attention to the ancient cultures that bordered on Greece. If these are the scholarly grounds for the dominance of classical antiquity in this area, then it is time for research to be extended to other ancient cultures. In an age of shrinking distances, increasing international communication, and global political pluralism, the backward glance of the historian and archeologist must also rise above their narrow Eurocentrism.

The roster of behavior patterns in sport that has been passed down to us is neither eternal nor definitive. Historical self-awareness means a tolerance for different solutions as well as an openness to change. By no means, however, do I intend to maintain that knowledge of Egyptian relationships can solve such problems of modern sports as political interference, commercialization, doping, or the gigantism of the Olympic Games. Nonetheless, concern for the sports of ancient Egypt is more than simply the accumulation of dead facts.

In many respects, Egypt of the pharaohs is a case study in sport history:

1. From no other culture do we possess older visual representations and written accounts of sport, that is, historical evidence in the full sense of the term. It might even be maintained that humankind's oldest sources for sport history have come from Egypt. Nearly five millennia separate us from the era documented in these sources. It might, incidentally, also be said that this fact is relevant to the question of the origins of sport. This is, however, a problem not pursued in this present study because it requires comparative materials from other cultures and other disciplines, for example, the historical study of human behavior (ethology). It is by no means my intention to claim that Egypt is the land where sport originated.

2. The sources stretch in unbroken continuity for nearly 3,000 years and offer a rare opportunity to consider sport as an aspect of cultural history. This takes on a special importance in establishing future strategies for the scholarly study of Egyptian sport history.

3. In regard to sport, Egypt was for approximately twelve hundred years, from the beginning of the third millennium B.C., virtually an island. Cut off by the geographical isolation of the Nile Valley from perceptible outside influences, Egypt was able to develop without interference. The first great cultural contact with the outside world was a consequence of the invasion of the Hyksos (seventeenth century B.C.), which disrupted the development of Egyptian sport and strongly influenced the royal dogma of the eighteenth dynasty.

4. Compared with the sources available from comparable cultures, like that of Mesopotamia, those from Egypt can be considered abundant. This will become evident as we proceed in our analysis.

5. Even though important aspects of ancient Egyptian culture were transmitted by way of the Greeks to the West and thus to the modern era, that which separates us from the Egyptians is at least as striking as that which links us. Comparisons of Egyptian culture with our own reveal enormous differences that can be most precisely seen in a series of contrasts. We see a society remote from our conception of reality. For this very reason, the opportunities for comparison are excellent. With specific regard to sport, this means that the study of a completely different, contrasting set of conditions and appearances allows us a deeper understanding of the role and situation of sport in our own society.

A brief commentary on the division of the materials in this book may be helpful to the reader. It seems essential to me to instruct the reader about the sources from which I obtained my conception of sport in the age of the pharaohs. Thus the chapter that follows this introduction is an initial systematic effort to order the relevant literary, visual, and archeological materials. Those for whom contents are more important than questions of methodology should begin in medias res and move directly to chapter 3. There I emphasize what few now realize, namely that sports were a means by which the most famous Egyptian monarchs presented themselves to their people. At times, sport played a significant role within the framework of royal dogma. From the beginnings of documented history this role corresponded to the Egyptian belief that the pharaoh was the guarantor of the lives of his subjects. His obligatory and, in the ideal case, actual physical strength was that of a warrior and a hunter as well as an athlete. This was especially important in the thought of the eighteenth dynasty. In the form of a run, which proved the physical qualifications of the king and might even have had magical effects, sport was throughout Egyptian history a central part of the most important of royal festivals, that celebrating the jubilee.

Chariots and composite bows, weapons introduced into Egypt by the first of their foreign rulers, the Hyksos, not only shattered the social structure of Egyptian society at the start of the eighteenth dynasty, but also helped to make chariot driving, horse handling, and archery the demonstration sports of the New Kingdom monarchs. Archery has been described in such detail that we can follow the improvements in the archers' performance much as we can observe of the progression of modern sports records (although the ritual component of Egyptian archery precludes direct comparisons of the two phenomena).

Chapter 4, which concerns the sports of the private persons (all those who did not participate in royal sports), covers a number of topics. The first of these is a run attested by a recently discovered text (the Running Stela of Taharqa), important not only for substantially raising the significance of Egyptian sport in comparison to that of other ancient civilizations but also because it proves that we can by no means close the book on further research. Archeological research can at any time unearth further finds like this inscription. The section on jumping has an unusual facet which gives it an additional value: an Egyptian archeologist was able to decipher an apparently inexplicable ancient depiction by calling upon memories of his own childhood play, thus solving the puzzle.

As one would expect from their appearance at the dawn of civilization, combat sports are especially well documented. Wrestling, for instance, has been documented with unique thoroughness in the famous wall paintings of the princely tombs at Beni Hasan. Stick-fighting too can be clearly seen, but boxing appears only in schematic form. The Nile and its numerous tributaries and canals were an ideal place for water sports and sport-like activities. The Egyptians' ability to swim is well attested, as is their rowing, which had its own special technique. In contrast, however, to fishermen's jousting, which can be shown to have occurred as an improvised contest between boats' crews, swimming and rowing were never (or scarcely ever) done competitively.

To this point, the narrative has been structured on the basis of persons—kings and commoners—but subsequent chapters are ordered by sport disciplines, most of which were pursued by both social groups. Before turning to the disciplines, however, I have set aside a chapter to demonstrate the fact that athletic contests were indeed a part of the Egyptian concept of sport, a contention that has long been rejected by those who claim uniqueness for Greek sports and deny the existence of the *agon* (sport festival) beyond the borders of Hellenic culture. In fact, the conception of athletic contests was so strongly rooted in ancient Egypt that sports played a role in Egyptian myth, where they decide the quarrel of the gods over the rulership of the world. The pharaoh stood apart from the sphere of athletic competition because his unmatched superiority was, in theory, not to be questioned. Even in this area, however, Amenophis II (eighteenth dynasty) was exceptional; he can be considered *the* ideal athlete upon the Egyptian throne.

The domain of games, discussed in Chapter 6, can be divided into ball games, children's games, and board games. In addition to simple games of catch and juggling, ball games also appear in Egyptian cult. Numerous graves from the Old and Middle Kingdoms show lively scenes of children's games, some of which are still played today. The favorite among board games was Senet, played on a field consisting of three rows of ten "houses" each. It probably had a symbolic significance related to the resurrection of the dead. In addition to variants of Senet, the "snake game" and the "sticking game" were important and survived for centuries after the end of pharaonic culture.

From Egyptian dances, I have selected those characterized by acrobatic forms that gave them an athletic aura. The chapter on acrobatics includes a discussion of a climbing scene from the cult of the god Min; it reminded the Greek historian Herodotus of the agon of his homeland.

Hunting, the theme of Chapter 7, was unquestionably a favorite recreational pastime. Originally the privilege of royalty (lion and wild bull hunts always remained so), hunting became a part of aristocrats' world as early as the Old Kingdom. Within the scope of this book, hunting is relevant only to the degree that it was not done primarily for its contribution to the food supply. In big-game hunts the king was able to demonstrate his strength and exercise his protective function. Swamp hunts, a combination of bird hunting with a kind of throwing stick and fish spearing, not only stimulated Egyptian artists to masterful works of art but also provided materials for writers. The fascination of these swamp hunts, bound up as they were with experiences of nature, was depicted in nostalgic tones that moved the high officials of four thousand years ago and still touch those of us who live in the modern age.

Chapter 9, which concludes the book, contains a brief account of research in the field of Egyptian sport studies from the Renaissance to the present day.

2　The Sources for Ancient Egyptian Sports

The materials from which we wish to fashion our image of sport and related activities in ancient Egypt are available in many forms. Every source providing information on life in the Nile Valley in pharaonic times can also contain details essential to a history of ancient Egyptian sports. Thus it is that the historian who ventures into this area of specialization must, if he is to be equal to his task, familiarize himself with the entire field of Egyptology. In addition, as will become increasingly clear, the historian who pursues the ideal of full comprehension must consider other fields as well as Egyptology.

Egyptian Sources

If we limit ourselves initially to Egyptian sources, we can divide them into (a) properly Egyptological sources coming to us from Egyptian antiquity and (b) sources drawn from later periods of Egyptian history. An example of the latter is Coptic texts, which we can expect to contain survivals of earlier folkways. For these texts, Coptology—the study of Christian Egypt, a field presently in the process of establishing its independence from Egyptology—is the appropriate academic discipline. Here, too, one discovers visual sources: Coptic materials picture sports such as chariot races, boxing, swimming, and dancing. The scholarly investigation

Table 1. Sources for Ancient Egyptian Sports
_____

Egyptian Sources

  I. Ancient Egyptian Sources
     1. Equipment
       a. Balls
       b. Board games
       c. Children's toys
       d. Chariots
       e. Simple and composite bows, with arrows, quivers, etc.
       f. Throwing sticks
       g. Harpoons
       h. Fish hooks
     2. Visual representations
       a. Temple walls
       b. Tomb walls
       c. Stelae
       d. Sculptures
       e. Miniatures
     3. Written accounts
       a. Inscriptions (temple and tomb walls, stelae, etc.)
       b. Papyri and ostraka
     4. Sports venues
       a. Tracks
       b. Archery sites
       c. Ponds for swimming
       d. Hunting preserves
 II. Coptic Sources
     1. Written accounts
     2. Visual representations
III. Arabic sources
IV. Modern Egyptian folk culture

Non-Egyptian Sources

  I. Mesopotamia
 II. The Hittites
III. The Phoenicians
IV. Ancient Israel
 V. Greece
_____

of survivals of ancient Egyptian sports in Nilotic Christianity has only begun.

Since morals and customs have scarcely changed in this tradition-oriented land with its nearly constant living conditions, one must also consider the era that began with the Arab conquest of Egypt in A.D. 641. Islamic and Arabic studies both offer the potential for new discoveries from the long epoch of Islamic culture. A specific example of the strength of tradition is the fact that one can solve a puzzle from an Old Kingdom grave painting by means of a still-current children's game, *khazza lawizza* (fig. 31), a game that has been played over a period of four and a half millennia.[1] Similarly, the age-old sport of stick fighting survives in the popular culture of modern Egypt. In such cases, ethnology is the discipline that assists the historian.

We return to the Egyptian sources of the age of the pharaohs, with which we shall be most concerned. Those that document sports can be divided into four large categories which, ideally, supplement one another. Ranked according to how vividly they present the evidence, they can be listed as follows:

1. Sports equipment
2. Visual representations of sports
3. Written accounts of sports
4. Sports venues

Of course, one could reorder these categories to give more weight to the precision of verbal information than to the more ambiguous visual evidence, but sport is inherently kinetic. Visual evidence tends to be the most informative.

What this means ideally, if we take the example of chariot races, is that we have the original chariots (category 1), know the place where the races occurred (category 4), have reliefs depicting the races (category 2), and know the names of the victors (category 3). But this example is a fiction. Not even the sources for Greek sports, which are better than those for Egypt, fulfill category 1 and provide us with original chariots (although we do have them in Egypt!). No single Egyptian sport phenomenon has been attested by all four categories of evidence, but the concurrence of three categories is rather frequent. A number of texts and pictures (figs. 15, 17–19) portray the pharaoh riding his chariot and shooting arrows with his bow at a target. Original chariots (fig. 18), bows (fig. 14), and other equipment appropriate to the sport have also survived. Many examples of the popular board game Senet have come down to us (figs. 86 and 88), and scenes of men and women playing the game are found in many graves of the Old Kingdom (figs. 91 and 92), often with inscriptions. In addition, we have three papyri with a "Great Board Game Text." Such examples might easily be multiplied.

Sports Equipment

If we limit ourselves to ancient Egyptian objects used exclusively for sports, we can name balls (figs. 75–76) and board games (figs. 86 and 88). Only the latter have been systematically studied.[2] Many museums, however, own balls made of leather-covered reeds or of faience, which is quite fragile. Although collecting them required a great deal of effort, they tell us little about Egyptian ball games and for this reason they merit little attention. In this context, children's games and toys that have come down to us, for example, the "snake game" (figs. 93 and 94),[3] should be mentioned.[4]

Among the items of sports equipment we must include those objects which are occasionally rather than exclusively used for sports. A chariot, for instance, could be used in warfare, and then in a hunt, and then in a sports contest. The boundaries that determine use can shift. We are fortunate to have six chariots from the grave of Tutankhamon (eighteenth dynasty), one owned by the father-in-law and mother-in-law of Amenophis III (eighteenth dynasty),[5] and an eighth specimen, now exhibited in Florence, from a private grave in Thebes (fig. 28). Together, they offer sport historians a valuable visual impression of an object important in many cultures, some of which had chariot races, but which is no longer extant except in Egypt. These chariots appeared in the Nile Valley shortly before the New Kingdom, that is, in the sixteenth century b.c., when the Hyksos arrived from Syria and Palestine and successfully employed them against the Egyptians. In addition to this weapon, the chariot-borne Hyksos archers also brought with them the composite bow, which considerably exceeded the potential of the simple wooden bows that had been used previously. As sport bows they were used to shoot at targets; as hunting bows they greatly increased the hunter's range. In time of war, the same bows were, naturally, dangerous weapons. Once again, the tomb of Tutankhamon is the most prolific source for both composite (fig. 14) and simple bows.[6] In addition, the site contains accessories needed by the archer—many different varieties of arrows, bracers (forearm guards) to soften the painful snap of the bowstring, quivers and bow cases. Elsewhere, archeologists have found finger rings, which presumably eased the archer's effort. In addition, original targets have been preserved (fig. 21), but not from Egypt. (They will be briefly discussed among the non-Egyptian sources.)

Also included among sports equipment are wooden throwing sticks used for bird-hunting in the papyrus thickets of the valley, a favorite pastime of the Egyptian nobility. Here, too, the tomb of Tutankhamon is our best source of information (although archeologists have not yet published the results of their investigations). Harpoon tips used by hippopotamus hunters and fishing hooks round out the repertory of surviving sports equipment. Boats of the sort found next to the pyramid of Cheops (fourth dynasty) are not considered as sports equipment here, but the Sphinx Stele of Amenophis II (eighteenth dynasty) does report that one of the great athletic achievements of the pharaoh was that he, without help, was able to steer a giant boat.[7]

Visual Representations of Sports

Systematic classification of visual representations of sport motifs is not easy. One can classify them on the basis of the site where they were found or, just as easily, by the techniques used to make them. My choice of categories was made with an eye to practicality.

1. Temple walls
2. Tomb walls
3. Stelae
4. Sculptures
5. Miniatures

As with my classification of sports equipment, a few examples will be useful for clarification. Although none of the great temples of the eighteenth dynasty has survived, except for the festive temple of Tuthmosis III in the architectonic complex of the great Amun Temple at Karnak, the funerary temple of Ramesses III (twentieth dynasty) is eloquent evidence for temple wall representations. On the walls of this very well preserved construction are not only pictures of sport contests between Egyptians and foreigners (figs. 48–49, 54) but also some striking pictures of the pharaoh as a connoisseur of horses (fig. 23). In addition, he is immortalized as a hunter by imposing compositions on the walls of the first pylon, where he attacks wild bulls with his lance (fig. 117) and slays lions with bow and arrow (fig. 121). The temples also contain numerous scenes of the ritual run which was a part of the pharaoh's jubilee celebration (figs. 2, 9).

The many different decorative themes of the tomb, site of the life beyond, were tied to the central canon of the religious perceptions of the age, but to a limited degree there was also room for the personal wishes of the deceased, many of which were related to sports. A good example of this is the grave site of Prince Min of This, who arranged to have himself portrayed instructing young Amenophis II in the art of archery (fig. 15). In addition to the tombs with their stereotypically repeated scenes of fish-spearing and bird-hunting, I should also mention the graves of the viziers of the Old Kingdom, Ptahhotep (fig. 81) and Mereruka (fig. 80), whose tombs in Saqqara contained a wealth of children's toys, and the Middle Kingdom graves of the princes of the "Nome of the Antelopes," with their textbook-like illustrations of wrestling, the sport specialty of Middle Egypt in that era (Figs. 38–42). In fact, the sport scenes of Egyptian graves outnumber all our other sources.

The third group, the stelae (monuments with inscribed texts and, usually, pictures), are best represented by the so-called "Shooting Stela" of Amenophis II (fig. 17), which may well have the most beautiful portrait of a sportsman king, and a stela of Sethos I (nineteenth dynasty), in which he appears as a hunter shooting his arrows. Stelae are also relevant under the next rubric.

When we speak of sculpture, we must not think of the proportions of Greek statues. The Greek artist's representation of the actual athlete, developed in numerous statues—for example, the charioteer of Delphi, the Doryphoros of Polykeitos, and Myron's Discus-Thrower—was never a motif for Egyptian sculptors. The plastic arts of ancient Egypt did indeed shape beautiful bodies that demonstrated the harmonious proportions of their limbs, but the image of the king was never that of the trained athlete even when it was convincingly vital. One can nonetheless classify as thematically athletic the portrait of Tutankhamon as hippopotamus hunter (fig. 113) even if the intention of its creator gave it a function quite different from that of Greek athletic sculpture. Statuettes like those of wrestlers or female acrobats (fig. 102) enlarge this group.

Whatever art or artifacts cannot be subsumed under these categories of visual representation have been brought together as "miniatures." Although this rubric seems at first glance a kind of grab-bag, these objects can also be ordered systematically within the category. We have here ostraka, that is, larger chalk fragments or pottery shards, which were used as inexpensive material for the representation of quite various themes.[8] It is no surprise that many of these scenes include sports. In this fashion, wrestlers and stick-fighters have been immortalized in a hasty sketch (fig. 55). Some of these works in miniature, like the representation of a female acrobat now in the Turin Museum (fig. 101), achieve a high aesthetic level. A sharply delineated group is made up of anointing spoons used in cultic daily ritual.[9] A great number of them are shaped so that the carved figure of a naked girl serves as the handle of a spoon. The figure is conventionally said to be a swimmer, an interpretation that seems confirmed by the object's piscine or duck-shaped bowl (figs. 60–61).

Boxes or chests of the sort found in profusion in the tomb of Tutankhamon are frequently ornamented with hunting scenes. These, too, should be included in any enumeration of representations of sport. Less certain is the status of model rowboats, which are plentiful, or miniature scenes of board games, of which we have at least one. Thousands of scarabs and related carved objets d'art, such as gems and scaraboids, have been preserved, and they, too, form a subcategory of miniature art.[10] Within the enormous variety of their themes, sport-related ones are quite frequent. Mostly these concern the kings as they hunted or as they, true to the dictates of the royal dogma, triumphed in sports and thus guaranteed the cosmic order. This mandate the pharaoh fulfilled as victorious warrior, as successful hunter, or as unrivaled athlete.

It may be that some visual evidence of sport in ancient Egypt has escaped our nets. An interesting bowl with swimming maidens, for instance, is difficult to categorize (fig. 62). Nonetheless, I am convinced that the suggested classification corresponds realistically to the source materials.

Written Accounts of Sports

When we recall that Egyptian culture had developed a complicated script by the beginning of the third millennium and used this invention extensively and lovingly until Egypt ceased to exist as a culture, we should not be surprised to come upon documentary evidence of sports.[11] Just as visual representations mirror the sport interests and passions of this epoch in Egyptian history, so does the written record allow inferences about the role of sport in this early civilization. These surviving written documents extend over the entire three thousand years of Egyptian history, and despite their conventional formulations, they help us to follow the historical development of this cultural domain. The written sources, which are less ambiguous than the visual evidence, can be divided into _epigraphic_ and _papyrological_ sources. This classification follows from the time-tested structure of classical philology and can be applied with little difficulty to Egyptian sources.

The _epigraphical texts_ (i.e., inscriptions) often accompany visual representations, which means that the Egyptian documents relevant to sports history are frequently a synthesis of picture and text. This is clearly advantageous for the historian, who can now compare and evaluate both kinds of information. For instance, the sport scenes in the funerary temple of Ramesses III in Medinet Habu are accompanied by inscriptions typical of those found on other temple walls.[12] The numerous reports of the Battle of Kadesh, where Ramesses II (nineteenth dynasty) proved himself a superb and obdurate fighter, should also be noted by sport historians.[13] In addition, written accounts found in tombs often add autobiographies of the deceased to the brief captions for the visual representations. When these are formulated like those of Prince Kheti of Siut (First Interregnum), which tell us how the deceased enjoyed his swimming lessons, they qualify as first-rate documentation for sport history.[14]

Stelae texts are splendid purveyors of information about royal sports.

Stelae of Tuthmosis III from Erment[15] and from Gebel Barkal (fourth
Cataract of the Nile)[16] are noteworthy, but the Sphinx Stela of his son
Amenophis II[17] which transmits to us the portrait of the perfect athlete, is
even more important. His Shooting Stela (fig. 17) and the Running Stela of
Taharqa (twenty-fifth dynasty)[18] drive home the truth that written sources
can be especially fruitful. It is interesting in this context that one stela
informs us that the Egyptian artist had sport motifs in his repertoire.[19] We
also have small objets d'art like the oversize commemorative scarab of
Amenophis III, which report of his successes as a lion hunter and a wild-
bull hunter (fig. 115).[20] Only in exceptional cases do the inscriptions on
obelisks mention important sport information, but the Antinoos Obelisk
from Roman times does mention the funeral games carried out in honor of
the emperor Hadrian's dead lover.[21]

Papyrological sources make up a second branch of written remains. It is
common knowledge that the Egyptians extracted the pulp of the papyrus
plant, pressed and smoothed it, pasted the sheets together in rolls, and
thus created the writing material whose name lives on in our word *paper.*
The Egyptian word derives from the ancient term *p3 pr '3,* which means
"monopoly of the pharaoh." On such papyrus rolls, which have survived
over millennia thanks to the dry Egyptian climate, longer texts were inscribed. Among the literary works transmitted in this form are some with
sport themes—for instance, two now preserved in Moscow that describe
hunting excursions. Their modern editor has entitled them "The Pleasures
of Fishing and Fowling" and "The Sporting King."[22] Unfortunately, their
state of preservation is not especially good; there are numerous lacunae in
the text. Since papyrus was quite expensive, the Egyptians often preferred
to use pottery shards for their written communications.

Passages from other literary works also contribute to Egyptian sports
history. Among them are the rowing episode from the Westcar papyrus,[23]
the description of a duel from the "Story of Sinuhe,"[24] the suitors' contest
from the fairy tale "The Enchanted Prince,"[25] and the episodes of competition from the history of the quarrel between Horus and Seth.[26] In this
connection it should be mentioned that the dry sands of Egypt have also
preserved important papyri from the Greek and Roman periods that are of
great significance for the history of Hellenistic gymnastics and sports competitions.[27]

Sports Venues

Where sport takes place is a function of the characteristics of the
individual sport disciplines, the interest of the spectators, the ambition of
the administrators, and the skill of the architect. Out of this configuration
come the sites that are available for sport events. It was the same then as

now. The Greek gymnasium, which every polis possessed, the stadium, and the hippodrome are imposing examples of sport architecture.[28] In Rome, the circus, the amphitheater, and the baths were typical stages for sports, even if the thought of the Colosseum and its gladiatorial fights rubs us the wrong way.[29] The ball game courts of the Mayas and Aztecs, the tilting yards of the Middle Ages, and the Persian polo fields and "strength-houses" (*zurhane*) should suffice to suggest the universal scope of sport architecture.

One might suspect, therefore, that traces remain of Egyptian sites as well, but this is not the case. The Egyptians, who left behind so many extraordinary architectural monuments, were masters of improvisation when it came to sport venues. No hippodrome was built for kings who galloped off in their chariots; ballplayers were not confined within a playing field. Still, Egypt did have one of the most significant sport facilities the world has ever known, probably the oldest of its kind: the track on which the pharaoh performed the ritual run of his jubilee festival. The track that is part of the burial site of Djoser (third dynasty) is constructed in stone and has outlasted the millennia (figs. 4, 6 and 7). We can assume that the stages which were erected for the actual jubilee festival, and which were subsequently disassembled, were accurate models for the two hemispheres that enclosed the track itself.

There are hints in the texts that point to sites for archery as well.[30] One text refers to the instruction in archery received by young Amenophis II "in the great hall of the pharaoh at This."[31] The "great hall" is presumably a reference to the royal reception hall of the princes, temporarily usurped for sporting purposes. The rectangular garden ponds of the Amarna Period (eighteenth dynasty), which resemble modern swimming pools, can also be included under this rubric, if we allow the assumption that they were used for sports. Finally, since hunting is here considered part of Egyptian sport, we must note that there were many hunting preserves artificially bounded by nets and railings. We know about these royal preserves from both literary and iconographical evidence and can locate one of them on the basis of its remains.[32]

Non-Egyptian Sources

In addition to the sources derived from the Nile Valley itself in pharaonic times, which bear immediate witness to past events, one must weigh the evidence for ancient Egyptian sports transmitted to posterity by neighboring cultures. Foreigners who came into contact with Egyptians, merchants who brought their wares to Egypt, prisoners who involuntarily

witnessed Egyptian life, travelers attracted to the wonders of Egypt by
curiosity or a zeal for knowledge—all these are potential informants on the
state of Egyptian sport. If due caution is exercised, substitute materials
from neighboring cultures can illuminate phenomena which, in Egypt,
remain in the shadows, provided, of course, that we are certain that the
phenomena in question occurred at all in the Valley of the Nile. Only traces
of the instructions for training Egyptian chariot horses have been preserved, for example, but the Hittite text of a certain Kikkuli, from the
fourteenth century B.C., survives to fill in the desired picture.[33]

Thanks to its sheltered geographical situation, Egypt experienced no
extensive periods of warfare before the invasion of the Hyksos in the
seventeenth century B.C. Once the lively cultural exchange with the outside
world began, in the early years of the New Kingdom (ca. 1500 B.C.), peace-
ful and bellicose interactions with Syria, Palestine, and Mesopotamia introduced testimony, in various cuneiform scripts, to which we must be attentive. Although a knowledge of the Akkadian and Hittite languages would
be useful, I must, by admitting my inability to read them, disappoint the
reader who hoped for a rich flow of information from these sources.
Fortunately, reliable translations do exist for many of these texts, and the
iconographic documents have been published. Since Akkadian was the
diplomatic language of the ancient Near East, the correspondence that the
eighteenth-dynasty kings had with their counterparts and vassals to the
east captures for us some of the atmosphere of court, resplendent with
horses and chariots.[34] To the best of my knowledge, however, there are no
direct references to ancient Egyptian sports in the Mesopotamian and
Hittite sources. We can, however, introduce contemporary evidence from
the Tigris and Euphrates and from the Hittites to draw comparisons with
Egyptian conditions.[35] A recent find from late thirteenth-century Phoenicia arouses hopes for further material from that area. The raising of a
copper-bearing ship that sank off Cape Gelidonia on the Turkish coast has
delivered to us numerous copper ingots in the shape of ox hides which,
according to literary and pictorial documents, were used as archery targets
by the pharaohs of the New Kingdom (fig. 21).[36] Reports of the pharaohs'
spectacular achievements would normally have gained greatly in credibility because of this archeological find, but—as we shall see—attempts to
simulate their feats have left the experimenters skeptical.[37] Ancient Israel,
with its painfully direct knowledge of the land of the Nile, provides us with
occasional notes on Egyptian sport in the broadest sense of the term (e.g.,
the export of horses, the royal baths), but this source leaves much to be
desired.

Given the present state of our knowledge, we can say that the most
important non-Egyptian sources for sports in pharaonic times derive from

Greek authors. Although the palace archives of the Mycenaean age, written in so-called Linear B, are not likely to be of much use in the future because they are predominantly economic lists, Homer (eighth century B.C.) offers an often misunderstood reminiscence of the archery achievements of the pharaohs of the New Kingdom, which surely proves that they were known beyond the borders of Egypt.[38] The axes through which Odysseus shoots to best Penelope's suitors are analogues to the copper plates through which the pharaohs sent their arrows (fig. 16). The qualification for the feat was the ability to bend the bow, and the solitary success of Odysseus clearly parallels that of Amenophis II. Around the middle of the fifth century B.C., the Greek historian Herodotus was driven by his thirst for knowledge to voyage from his native Halicarnassus in Caria and to tarry a number of months in Egypt. Although he had the impression that only one city staged sporting events comparable to the agones of his homeland (ii 91),[39] he nonetheless reported many details of a second Egyptian sport ritual in Papremis (ii 63).[40] He also told of a delegation sent at the beginning of the sixth century by the officials of the Olympic Games in order to interrogate the wise Egyptians and to obtain their help in revising the rules of competition (II 160).[41] The suggestion for reform made by the Egyptians proved that they had a good sense of actual athletic practice. By the first century B.C. Diodorus included the athletic education of the rulers of the Middle Kingdom as a part of his universal history (I 53).[42] Perhaps this is, for now, a sufficient sample from Greek literature. Since it was Greeks who settled in Egypt and ruled the land, we shall not discuss the lively story of the naturalization of Greek sports in the Egypt of the Ptolemies (332–30 B.C.) nor the further development of Greek sports during Roman rule (after 30 B.C.). In conclusion, it should be noted that the works of Latin authors do not mention the sports of ancient Egypt, presumably because of their distance in time from the age of the pharaohs.

This is the material basis for the history of Egyptian sports. The process of building from it can begin.

3   The Athletic Kings

Conception of History and Royal Dogma

To the degree that it is something other than a bare account of everyday affairs, Egyptian history has come down to us in its official version, in chronicles, reports of military campaigns, and the historical inscriptions of the kings. This selectivity influences our view of the royal sports. Unlike Greece, where as early as the fifth century B.C. critical historians like Herodotus and Thucydides were analyzing events with more or less modern criteria, ancient Egypt had no "private" historiography. For this reason, the famous maxim of Ludwig von Ranke, to recreate the past "as it actually was," cannot be applied without modification to the royal inscriptions. They report the course of events as they, ideally, *had* to have been. Just as the world view of the Middle Ages differs from today's, the concept of history in early civilizations was determined by values quite unlike our own. Their historical vision, their perspective, filtered events so that, as E. Hornung[1] has remarked, their histories were stamped far more by ideology than modern histories are,[2] and it was an ideology that remained constant throughout Egyptian history, from Menes, the first king, to the Roman emperors.

For the Egyptians' official view of history, it was not the unique that determined events but rather the ever recurrent, the typical rather than the individual. In historical events, persons and things play a clearly circumscribed role: the king guarantees the order of the world, which he must defend against enemies rising up out of chaos. The gods grant the king his victory over these enemies who have attacked the order of the world. The Egyptian understanding of the world was such that historical sequences were conceived as cultic drama festively enacted upon the world's stage.[3] Officials and priests are the supernumeraries. Hornung's phrase *pharaoh ludens*, borrowed of course from Johan Huizinga's concept of *homo ludens*,[4] is, at a higher level, an appropriate tag for the king's self-concept. Ritual and ceremony occupy the center of this conception of history while real events, the historical facts, are simply not the stuff of Egyptian historiography. The king celebrates "history as festival." One looks in vain through Egyptian sources for visual or written references to a royal defeat. Such references were incompatible with the Egyptian conception of history, but in no way was this intended as a falsification of history. The conventionally composed reports of victory, like those in the chronicles of Tuthmosis III, are ideologically related to medieval chronicles of the well-ordered world.

The peculiar nature of the Egyptian conception of history colors royal dogma, the ideal portrait of the king, who is the central figure of Egyptian society. Whatever is imagined or thought about the continuity of the world's order, the existence of the state, and the welfare of individual Egyptians is thought or imagined with the king in mind;[5] upon him life depends. In Egyptian thought the decisive role is played less by the personality of the king than by the throne. The moral duty of whoever occupied the throne at any moment in time was to provide the human material from which the *Maat*, the divine personification of truth and righteousness, might be fashioned. Pharaoh guaranteed the blossoming of the cosmos and the harmony of the world. He alone of all humankind had direct intercourse with the gods because only he was given the ability to share in their mighty power and, as their representative on earth, to maintain creation exactly as it had been when the gods handed it over to him. The necessary communication between the king and the gods took place through his person and also through his priestly deputies who performed daily sacrifices in his name in the temples of Egypt and who spoke daily prayers in his stead.

Naturally, the function of the king as guarantor of the life of the underlings entrusted to his care demanded overwhelming physical strength, which was given to him by virtue of his office. The king as unconquerable warrior-hero steps into action when enemies threaten Egypt—that is, in a national crisis—but he also performs mighty athletic feats, as best illustrated by the Sphinx Stela of Amenophis II. His intervention in a crisis brings the disjointed state of the world back to its proper form. Thanks to his natural superiority, he casts out the forces of chaos. When he appears in the tumult of battle, success is the only possible outcome. His exclusive role is that of the radiant hero, claimant of victory. Once he arrives, his enemies flee. His superiority is unquestionable. His enemies are fated to defeat while he celebrates one triumph after another. In this conception of the king, there is no place for failure. Tragedy is an unknown term. That he wrestle another as an equal is unthinkable. The persona of the tragic hero who remains true to his values as he struggles vainly against his fate, that is, the hero described in C. M. Bowra's widely renowned study *Heroic Poetry*, is the very opposite of the sovereign, all-conquering pharaoh.[6] Because of this indubitable royal superiority, Egyptian depictions of battle generally do not represent the pharaoh in one-on-one combat. Exceptions, such as the depiction of the victory of Ramesses II (nineteenth dynasty) in a duel against an opponent nearly equal in size, confirm the rule.[7] One might also reckon this representation among the scenes of triumph that show the pharaohs "vanquishing the enemy."[8] Furthermore, this same conceptual set explains the king's absence from one-on-one contests in sports. The deepest meaning of Egyptian history is the repetition and reinstatement of the divinely ordained order of the world, an ideal that cannot be achieved to perfection but which, as *perpetuum mobile*, sends events on their winged way.[9]

Of course, this apparently quite static picture of the king, sketched here with a few strokes, underwent changes in the course of Egyptian history. I have limned the ideal picture, which appears more or less clearly depending upon the historical circumstances. It was more strongly cultivated in times of domestic stability and domination of neighboring states than during periods of Egyptian weakness and impotence. A somewhat simplified formulation is that the Egyptians had to dispense with this exalted dogma during the Intermediate Periods between the Old, Middle, and New Kingdoms, when the king's power failed to reach very far beyond the palace. In such periods, his faded glory appeared mainly in the inscriptions of the nomarchs, whose authority over their territories substituted for the absent power of the king.[10]

Doubtless, the origins of this conception of the athletic king reach back into Egyptian prehistory. Unable to date these origins more precisely, we can trace them only from the evidence of later times. The prehistoric chieftain had the task of protecting his clan and securing its physical survival. For nomads on the borders of the desert and on the savannahs, which were then coming into being, this meant succeeding as hunters and as providers of an ample supply of meat. It also meant the ability to overcome large animals like lions and elephants, dangerous despite the fact that they were, in historical times, numerically on the decline. In this last function, the leaders of emerging agricultural society were compelled to defend their area of settlement and its population against the incursions of hippopotamuses and crocodiles. Only the germ of sport in the true sense, in contrast with the unambiguous practice of sport by the kings of the eighteenth dynasty, was present in prehistoric times. When the raison d'être of hunting ceases to be the mere provision of food, when hunting is no longer a form of self-defense, sport begins. When, in order to prove his superiority and to ward off the forces of chaos, the chieftain seeks to meet the ferociously powerful animal in a one-on-one contest for survival, he has moved toward that domain which we now refer to as sport. Easiest to comprehend are those sport-related elements from the prehistory of a ritual that, in historical Egypt, became a central ceremony of the royal festival, that is, the jubilee celebration. The next section discusses this festival.

The true blossoming of pharaonic sport came in the eighteenth dynasty. Tuthmosis III, his son Amenophis II, and Amenophis's son Tuthmosis IV, gave birth to a sports tradition that had its renaissance toward the end of dynasty, during the reigns of Tutankhamon and Ay.[11] The eighteenth dynasty's conception of kingship was marked by unprecedented historical events. Immediately before this eighteenth dynasty, for the first time since the establishment of the Egyptian state, a foreign power was able to invade the Nile Valley and occupy large sections of Egyptian soil. Modern scholars follow the Greek historians and conventionally refer to these invaders as the "Hyksos," but the term applies, strictly speaking, only to the ruling class.[12] (It means "Rulers of Foreign Lands.") The Hyksos were an offshoot of those half-nomads who had from time immemorial threatened Egypt from the northeast. The pharaohs of the Middle Kingdom had erected a defense against them in the form of the "Wall of the Ruler," a loose chain of sentry posts in the desert, the purpose of which was to hinder and to report hostile attacks.

In the seventeenth century B.C., the Hyksos were already in possession of a weapon just being introduced into the ancient Near East—the light two-horse war chariot, which quickly developed into the status vehicle of the ruling class. It was to be found in many regions of the ancient world.[13] Initially, chariot-borne warriors were able to impress their opponents by the novelty of the weapon or by the fierceness of their attack, but the surprise soon wore away as horse and chariot became more familiar and as it became clear that not every terrain was fit for chariot assaults. The chariot was suitable for level plains such as steppes and savannahs, but it was of only limited use in mountains, forests, and deserts, and Egypt's many canals were also a hindrance.

As they drove their chariots, the Hyksos availed themselves of another novel weapon, the composite bow, which made their warriors demonstrably superior to the Egyptians.[14] For the first time in its history, the Land of the Nile became subject to the will of foreigners. To bring a swift end to this shameful state of affairs was the Egyptians' highest priority, and the king's responsibility was the heaviest. Strength was now mobilized that had from the beginning lain dormant in the kingdom but which had seldom been called into action. Those virtues of rulership that had always been attributed to the pharaoh were now activated: daring, courage, and strength. As a youthfully handsome warrior he stood at the head of his army and encouraged his soldiers, a true leader whose appearance was like that of Month, the god of war.[15] The war for independence from the Hyksos was begun by Seqenenre (seventeenth dynasty). The lethal wounds found on his mummy suggest that he lost his life in the battle against the occupiers.[16] His successors, his brothers Kamose (seventeenth dynasty) and Ahmose (eighteenth dynasty), continued successfully what Seqenenre had begun. Around the middle of the sixteenth century Egypt was once again, after a hundred years of dependence, a sovereign kingdom in a position to make the most of the geopolitical opportunities of the moment. Yearly campaigns of conquest were sent into the Near East, especially by Tuthmosis III at the beginning of his reign to prevent a repetition of the invasion by the Hyksos.[17] With Tuthmosis, one of the great men of Egyptian history, begins the age of the athletic monarchs.

Exactly how royal sports emerged during the eighteenth dynasty is unclear, but we can be fairly certain about the milieu in which they developed. It was the bellicose spirit elicited by Egypt's historical situation that pointed the way to royal sports. Just as the battle-tested heroes of Homer proved themselves to be superb athletes, as demonstrated in the funeral games for the fallen Patroclus in book 23 of the *Iliad*, sports were also a by-product of the pharaoh's military preparedness. This in turn was the result of constant military training, and therein lies a formal similarity between warfare and sports because they both, of course, require constant training. Ancient Greece can once again provide a useful parallel example. A precondition for the rise of the polis in the seventh century B.C. was the ability of the citizens to defend themselves, which was ensured by the constant readiness for combat on the part of the hoplite infantry phalanx that replaced the chariot-borne warriors of the Homeric age. This military development explains not only the renewal of panhellenic games at the beginning of the sixth century in Delphi, Nemea, and on the Isthmus of Corinth but also the introduction of the hoplite race at Olympia in 520 B.C. and the construction of gymnasia throughout Greece.[18] The gymnasium was originally nothing other than a site for the military training of the young men of the polis. Only later did it evolve into the place for sport, and later still—if one follows the history of the gymnasium to the present day—did it become an institution whose function in central Europe is almost completely intellectual (while, at the same time, the term *gymnasium* has kept its athletic significance in the English-speaking world).

The foremost ceremonial sport of the eighteenth dynasty was target archery from a moving chariot, a sport that corresponded to the military techniques of the time and was quite compatible with royal dogma. This sport owed its existence to the introduction of "modern" weaponry—the chariot and the composite bow—which quickly evolved into royal sport equipment, with the chariot serving as the superior status symbol. To drive it demanded as much skill as archery did, and there was in addition the need to train the horses. Sport seemed almost immediately to become a central concern of the kings of the eighteenth dynasty, and just as immediately, at the end of this epoch sport lost its importance as a part of royal dogma. Although we can easily imagine that sport might have been ideologically important for the nineteenth and twentieth dynasties, little was left of its earlier function aside from a penchant for horses and some generally weak reminiscences.

It would be a one-sided account that did not point out that the royal sport of the eighteenth dynasty had another typical purpose beyond its function as a part of royal dogma. As the texts repeatedly emphasize, sport was also enjoyable. Already at the start of the eighteenth dynasty, an inscription reported that archery was a source of pleasure to the crown prince.[19] The same is said in the annals of Tuthmosis III.[20] In addition, it is said of him that he enjoyed hunting.[21] Amenophis II, who excelled in his performance as an archer, "experienced this pleasure before the entire land."[22] Tuthmosis IV (eighteenth dynasty) was said expressly to have enjoyed hunting and sport.[23]

Running and the Jubilee Celebration

What exactly the Egyptian designation for the jubilee celebration, ḥb-sd, means is unclear, but that celebration was one of the kingdom's most important festivals. It is also known in the Egyptological literature as the Festival of Sed,[24] the Festival of Renewal,[25] and the Ritual of Renewal.[26] The problems of interpretation posed by this event have rarely been discussed despite the rich documentation handed down to us. Its origin lay in the predynastic period while witnesses to the event fell silent only with the end of Egyptian culture itself. There is unanimity about the function of the festival: "We are concerned with a festival through which the physical and magical power of the person of the ruling monarch is renewed."[27] A recent, methodologically exemplary work by Hornung and E. Staehelin has placed the research into this festival on a new basis.[28] Thanks to the larger complexes of partially preserved sites, including the sanctuary of the Sun built by Niuserre (fifth dynasty) in Abu Gurob, the festival temple of Tuthmosis III in Karnak, and the Bastet Temple of Osorkhon II (twenty-second dynasty) in Bubastis, it is possible to reconstruct the most important episodes of the festival.[29] The dramatic papyrus of Ramesses and depictions of the first jubilee celebration of Amenophis III, from the grave of Kheruef in Thebes, have also contributed to our understanding.

The festival was first celebrated on the thirtieth anniversary of the reign when the strength of the aging king had diminished and his might had shrunk. From this point on, it recurred at three-year intervals. The dismissal of a ruler after the passage of a generation seems sensible: the old chief must step aside to make room for his young successor, who, at the peak of his vitality, can defend the clan physically and magically.

The function of the rituals of the jubilee festival was to effect a regeneration of the king's might, to put the pharaoh in a condition to fulfill his office. Rejuvenated and equipped with new powers, he can confront his own successor. Not every mention and depiction of the festival is witness to its actual occurrence, but even oblique references confirm the immense significance of the ritual for the kingdom.

The ritual run was an important part of the jubilee celebration and has been considered by most researchers to be the center of the cultic occurrence and the core of the ceremony. H. Kees calls it the "chief characteristic";[30] W. Helck speaks of "its core, the 'Seizure of Possession Run.'"[31] P. Munro characterizes the run as "one of the central scenes of the Festival of Sed";[32] for Hornung and Staehelin, the run stands "at the mid-point of the Festival of Sed."[33] In relation to a structure, which will occupy us further and in more detail, J. Brinks comments, "The running stations built into the 'Great Court' of the Djoser complex characterize it as the central structure in the sequence of events of the Festival of Sed."[34]

This run, an essential stage in the ritual progression of the festival, can only with great effort be followed through its historical evolution. In many of the later representations, ideas are mixed together that were originally unrelated. As diachronic leitmotif two sets of three semicircles are to be seen flanking the king, who is portrayed in full stride, so that three semicircles appear before him, three behind him (fig. 1). Although these semicircles usually appear ankle-high, they occasionally occur at the waist (fig. 2). It seems plausible to see in them elements standing in some close relation to the path of the run, perhaps as markers. They might have indicated the borders of the terrain the king had to round. In this fashion they might have given material expression to the thought of a renewed seizure of the royal domain. If we extend this notion we arrive at the conception of the run as what Helck called a "seizure of possession run," a term he coined in

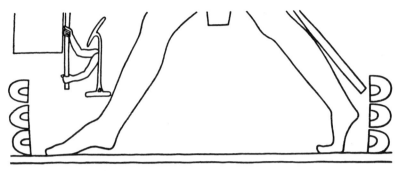

1 *Arrangement of the bases in representations of the ritual run of the jubilee ceremony*

referring to the initiation ritual of the nomadic chieftain of the western Sahara who circles his clan in order to make visible his claim to power and thus to take possession of his "world."[35] From this same conceptual universe of the early hunters comes the upuaut-standard, crowned with a dog's head, that can appear next to the running king. As "pathbreakers" (upuaut) the hunting dogs accompany the lord of the hunt. Running is of course a characteristic of the hunting pack.

According to another explanation, the three semicircles represent watering places, but this seems improbable, despite the fact that water, whose very existence presents a sharp contrast to the aridity of the desert, played

---

2 *Queen Hatshepsut (eighteenth dyn.) running, block from Karnak*

an important role in Egyptian life.[36] B. H. Stricker's theory should also be

mentioned in this connection. In his view, the two sets of three semicircles
symbolize the hemispheres of the earth and the run has cosmic significance because the pharaoh imitates the course of the sun. According to
Stricker, the run took place between the two sets of semicircles. Furthermore, he derives the architectonic concept of the Roman circus (i.e., hippodrome) from these Egyptian markers.[37] Easier to accept is an interpretation that attributes to the semicircles the value of boundary markers
defining the borders of a ruler's domain.[38] Although the discussion of
their function continues, archeological research at the pyramid complex
of King Djoser has ended speculation over the physical appearance of the
markers (fig. 3). During the 1930s, in the course of his investigations at the
great courtyard to the south of the oldest pyramid in Egypt (fig. 4), which
unlike its successors has a characteristic step form, the French architect J.-P.
Lauer came upon two constructions that until then had been known only
through reliefs.[39] From their form it is clear that they must be the markers
that one sees in the representations of the running king during the Festival of Sed. Surprisingly, only pairs of semicircles came to light instead of
triplets, although every known picture of the running king showed two
groups of three each. As was the case with the representations, the two
straight sides faced one another while the rounded sides pointed outward.
From a bird's-eye view or from the uppermost step of the pyramidal structure, one might have the impression that two oversized letters B, each the
mirror image of the other, had been laid out on the ground (fig. 5). The
distance between the approximately eleven-meter-long straight sides of

---

3 *Step Pyramid of Djoser (third dyn.), Saqqara, viewed from the Valley Temple of Unas*

4 Courtyard of the Step Pyramid of Djoser (third dyn.), Saqqara

5 Djoser's running track at Saqqara A. Step Pyramid, B. Altar, C. North turning base, D. South turning base

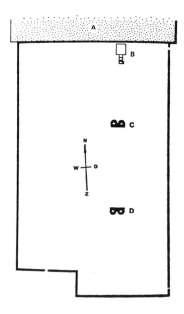

each **B** shape came to about fifty-five meters, a distance that corresponds rather closely to one hundred Egyptian ells. These double semicircles were bordered by an oblique bank of solid stone that can be observed even now (fig. 6). It looks as if the angle of the bank went outward from the straight sides.

Clearly we have here the world's oldest sports facility (ca. 2600 B.C.), although one must qualify this claim with the reservation that the running track was an element of the royal funerary complex and not the stage for the actual run that took place during the Festival of Sed. The pyramid, surrounded by a massive wall in niche style, imitated the royal palace, and the various cult-associated courts were supposed to have made it possible for the deceased ruler, now become Osiris, to continue his earthly role (fig. 7). In the same way the running track, constructed in stone to last through the ages, gave the king the opportunity to celebrate "millions of Festivals of Sed" in the hereafter. This tomb complex permits us to make inferences about the facilities constructed for the actual ceremonial run of the jubilee festival and removed again after the festival's termination. There is no need to assume any significant difference between the tracks on the basis of their different purposes. The north-south orientation of the track optimally reinforced the symbolism of a run to and from the farthest points of the pharaoh's domain or—grander yet—to and from the geographical ends of the earth. The realm's sacred buildings, positioned near the middle of the running stretch, might have signified the presence of spectators from all

6 *Turning base of Djoser's running track at Saqqara*

7 Funerary complex of Djoser (third dyn.), Saqqara, model constructed by J.-P. Lauer

over the land of Egypt, before whom the king exhibited his newly acquired powers and his repeated claim to rule. The discrepancy between the iconography's three pairs of semicircles (fig. 8) and the two pairs found in the great court of the tomb complex of Djoser seems less problematic when we consider that there is some evidence of the existence of a second track

8 Wooden panel of Dewen (first dyn.) with representation of running

in the so-called festival court. There one of the two missing semicircles has been found, silently inviting the runner to circle it.[40] In any event, one must take seriously the fact that the numerous representations of the run during the Festival of Sed all, with the exception of one nearly two thousand years later than the time of Djoser, differ from the single example of the three-dimensional find in that pharaoh's tomb complex. And Djoser himself is thrice pictured in his tomb's niche reliefs as he rounds the customary triad of semicircles (fig. 9).

The ceremonial run during the jubilee celebration was already the source of considerable confusion even in the first dynasty, as one can see in two scenes engraved upon a seal of King Dewen.[41] Wearing the crown of Upper Egypt the king runs toward a sitting baboon, taken by Helck to be the representation of an ancestor or predecessor, who offers the runner a drink that presumably will have a magical effect upon the physical vitality

9 Relief with Djoser (third dyn.) running, Saqqara, south grave

of the king. In an adjacent scene, the king wears the crown of Lower Egypt and runs in the company of the bull of Apis (fig. 10). The symbolic basis of this run is that the bull, personification of fertility, will influence the fields by magical analogy, so that the vegetation flourishes. The pharaoh shares in this potential power and simultaneously transmits it to the fields.

This is not the place to pursue further complexities of the matter, but the existence of New Kingdom rituals—vase runs, oar runs, and bird runs—can be briefly mentioned.[42]

Two further aspects are worth mentioning. The run that occurred as part of the jubilee ceremony was the act and the ritual demonstration of a unique person, the king. The thought of a competitor was out of the question because, as already noted, the royal dogma tolerated no rival to the king. Furthermore, D. Wiedemann has called our attention to the fact that a run can be magically effective because it lends itself to a kind of trance that carries the runner to a "higher level of consciousness."[43] That might be the case for extreme distances, but the jubilee's ceremonial run seems, as far as we know, to have involved only a hint of physical exertion. The run achieved its purpose as ritual when it was symbolically completed. In this connection, the shortness of the track found in the tomb complex of Djoser is notable. Although the great southern courtyard had space for a longer track, the actual distance is hardly more than 140 meters. It is difficult to imagine that this short distance was run in many rounds, quite apart from the fact that the aging king was no longer able to achieve great feats of endurance. For these reasons, the latest biochemical discoveries referring to the appearance of opiate-like substances in the bodies of marathon runners are not immediately applicable to the situation of the Festival of Sed runner.[44]

The king's run during this ceremony had its counterpart in a ritual of the coronation ceremony, which is not surprising in light of the fact that both festivals were closely associated with the ruler's assumption of dominion.

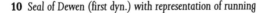

10 *Seal of Dewen (first dyn.) with representation of running*

11 *Club head of Narmer (predynastic) with running scene*

Indeed, it would be surprising if the run that forms the core of the jubilee ceremony did not occur in the festival which the jubilee imitates.[45]

W. Barta's vividly imagined reconstruction of the festival places the running ritual as the fifth stage of the ritual process—after purification, proclamation, mounting the throne, and ceremonial "uniting of both lands." The run took place as "the rounding of the walls" of the palace, whereby the king lay symbolic claim to his domain. But the run could just as easily be seen as proof of the physical qualifications demanded by the office of the monarch.[46] The running episode depicted on the Sphinx Stela of Amenophis II from the beginning of his reign can be understood in this sense.[47]

A run postulated by Helck might have represented a bridge between the royal run of the jubilee celebration and that of the coronation. Helck traces the cultic run at the renewal festival back to an old ceremony "the midpoint of which was a so-called Seizure of Possession run in which, formerly, the most capable prince competed in a contest to qualify himself as the successor [to the throne]."[48] The author gives no evidence for this belief, but he obviously had in mind a very early representation of the Festival of Sed carved on the head of a club owned by King Narmer of Hierakonpolis. Three persons are shown running between the bases (fig. 11), but the king is not among them. Another, less plausible explanation is that these runners are oasis dwellers carrying out a fertility ritual.[49]

Similarly, more than two thousand years later, three runners were depicted in the festival hall of Osorkhon II, where the king is enthroned in his baldachin.[50] There is a parallel to this theory of a successors' race in Greek mythology, when Endymion of Elis, whose territory includes the site of the Olympic Games, arranges the succession by having his sons run a race. The victor, Epeios, becomes the next ruler.[51] A similar conception lies behind the suitors' races in which the victor frequently wins not only the hand of the princess but also the right to follow her father as the next king. Greek mythology provides may examples of this type of competition.[52] The oldest evidence of such a suitors' contest, however, can be found in Egyptian literature.[53]

In conclusion, we can agree with Wiedemann that the significance of the king's run during the jubilee festival was threefold:[54]

1. After a reign of thirty years, (after a full generation) the aging king was obliged to prove the adequacy of his physical powers, because a feeble monarch would have been a danger to the entire cosmos.
2. Simultaneously, the completion of the run magically renewed the king's might and power.
3. The king's run laid claim to renewed possession of his domain (seizure of possession run). The running ritual of the jubilee festival was thus a repetition of the run that had occurred when the king assumed power.

Target Archery

No Egyptian sport is as well attested as target archery. From representations, texts, and original equipment we can form a quite vivid picture of the royal exhibition sport of the eighteenth dynasty.

The bow was used in prehistoric Egypt both as a weapon and as a hunting tool. Troops of archers, a fixed part of the Egyptian army, must often have practiced marksmanship by shooting at targets (as a representation perhaps dating from the end of the Old Kingdom suggests [fig. 12]).[55]

The emergence of sports archery at the beginning of the New Kingdom is explicable not only in terms of the king's lively interest in athletic manifestations but also as a result of the arrival of the composite bow, an

---

12 *Target posts with affixed arrows, Old Kingdom (?), block from Lisht*

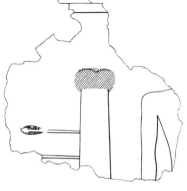

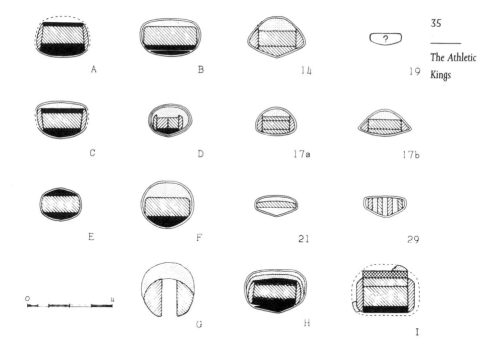

13 Cross-sections of composite bows, New Kingdom, predominantly from the tomb of Tutankhamon (eighteenth dyn.)

innovation already used by the Hyksos in their conquest of the Nile Valley. We cannot exclude the possibility that this superior weapon played a major role in the military success of the Semitic intruders. The bow's construction, combining various elements such as hard and soft wood, horn, and animal sinews, was quite complicated,[56] and the lime used in making the bow required an entire year to dry (fig. 13).[57]

The masterpieces created by Egyptian craftsmen were often highly decorated and distinguished by great flexibility. Far superior to the conventional type of bow fashioned from a single piece of wood, the composite bows loosed arrows capable of deep penetration and greatly improved accuracy. The masterful publication of material on the nearly three dozen composite bows found in the tomb of Tutankhamon provides us with a splendid look at the materials (fig. 14).[58] The double curvature of the unstrung bow is striking. When the bowstring, made from quadruply twisted animal intestines, is drawn, the bow takes on a characteristically triangular shape. The bows' finely achieved decorations were truly worthy of their royal owner.

Two pieces are especially noteworthy as curiosities: a doubly strung bow with a second string that made it into a kind of reserve weapon,[59] and an extremely small bow that resembles a child's weapon.[60] The composite

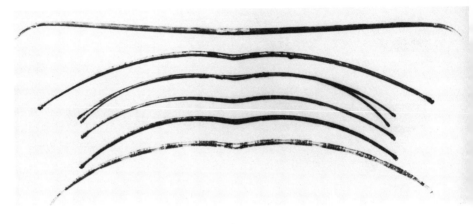

14 *Tutankhamon's bows, double bow third from top*

bows found in the tomb of Tutankhamon are up to 1.4 meters long, but the median length is approximately 1.1 meters, which is quite compatible with the average bow depicted in representations of archery from the eighteenth dynasty and, indeed, from the entire New Kingdom.

The degree to which the bows were used for the sport of archery cannot be determined any more than we can distinguish between bows used in hunting and those used in warfare. Royal sport archers were already present under Tuthmosis I, when a prince boasted of archery as a pastime appropriate to his status.[61] Truly impressive accounts began in the reign of Tuthmosis III, who consecrated a stela in the Temple of Erment upon which a "list of brave victories" is carved. The royal archer was distinguished as follows:

> He shoots at a copper plate because every (wooden target) is pierced like papyrus. His Majesty provided an example of this at the Temple of Amon with a target of hammered copper, three fingers (thick). His arrow was in the target which it struck. Thereby he (the king) allowed a penetration three hand's breadths beyond so that his progeny might wish for the strength of his arms in bravery and force. I say to you (?), in truth and without falsehood, what he did in view of the entire army, without boastfulness.[62]

The true master archer, however, was Amenophis II, who claimed in other ways as well to have been the greatest athlete ever to have worn the Egyptian crown. His career as athlete and in particular as archer can be traced in detail from his youth to his death—the sources are unusually ample not only for the pharaohs but generally for the world of sports everywhere in the second millennium B.C. The foundations for his athletic mastery were laid by his father Tuthmosis III, who inaugurated the eighteenth dynasty's remarkable sports tradition. As archery instructor for the young prince he chose Nomarch Min of This, immortalized by the honors ascribed to him in his tomb. He and the boy Amenophis are depicted in relief as the nomarch conducts the archery lesson (fig. 15).[63] Although the scene has since been badly damaged, it was still recognizable enough at the time of the tomb's discovery for early-nineteenth-century reconstructions to earn our confidence. The nomarch corrects the young prince's posture, turns him towards the target, and gives directions that are repeated in the inscription: "Draw your bow to your ears! Make [strong] your two [arms(?)]! Big . . . arrows . . . your . . . Prince [Amen]ophis. You act with your [force and strength]."[64] Such professional instructions and the presumably numerous hours of practice made of the young king an extraordinary expert whose impressive athletic achievement is immortalized upon the Sphinx Stela:

> He drew three hundred strong bows in order to compare the work of their makers and to distinguish the incompetents from the craftsmen. He came and said, "May each do as I have commissioned him to."[65] He strode upon the northern archery ground and found prepared for him four targets of Asian copper, a hand's breadth thick. Twenty ells (about 10 meters) was the distance from one post to the next. His Majesty appeared in his chariot like the god Month in his strength. He

15 The god Min teaches archery to the young Amenophis II (eighteenth dyn.)

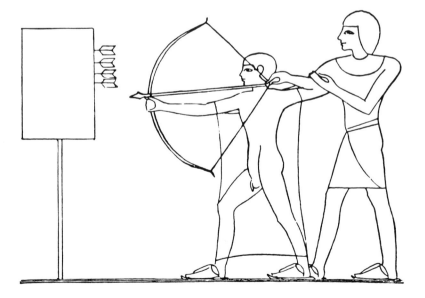

seized his bow and grasped four arrows at once. He drove off and shot like Month in his battle dress, and his arrows penetrated the targets. Then he attacked the next post. This was a deed never done before whose report none had ever heard: one arrow was shot at an ingot of copper, and it transfixed the plate and fell to the ground on the other side. [An impossible feat] except for the king, radiantly mighty, whom (Amun) has made strong, King of Upper and Lower Egypt, Aacheperure (Amenophis II), heroic as Month.[66]

The drawing of three hundred bows, an exhausting enterprise, demonstrated not only the king's strength but also the critical expertise of the pharaoh in whatever concerned the bow. He discovered an appropriate way to introduce the central event through a test of his overstocked arsenal of weapons. He must have had a number of archery practice fields because the geographical lay of the named site is precisely given.

The archery performance can be imagined to have proceeded as follows: Continuing the lessons of his youth under his weapons teacher Min, who taught him the normal technique of standing archery, Amenophis became a perfect shot who mastered the complicated technique of shooting from a moving war chariot. Four targets are set up; four arrows suffice for the king, who has a sure hand. When the targets, set up a good ten meters from one another, stand in a row, then, theoretically, an automatic sequence occurs—placing the arrow, drawing the bow, aiming, shooting—in which all four arrows can be loosed during a single passage of the chariot.[67] In addition to the accuracy required for such a feat, the text explicitly mentions the penetrating force of the arrows. They pass through the plates and drop to the ground on the other side. The choice of exactly four arrows could be connected with the fact that the coronation and jubilee rituals include the shooting of arrows in all four compass directions—an act symbolizing the king's claim of dominion. We may have here an artful allusion to the recent coronation celebration of the young successor to the throne.[68]

Word of this truly extraordinary athletic performance by the Egyptian king spread beyond the borders of the Nile Valley. Walter Burkert has recently maintained, quite persuasively, that this text, along with another to be discussed in a moment, provided the ultimate source for the archery contest in the Odyssey.[69] After his long and often-interrupted journey home to Ithaca, Odysseus in disguise learns that his wife, Penelope, thinking him long dead, and importuned by her suitors, has arranged for an archery competition whose victor will win her hand and succeed to the island's throne. Odysseus himself had advised her to take this step. None of the suitors is able to bend the powerful bow. As it says in the text of the Sphinx

Stela, "There was none among them who could draw his bow."[70] Odysseus alone can do this. No sooner does he bend the bow than he fires off the master shot that flies through the twelve holes in the handles of the twelve axes. This performance is the immediate prelude to Odysseus's revenging himself upon the suitors and reclaiming his rightfully inherited position.[71]

The context of the Sphinx Stela makes clear that the pharaoh's brilliant feat of archery qualified him for rule. Scholars have sought to explain Odysseus's bravura performance with complicated philological and ballistic considerations and speculations, which have proven to be far-fetched and unpersuasive, but Walter Burkert has recently demonstrated the dependence of this archery motif upon the Egyptian sources of the eighteenth dynasty. The copper plates that served the Egyptians as targets and that were allegedly transfixed by the arrows were outwardly similar in form to the axes through whose handles the Homeric arrow flew. A Greek πέλεκυς is scarcely different in its outline from the copper ingots produced by the Egyptians of the New Kingdom. The difference was merely that the edges of the double axe were convex while those of the plates were concave (fig. 16).

In the course of the "dark ages" of Greek history (twelfth century to ninth century B.C.), there came to be a confusion between the ultimate Egyptian source and its Greek interpretation so that Homer's verses concerning the archery test make an unintelligible mess out of an originally clear state of affairs. Quite apart from the twofold connection of the *Odyssey's* archery-test motif with Egyptian sources, one can also point to the role of the bow, whose function in both cases approaches that of an emblem of dominion.[72] Furthermore, latent knowledge of Egyptian archery achievements survives in other Homeric episodes. In the archery contests staged as part of the funeral games in honor of the fallen Patroclus, the victor is rewarded with axes whose form was presumably the same as that of the axes used in the *Odyssey* (*Iliad* xxiii 850–53).

The passage already cited from the Sphinx Stela has proven to be an

---

16 *Copper ingots and Greek double axe (pelekys)*

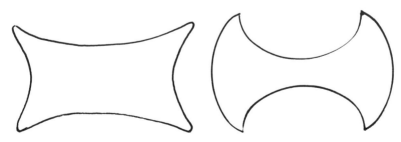

impressive literary portrayal of the king's masterful archery. The text can be supported by an equally impressive visual representation in the form of a relief cut into a block of granite and built into the third pylon of the imperial sanctuary in the Temple of Amun at Karnak (fig. 17).[73] This relief, whose combination of picture and explanatory text forms a nicely balanced synthesis, is one of the loveliest sources for Egyptian sports. It deserves a leading place among the masterpieces illustrating a world history of sports.

The famous relief, which protrudes from the larger architectural whole and acts as a pendant to a battle scene, shows the pharaoh firing his bow at the copper target. Upon the light two-horse war chariot, shown in full career (indicated by the "rearing gallop"), the king stands with drawn bow, arrow laid against the bowstring. As was conventional in representations of chariot-borne kings, he is shown without his charioteer. The reins are wound about his waist. He aims at a post erected as a target and already impaled by a number of arrows. The infallible accuracy of the charioteer-warrior is indicated by the fact that the already-fired arrows are lodged in the target at equal spatial intervals. The remaining arrow will complete the design. The inscription carved into the upper portion of the scene com-

17 *Archery Stela of Amenophis II from Temple of Amun, Karnak*

ments: "The perfect god, mighty in his strength, who acts with both arms in the presence of his army, powerful with the bow; who shoots accurately, without an arrow going amiss; and he shoots at the copper ingots, as befits his strength, transfixing them like papyrus, without a thought of any wooden (target); whose strong arms have no equal; (like the god Month) when he appears upon his war chariot."[74]

According to this text, the evidence of the king's archery must have consisted exclusively of the transfixed copper plate that we see propped against the post. It also seems as if other arrows had struck the upper part of the post, but no copper plate is visible, and the cords wrapped about the middle of the post are also puzzling.[75] The text referring to the copper ingot transfixed by five arrows can be translated as follows; "The great copper target from the land of copper, three fingers thick, at which His Majesty shot. The mighty one penetrated it with numerous arrows, and he shot so that three hand's breadths protruded from the other side of the target; he who is always accurate whenever he aims and shoots, the heroic one, the possessor of strength. His Majesty undertook this amusement in view of the whole land."[76]

Among the Egyptian documents concerned with archery, this scene, composed with a sure sense of space and with perfected technique, joins together with the concentrated, picture-oriented text to form an artistic high point. Conceptually, this monument is surpassed by only one source, whose content violates Egyptian conventions for representation in that the pharaoh, normally withdrawn from the sphere of merely human existence and elevated by the royal dogma to the rank of triumphant victor, here risks his unshakable superiority in an athletic contest. This unique occurrence is commemorated in the form of an inscription found in Medamud (in the neighborhood of Luxor), where stood a sanctuary to the war god Month. The text, although only partially preserved, permits the following interpretation of what occurred: "[His Majesty shot at a copper target] 3/4 [of a hand's breadth] in thickness. He pierced it with the first arrow so that 7/9 of the shaft of the arrow which was in the target protruded beyond the other side. . . . He said, 'Whoever transfixes this target to the extent His Majesty's arrow did, to him belongs these things.' Whereupon they began to shoot at this target."[77]

Thus pharaoh set the standard for the contest with his first attempt and promised to any who might equal his performance prizes which were not described in the text but which may have been pictured. Those who were challenged did their best, but they must quickly have recognized the hopelessness of their athletic ambition. There is no other way to imagine the outcome of the contest. Yet even this unusual configuration, which violates the canon of Egyptian thought, is compatible with the image of the

immensely superior king. The more visibly his deeds matched the dog-
matic prescriptions, the brighter shone his fame. The individual athletic
mastery of Amenophis II, to whom this anonymously transmitted document is unquestionably to be ascribed, was so superior, especially in target
archery, that it even effected this modification of the highly conventional
depiction of the king. Amenophis II could be shown to have risked his
royal prestige because there was, in reality, no risk at all. The discovery of a
bow in the royal tomb, although nothing very unusual when seen in light
of the number found in the tomb of Tutankhamon, rounds out a "sports
career" that was unequalled—and not just in relation to Egyptian monarchs.[78]

The tradition of the archer-kings declined noticeably after Amenophis
II but did not disappear entirely until the nineteenth dynasty. Tuthmosis IV practiced archery in the desert near Memphis, but the brief mention in his Sphinx Stela provides few details.[79] Although Amenophis III
(eighteenth dynasty) was a mighty hunter who must have been a good
archer, we do not know whether or not he shot at targets. For the religious
fanatic Akhenaten (eighteenth dynasty), no sport activities have been documented.[80] Tutankhamon's arsenal of bows and arrows may have been
used for sport,[81] but there is no iconographic evidence of this unless the
archer who appears in a sketch seated before the king, also seated, is
supposed to represent the young deceased pharaoh.[82] Some lovely scenes
do show Tutankhamon using his bow in hunting.[83]

Tutankhamon's successor, Ay, appears once again in the customary manner. In a relief upon a piece of gold leaf, perhaps a decoration from a
chariot, we see him in the familiar pose of the archer aiming at the target
(fig. 18). Hounds and fan-bearers are the escorts worthy of Ay's rank, and

18 *Ay (eighteenth dyn.) shooting his bow at a target*

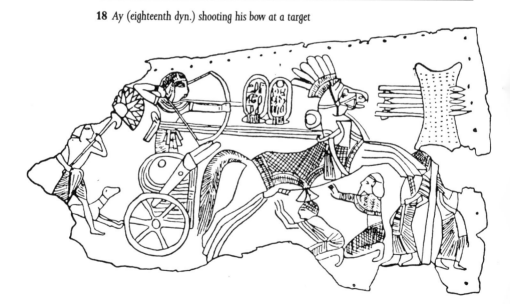

19 *Cylindrical seal: Ramesses II (nineteenth dyn.) shooting at a target*

the foes begging for mercy, two of whom are bound to the post that bears the target, recall an episode from the Syrian campaigns of Amenophis II (preserved upon a stela from Memphis). After the surrender of the city of Kadesh and the oath of submission of its prince, the king demonstrates his might and power by exhibiting his extraordinary ability as an archer. Shooting at two targets, he quiets his enemies and nips in the bud any desire to revolt.[84]

We cannot rule out the possibility that a cylindrical seal found in Palestine served a similar propagandistic goal (fig. 19). It depicts Ramesses II standing and shooting at a target to whose post two captives are bound as in the scene with Ay. Although later periods have also left us impressive scenes of royal archery in which the pharaoh appears as a mighty archer-warrior, the theme of sport archery disappears after Ramesses II.

It is also worth mentioning that the standards of Egyptian archery are attested by many pieces of equipment that are useful and even indispensable for the practice of archery at a high level of proficiency. The astonishing quality of the bows themselves has already been mentioned. Not less informative is the variety of shapes among the arrowheads, which allowed the archer to choose exactly the right arrow for any given circumstance.[85] Not only were there quivers for the arrows but also special cases to protect the valuable bows. Such bow cases are often visible on the "baskets" of chariots. Their upper parts, made of leather, folded limply when the archer used his bow. There were entirely stiff containers for bows, like the splendid one found in the tomb of Tutankhamon, with rich decorations and hunting scenes. These containers, which also had devices for fastening them to the chariot, were exceptions.[86] There were also special chests for storing bows in an arsenal.[87]

Like his modern counterpart, the Egyptian archer had to deal with the problem of the released bowstring's painful snap against his arm; the solution, then as now, was to protect the sensitive parts of the forearm and the wrist with padding developed for this purpose. This protective device is often depicted, as on the Archery Stela of Amenophis II (fig. 17), and many originals have been unearthed.[88] These protective bracers were made of leather, perhaps also of horn.

There is then every indication that Egyptian archery was well developed and that it included a strong emphasis on the sport component, but we still need to say a few more words about the performances of the archer-kings. Could the archers of that time really transfix copper plates? Can we be sure such plates ever existed? The first thing to be established is that the plates were also represented in other contexts where they were clearly perceived as imported goods or—from an Egyptian perspective—as foreign tribute. Attestations of them extend in time from the reign of Hatshepsut (eighteenth dynasty) to that of Ramesses III. The depictions can be divided between scenes of carriers and scenes of smelting and storing the raw material.[89] The usual form of the plates, presumably to lessen the problems of transportation, was the "ox-hide," cast at Asian and Cypriot production sites. Among these depictions, an especially enlightening one from the tomb of the official Rechmire shows a carrier with a plate on his shoulder, the usual mode of transportation, and with a bow in his free hand (fig. 20). From other cultures at the eastern end of the Mediterranean come further representations of such copper plates and also archeological remains that suggest that these objects were coveted items of coastal trade. The discovery of a late-thirteenth-century Phoenician trading vessel wrecked on the tricky cliffs of Cape Gelidonia on the south coast of Asia Minor led to the recovery of thirty-nine original plates which can now be inspected in the museum at Bodrum (the ancient Halicarnassus). They differ considerably in size. On the average, they are about 65 centimeters long, 40 centimeters wide (at the narrowest point about 25 centimeters), and 4 centimeters thick. The average weight is about 20 kilograms (fig. 21).[90] Interestingly, the cargo of the ship also included another sort of copper plate, rounded with a flat and a curved side, a form that one might call half-lens-shaped.[91] Apparently the unworked copper was shaped into more than one convenient form for offering on the market. This latter shape enables us to glimpse sport history from yet another angle. In the shape of these plates is foreshadowed the *solos*, a discus-like object thrown in one of the contests that made up the funeral games in honor of Patroclus

20 *Copper ingots as imported goods, tomb of Rechmire, TT 100 (eighteenth dyn.)*

in book 23 of the *Iliad*. Greek athletic practices eventually refined the *solos* into the discus.[92]

It cannot be disputed that the copper targets at which the Egyptian kings aimed really existed and were widely distributed throughout the domain of Egyptian culture. It seems less credible that these copper plates could be transfixed by the arrows. The various results reported, however, give the impression that they were based upon reality. Since it is impossible to use the original equipment for experimental purposes, the royal performances have been simulated with modern bows and arrows and targets

21 *Original copper ingots from a shipwreck off Cape Gelidoniya, thirteenth century* B.C.

fashioned from electrolyte copper (10 centimeters in diameter, 4.6 centimeters thick, Brinel Ophardness 80).[93] The arrows were shot from a distance of 3.5 meters.[94] In this and other experiments, the arrows penetrated only a few millimeters, which suggests the need for some skepticism in regard to the credibility of Egyptian accounts of the pharaohs' achievements. Real copper plates have yet to be used to conduct experiments to corroborate these results.

The Egyptian conception of history, however, dispensed with the central modern criterion of strict historicity; it was rather the case that the written word acted magically upon reality. The ideal king of the eighteenth dynasty was nonetheless a distinguished archer who was able to transfix with his arrows the copper plates imported from the lands of Egypt's traditional Asiatic enemies. In doing so, he may also have alluded, symbolically, to Egypt's superiority. It may well be that the later examples of royal archery degenerated into a hollow convention; nonetheless, behind the reports of Amenophis II, the archetypical Egyptian archer, lay more than a ritual gesture. With all due caution, one can still assume that personal preference and talent produced real sport achievements.

Driving Chariots and Training Horses

In the second millennium B.C. the two-wheeled, two-horse war chariot (fig. 22) arrived in the ancient Near East, proving itself not merely as a wide-reaching innovation in weapons technology but also as the cause of a social-historical revolution affecting the entire region, including Egypt.[95] The Egyptians' first acquaintance with the new vehicle was coupled with a painful experience because horse and chariot were in the hands of the Hyksos, whose seventeenth-century conquest of large parts of Egypt made them the first foreign rulers in Egyptian history.[96] Only when the surprise effect of the new weapon had worn off and the Egyptians were able to

22 *Chariot from a private tomb at Thebes (eighteenth dyn.), now in Florence*

construct their own war chariots was it possible for them gradually to expel

the intruders. The martial virtues necessary for the war of national
liberation—courage and technical mastery of the complicated art of
charioteering—remained indispensable through the whole period of the
New Kingdom. A new elite came to the fore, whose conduct was guided
by what we now refer to as achievement motivation—an elite that emphasized physical prowess.[97]

During the second half of the second millennium B.C., the aristocratic
culture of the entire Near East and of the eastern Mediterranean was abso-
lutely dominated by the ideal of the chariot-borne warrior whose situation
Helck rightly compares with that of the medieval knight. The aristocratic
charioteer considered his chariot the badge of his social class and displayed it as his status symbol. Mastery of the art of chariot driving, attain-
able only through constant practice, consisted of guiding the sensitive span
of horses, holding one's balance in the unsteady "basket" of the chariot,
and shooting arrows accurately from this shaky platform. Mastery of these
skills allowed the warrior to feel his position to be an exceptional one,
quite apart from his national identity. This common basis for understanding smoothed the diplomatic paths between the Egyptian king and the
Near Eastern courts. In diplomatic correspondence, formulaic questions
about the condition of horses and chariots often preceded information
about the well-being of the warrior.[98] A passage from the fairy tale "The
Doomed Prince" probably mirrored reality when, upon the arrival of a
chariot, the needs of the horses are met before those of their driver.[99]
Charioteering, transfigured by its aristocratic aura, had the glamor of a
sport. It is, therefore, quite surprising that there is no Egyptian evidence of
the chariot races which, outside the Nile Valley, play such a prominent
historical role.[100]

To the Mycenaean Greeks we are indebted for the first visual depictions
of chariot racing as a sport, and from them come the most beautiful poetic
accounts of the races.[101] Homer made such a race the poetic high point of
the funeral games for the fallen Patroclus (Iliad xxiii, 262–652). The race
surpasses in importance all the other contests staged by Achilles. This is
apparent simply from the extent of the account, which exceeds those of
the other seven disciplines combined (Iliad xxiii, 653–897).

Chariot races became a part of the program for the Olympic Games in
680 B.C., and the list of victors is packed with renowned names: Sicilian
tyrants, Athenian noblemen, Macedonian royalty, Roman emperors—all
sought the immortal fame that followed a victory in the hippodrome of
Pelops at Olympia. Chariot races in Rome's Circus Maximus were an attrac-
tion that won the favor of the masses,[102] and the ancient tradition underwent a late revival in the hippodromes of the Byzantine empire.

In Egypt, we encounter nothing of the sort. And yet the unusually good Egyptian sources for chariots give us the impression that we really are in a sphere colored in some special way by sports. The radiantly aristocratic aura of equestrian connoisseurship and the mastery of the charioteer's art reveal themselves as elements imprinted upon the monarchical ideal of the New Kingdom. Although the Egyptians have transmitted to us no training manual for horses like Kikkuli's text from the Hittite culture[103] or the anonymous directions from Assyria,[104] one can, nonetheless, confidently relate these detailed training programs to Egyptian conditions. In the royal stables, there were presumably experts in the care and training of horses who were the equals of their Asian colleagues. The pharaoh's engagement in this matter has been well captured in the Sphinx Stela of Amenophis II. Even before the long passage that relates the athletic abilities of the crown prince, his qualities as a horseman are summarized in a sentence: "He knew horses better than anyone else in this numerous army."[105]

A great part of this text, which better than any other expresses with powerful immediacy the athletic ambitions of an Egyptian king, is given over to the pharaoh's burning interest in horses and his mastery in horsemanship:

> When he was still a young prince he loved his horses and took pleasure in them. His heart was steady when he handled them, and he knew the character of every one of them. He was informed about training them and became an expert in this matter. One heard about this in the palace through his father Horus, the "Mighty Bull That Appeared in Thebes" (Tuthmosis III). The heart of His Majesty rejoiced as he heard this. He was jubilant because of what had been said about his eldest son, and he spoke in his heart, "He is the one who will (act) as Lord of the entire World." . . . And His Majesty said to those who were with him, "You shall give him a beautiful span of horses from His Majesty's stables in Memphis; you shall say to him, 'Watch over them, care for them, let them trot and calm them when they are unruly.'" Whereupon the king's son was commissioned to handle the horses of the royal stables. He carried out his commission. Reshef and Astarte were delighted with him as he did that which his heart desired. He trained horses whose equal was not to be found. They were tireless when he harnessed them, and when they galloped they did not sweat. He came secretly to Memphis and halted in the resting place of the Sphinx. There he tarried for a short time in order to drive about and behold the grace of the resting place of blessed Cheops and blessed Chephren.[106]

This episode refers to the youth of the future king, and it is clear that his masterful sports accomplishments predestined him for the brilliant office he held in the eighteenth dynasty. The entire text of the stela is in this style, and the sentences omitted from the translation also refer to his destiny as prince. Furthermore, the reaction of his royal father, Tuthmosis III, to the news of his son's successes demonstrates that he too was knowledgeable about the training of horses. The passion for horses here so palpably expressed is visually attested at the end of the New Kingdom in regard to Ramesses III. The king is portrayed in his funerary temple as he inspects his stables and points with his staff to a pair of horses (fig. 23). The inscription informs us that these are "the horses that he trained with his own hands."[107]

It is important to note that kings were not the only trainers of horses. The fact that it was part of the normal private life of the Egyptian to have his horses trained is weighty testimony to the significance of horse and chariot in the New Kingdom (fig. 24). Thus an overseer reports to his master, occupied away from home, about the conditions of his horses: "My lord's horses are well. I had their portion mixed before them, and the stable boys bring them the best grass from the papyrus thicket. I give them their daily feed and their yellow salve in order to brush them down every month. The stable master lets them go for a trot every ten days."[108]

23 *Ramesses III (twentieth dyn.) inspects his horses, royal funerary temple, Medinet Habu*

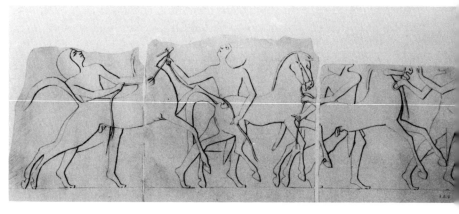

24 *Training Horses, tomb of Ipuya, Saqqara (eighteenth dyn.), Cairo JE 11420*

In comparison to the Asiatic training methods mentioned above, these minimal demands were thinkable only for those horses that were not yet in training but might have been reserved for future use. The light workout every ten days surely points to the future rather than to the present.

If one wanted to consider a weakness for noble horses as an index of athletic ambitions, one could name other kings with this weakness as well. Ramesses II planned to feed his trusty horses with his own hand, which can be understood in light of the fact that they did not desert him when his position during the Battle of Kadesh was truly desperate.[109] A lovely example of his passion for horses is also revealed by one of his rings, which is decorated with a pair of sculpted horses (fig. 25). King Piankhi (twenty-fifth dynasty) was a fanatic, a real fool for horses, who treated his enemies as they treated their horses. Thus he held it against the vanquished Prince Nimrud that he had let his horses starve during the siege of Hermopolis. Piankhi's weakness for horses was quickly bruited about. A report of his victorious campaign throughout Egypt against various alliances and minor princes contained a curious tip to the effect that the gift of horses might win for the defeated the favor of the victor.[110] It is no accident that the long text of a stela is crowned by a representation of the leading of a horse.

The use of a chariot in the spectacular demonstrations of royal prowess in target archery, discussed above, was undoubtedly an instance of sport in the true sense of the term. Here let it be recalled that deeds such as those of which Amenophis II boasted in his oft-cited Sphinx Stela, required not merely the absolute mastery of the composite bow but also, in equal measure, a masterful calculation of the behavior of the horses and the movement of the chariot, two unknowns in the equation. All this compels our admiration. Every mention of the king's chariot-borne target archery

50

simultaneously testifies to chariot driving as a sport, for which the visual evidence of the Archery Stela of Amenophis II is the most impressive proof (fig. 17).

A short passage from the Sphinx Stela of Tuthmosis IV has some of the excitement of a chariot race although it bears the stamp of royal dogma. The passage appears between the paws of the Sphinx of Giza and should not be confused with the memorial to the father of Tuthmosis, Amenophis II, which scholars refer to by the same name. The well-chosen text allows us almost to experience the intoxicating velocity of the chariot as it approaches the limits of what was then humanly possible: "He practiced and he enjoyed himself on the south and north sides of the desert plateau of Memphis, shooting at targets, hunting lions and beasts of the wilds, and he flew along in his war chariot, with horses swifter than the wind, with a single companion."[111]

In this brief depiction of the rushing span of horses, to which the king in the ecstasy of an exciting new experience gave free rein, the writer charmingly captures the sporting pleasure of such an excursion (fig. 26).

Although Egypt provides little material for the history of chariot races in the narrow sense, there is indirect evidence whose uniqueness merits close attention. In contrast to the chariots of other ancient cultures, which have long since mouldered away, eight Egyptian chariots survive, valuable tangible evidence that helps enormously to answer questions raised by other source materials. The chariots themselves compensate for the lack of direct statements about chariot races. One of these chariots, now in the Museo Archeologico in Florence, comes from a private tomb.[112] Another was owned by the parents-in-law of Amenophis III.[113] Six others come

25 Ring of Ramesses II (nineteenth dyn.) with horses

26 *Leaving by chariot, New Kingdom*

from the tomb of Tutankhamon.[114] Except for the first, all these chariots are now on display at the Egyptian Museum in Cairo. In addition to these eight intact chariots, numerous partly preserved chariots have been discovered.[115]

The Egyptian chariot-makers were masters of their craft (fig. 27). Their products are technically sophisticated and elegantly seductive. Wood is their basic material, the kind varying with the different functions of the different parts of the chariot. The chariot in Florence was constructed of seven different kinds of wood. The most important parts are the strikingly

27 *Chariot builders, tomb of Menkheperresoneb, TT 86 (eighteenth dyn.)*

large wheels (fig. 28), a meter in diameter and attached to an axle of nearly a
meter and a half; the basket in which the charioteer stood; and the shaft
together with the yoke, by means of which the chariot was set in motion.
The rims are made of several segments and are attached to the hub by four
or six spokes (fig. 29). In the picture carved into the Archery Stela,
Amenophis II drives a four-spoked chariot like the one in Florence, but all
the other surviving specimens are six-spoked chariots, which was customary after the experimental phase of chariot-construction. In the chariot of
Tutankhamon, the three spokes were bent in the middle into a V-shape,
making a six-part circle, while the chariot from the private tomb has four
struts.[116] The bent parts of the spokes were housed in a middle section
that, together with the lateral flanges of the axle, formed the hub.[117]

The astonishing thing which cannot be seen in Egyptian profile depictions, is that the hub extended on both sides by a third of a meter. By this
means, the track was beautifully stabilized. The floor of the basket consists
of a semicircular frame strung with a web of leather strips, which acted as
springs. The forward section of the basket, occasionally in the form of a low
partition, offered a handhold for the warrior and the driver. The shaft bent
sharply just at the front of the basket. The shaft must have been made of

28 Chariot detail,
Florence

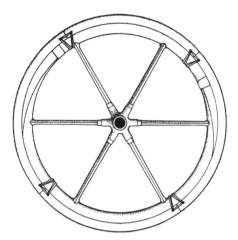

29 Wheel from Tutankhamon's chariot

30 Stela with Ani and charioteer, Cairo JE 34 177

elastic wood because the rearward placement of the axle transferred considerable weight to it when the chariot was in motion. The four-spoked
chariot in Florence weighs twenty-four kilograms, with the axle and
wheels together accounting for thirteen kilograms. If one ignores the two
ceremonial chariots of Tutankhamon, the other chariots give the impression of great solidity. One can easily imagine that they drove well even at
high speeds (fig. 30).[118]

Ritual and Record

In his interesting book *From Ritual to Record*, Allen Guttmann attempts to characterize the development of sports from antiquity to the
present.[119] The title is a kind of synopsis of the argument: while the sports
of antiquity were related to religious rituals, those of the modern age are
secular, a fact best exemplified by the modern concept of the sports record. However, the author has not paid sufficient attention to Egyptian
circumstances.[120] Had he done so, he might have realized that the sports of
the Egyptian kings of the eighteenth dynasty show in exemplary fashion
that the two elements—ritual and record—do not appear merely as mutu-
ally exclusive polar opposites in a historical development. It is true that the
sports achievements of the pharaoh took place without an opponent and
approached the status of ritual—like every action touched by the person of
the king. At the same time, however, this ritual contained the concept of a
sports record insofar as the royal activity was accompanied by the principle
of the "extension of the preexistent."[121]

This central concept of the Egyptian kingdom appeared in various
forms. The extension of the borders of the land through military conquests
is one, the most obvious perhaps, but in the nature of things confined by
boundaries (in both senses). Another form was the surpassing of the architectural achievements of one's royal predecessors, whether in monumen-
tality or in the number or unusualness of the individual parts of the structure. Hornung, to whom I owe not only basic thoughts about the nature of
the Egyptian kingdom but also these more recent observations, has even
traced the lines of such development in the layout of the royal tombs.[122] In
this area, moreover, the Roman emperors were unwitting imitators of the
pharaohs when they constructed their imperial fora so that the clash of
political programs became visible. For this phenomenon, A. Linfert has
coined the term *certamen principum* ("contest of the emperors").[123]

At any rate, the relatively static royal dogma was first set into motion by
external influences. In connection with the Hyksos' invasion of the Nile
Valley, seeds were planted which sprouted during the eighteenth dynasty
and then exfoliated into new forms.

To return again to Guttmann's thesis: He is surely correct to emphasize that the ritual element in sport was more pronounced in earlier times than in our own day, although even now it has not entirely vanished. And the American historian Richard D. Mandell has put forth a very enticing theory, according to which the modern sport record is considered to be an invention of the eighteenth and nineteenth centuries A.D.[124] Both Guttmann and Mandell have, from a similar perspective, rightly seen the general tendency of sport's historical development, and both have cited various publications by the German historian Henning Eichberg.[125]

Nonetheless, Egyptian sources from the eighteenth dynasty raise questions about their elegant and attractive theory. Can it be that these Egyptian kings, whose superiority in sports and in everything else was the main theme of official texts, were the exceptions that disproved the rule? Did they celebrate athletic rituals in the true sense of the word and allow alterations and reforms in the time-honored, change-resistant royal dogma—they who merely demonstrated their prowess and who, with the exception of Amenophis II, were too exalted for competition, who performed the ritual run during the Festival of Sed, whose jubilee celebration rarely incorporated new elements of sport ritual, whose hunts preserved an aura of traditional ritual?

In order to understand what is implied by positive answers to these questions, one must rid oneself of the notion that sport records always come in numbers with at least two digits after the decimal point. The achievement principle does not begin with modern industrial society because it is not at all dependent on modernity's technically advanced means of measurement. It is true that the administration of performances by means of a bureaucracy is a characteristic of industrial society, but it is just as true for the high cultures of earlier times. There is scarcely a land where the drive to register every item of economic activity can be followed as closely as it can in ancient Egypt!

If one reduces the concept of the sport record to its essence, it merely testifies that a hitherto unreached level of athletic performance has been witnessed and very accurately measured. Since the external conditions of the achievement are known and the equipment used is also measured and, as a rule, standardized, the performance can be repeated and surpassed at other times and in other places.[126] Exactly these criteria are reported in numerous accounts of the target archery performance of Tuthmosis III and his son Amenophis II. The text accompanying the archery target on the Archery Stela can be paraphrased as follows (with clarifying interpolations): "The king has shot at a copper ingot [with the admittedly good composite bow of the sort made in the palace workshops and the equally masterfully fabricated arrows of the "iron tip" variety]. The plate comes

from the land of copper [from whence it was brought from time immemorial by Phoenician ships]. The plate has the standard thickness of three
fingers. The arrow bored so that three hands' breadths of its length came
out the other side of the plate. The king achieved this several times before a
great crowd of spectators."[127]

A record signifies the surpassing of an achievement. And herein lay a
difficulty for the royal dogma because the king's achievement could not be
surpassed by anyone else's. This meant that the king was his own opponent, that is, that only he could surpass his own best performance. Another
possibility was to break the record of a previous king. We have instances of
both models. In short, Egypt furthered the concept of the sport record as
classically formulated by Guttmann: "The concept [of the record] is an
ingenious abstraction which permits contests between the living and the
dead."[128]

Tuthmosis III set the standard with an arrow that transfixed a three-
finger-thick plate by a distance of three hand's breaths. Precisely this
achievement was equalled by his son Amenophis II (as recorded on the
Archery Stela). Thus Amenophis devalued his predecessor's record, and a
kind of inflation set in when he repeated his performance a number of
times. A fragment from Medamud tells that Amenophis then broke his
own record with an arrow seven-ninths of which pierced a plate three
fingers thick. The new record was achieved on the first try. Finally, the
Sphinx Stela immortalized the ultimate achievement: despite the copper
plate's thickness of a hand's breadth (four fingers), four plates were completely transfixed in the first attempt so that the arrows fell to the ground.
The Egyptian text makes the significance clear: "It was a deed that had not
been done before, and a deed that none had heard of."

We cannot exclude the possibility that a later inscription attributes a
further improvement of the record to King Tutankhamon. Unfortunately,
the inscription carved into a block at Karnak is damaged at just the point
where we might expect information on the thickness of the target. It is
hard to escape the assumption, however, that one or several plates were
transfixed so that "his arrows went into the earth." If and in what way the
record of Amenophis II was broken must, however, remain a matter for
speculation.[129]

The evolution of the archery record is traced in table 2, which permits us
clearly to follow the progressive improvement of the record. By means of
the contest, about which we are poorly informed because the texts have
often been lost, the royal dogma was exploded.[130] Even if one doubts the
historicity of the performances, even if one considers the archery contests
to have been a ritual the purpose of which was to use targets imported
from Asia to render magically harmless the Asian enemy, the existence of

Table 2. Evolution of the Royal Records in Archery, Eighteenth Dynasty

King	Thickness of Target (in fingers)	Achievement (protrusion)	Special Characteristic	Spectators	Source
Tuthmosis III	3	3 hands' breadths	—	Yes	QT 14 (Erment)
Amenophis II	3	3 hands' breadths	Done repeatedly	Yes	QT 19 (Archery stela)
Amenophis II	3	7/9 of a shaft	Contest, first attempt	Yes	QT 20 (Medamud)
Amenophis II	4	Target wholly transfixed	4 plates, first attempt	Unknown	QT 17 (Sphinx stela)
Tutankhamon	Unknown	Target wholly transfixed	Several plates?	Yes	Urk. IV, (2047) (Karnak)

QT = Decker, Quellentexte
Urk. = Helck, Urkunden der 18. Dynastie

the concept of the record cannot be dismissed. Of course, this record is bound up with ideology, but both form and content are present. If one wished to take the point of departure of our discussion and push it to the extreme, modifying the dichotomized usage of the words ritual and record in accordance with Egyptian relationships, we might set up a new kind of synthesis and speak pointedly of "the record of the ritual."

To round off this discussion, it is appropriate to recall that the sources for Egyptian sports contain—surprisingly often—quantified information. Amenophis II, for instance, drew three hundred composite bows, a first-rate feat of strength; using a rudder twenty ells in length (around ten meters), without pausing to rest, he steered a ship manned by a crew of two hundred for a distance of three itrw (around 31.5 kilometers). This information is also found inscribed upon the Sphinx Stela, the source of our references to the unbroken archery records.[131]

Quantification appears elsewhere in the sources. A Syrian princess, the prize of a sports competition, was kept in a room whose window was seventy ells high. The victor had to leap up to the window (i.e., more than thirty-six meters).[132] The best runners described by the Running Stela of

Taharqa covered the distance, one hundred kilometers, in approximately nine hours.[133] Quantified results were given for hunting as well. Tuthmosis III hunted 120 elephants "en passant,"[134] 120 wild bulls in an hour, and seven lions "in the blink of an eye."[135] Amenophis III killed 102 lions in the first ten years of his reign.[136] On a single day his hunting booty came to fifty-six wild bulls, and his total for an additional four days was forty animals.[137] The degree to which these feats were conceived as records quantitatively surpassing those of his predecessor is unclear, because other achievements fail to equal those of Tuthmosis III. The royal duty to "extend the existent," which in some ways overlaps with the concept of the sports record, can also be expressed in hunting by claims that certain successes are unprecedented. This was the case for the elephant hunts of Tuthmosis III, and perhaps even more strikingly so in the unique details of his rhinoceros hunt, for which the king repeated in word and picture the dimensions of the slain animal's body.[138] This might also have been the case for the single reference to a royal ostrich hunt by Tutankhamon, depicted upon a fan.[139] These sources are, moreover, contemporary with the records set in archery and sometimes, as in the case of Tuthmosis III, refer to precisely the same kings. Except for the Running Stela, the sources all come from the eighteenth dynasty and provide a closely related context for the reports of record-setting.

4   Sports of Private Persons

Outside of the sphere of the kings, where the royal dogma limited sports to a few status-appropriate disciplines (cultic running, archery, charioteering, and—as we shall see—hunting), the life of private persons included a remarkably broad spectrum of sports activities. This alone allows us to assess the popularity of sports as leisure-time pursuits.

The evidence for the sports of private people derives principally from the archeologically rich finds in the tombs of the aristocracy, whose stone chambers have better withstood the ravages of time than the modest graves of simpler folk. Scenes of daily life painted on tomb walls reproduce for us the aristocratic milieu in which the deceased had lived their lives. Sports were one element among many that had gladdened their hearts. The possibility of spectatorship existed along with active sport participation; aristocrats observed the sport activities of the lower classes. Thus the Old Kingdom abounded with images of fish spearing whose contemplation must have been a source of special pleasure for the dead nobleman's spirit. It may also be that princely taste was responsible for the many wrestling scenes preserved for us in the Middle Kingdom tombs of Beni Hasan.

Considering the present state of research, one does best to classify and discuss the sports of private Egyptians on the basis of the individual sports disciplines. When the sources require it, they are subdivided further. A thorough social history of the sports of private persons is much to be desired, but the lack of preliminary studies makes such a history impossible at the present moment.

Running

Running seems to us to be a sport that can be practiced without extensive preparation or great technical skill. This was as true for the ancients as for us. If one approaches earlier times without preconceptions about their sport practices, one is likely to think first of all of running. This can be explained, of course, by the fact that the activity is such a natural one. Everyone can imagine that early hunters and nomads had to be remarkable runners simply because their lives demanded that they be. This mode of transportation was the only one available for quick movement when early man had neither domesticated animals nor invented techniques upon which to rely. What was more natural than that one man should have been stimulated to test his swiftness against another's?

We know, for example, that the Hittites staged races in which the great men of the realm competed for the honorary office of "holder of the reins of the royal chariot."[1] In Homer's *Iliad*, the footrace is—to no one's surprise—a part of the funeral games in honor of Patroclus (xxiii 653–99). The greatest of the Greek heroes take part in it, as in all the other contests. When Ajax slips and falls into a dung heap left by the slaughter of beeves, the spectators have an occasion for some hilarious amusement, which is the model for the oft-cited "Homeric laughter."

Modern researchers follow their ancient predecessors in believing that the first seventeen Olympic Games consisted only of footraces. To the original competition in a single race the length of the stadium (about two hundred meters) the organizers of the fourteenth games added a race exactly twice as long (the *diaulos*). In the fifteenth Olympiad, a distance race (*dolichos*) was introduced. Thus running alone dominated the first sixty years of the games.[2]

If one excludes from consideration the events of the royal jubilee festival, which had a very different significance, nothing in the history of Egyptian sports resembles this dominance of running. We are familiar with representations of running infantrymen from the Amarna period (eighteenth dynasty); they also appear in texts as pḥrr (runners).[3] Such runners also appeared in private life as the escorts of prominent men, whom they accompanied in their function as running bodyguards while high officials traveled in their chariots (which were also, like the runners, status symbols).[4] At various times, soldiers were awarded the honorary title of "swift runner," and texts sometimes seem to refer to this quality as if it were the result of a contest. We may, therefore, be justified in thinking that such contests occurred in practice more often than the evidence indicates. We may also conclude from our knowledge of Egyptian messengers that they were clearly well trained runners quite practiced in their specialized role.[5]

One searches in vain, however, through the visual representations of Egyptian life for depictions of footraces of the sort abundantly available in the form of Greek vase painting.[6] Where a number of runners are shown together, they are clearly footmen accompanying a chariot, a custom not restricted to the Amarna period (although the pictorial evidence derives only from this period). The frequent representations of royal runners cannot be classified as images of contests even if we do consider the king to be involved in sports (as was shown above in the section on running as an aspect of the jubilee festival).

A few years ago a source was discovered which, in the fullness of its details, its vitality, and the variety of its surprising statements, does a great deal to compensate for the relative sparseness of Egyptian documentation for running.[7] Indeed, we are undoubtedly justified in saying that this discovery should be ranked among the most important known sources for ancient Egyptian sports. I refer to a stone monument that originally fronted an ancient road leading, presumably, from the capital Memphis to the great oasis of Fayum. The memorial, identifiable by its typically rounded upper end, derives from the reign of King Taharqa (690–664 B.C.) and can be dated to the period between 6 December 685 and 5 January 684. The twenty-fifth dynasty, to which it belongs, had its origin in Nubia. Modern scholars, following the misleading example of Herodotus and other Greek historians, refer to the officials of this dynasty as Ethiopians. We must be clear about this misnomer to avoid false associations occasioned by the similarity of their athletic feats to those of recent Ethiopian runners.

The Egyptian text justifies our referring to the monument as the "Running Stela of Taharqa."[8] Because of its uniqueness and its general interest for sport history, I reproduce the text verbatim.

> [Sixth year, third month] of the season of šmw under the majesty of Horus "Great in Appearance," of the two queens "Great in Appearance," of Golden Horus "Who Protects the Two Lands," [of the King of Upper and Lower Egypt Nfrtm-ḫw-Rꜥ, of the Son of the Sun] Taharqa, beloved of Bastet Guest in Bugem, gifted with eternal life.
>
> His Majesty commanded that [a stela] be erected [at] the back of the western desert to the west of the palace and that its title be "Running Practice of the Army of the Son of the Sun Taharqa, may he live forever." His Majesty commanded that his army, raised up on his behalf, daily run [in] its five [sections].
>
> Accordingly, His Majesty said to the men: "How lovely that is, which my Father Amon has made! No other king has done the like. He has arranged for the decapitation of the Peoples of the Bow. The Nine Peoples of the Bow are bound beneath the soles of my feet. I am served by all that is encircled by the disc of the sun. The heavens

enclose no enemy of mine. There is none among my army who is not
toughened for battle, no weakling who acts as a commander of mine.
The king goes in person to Bia in order to inspect the good order of his
army. They come like the coming of the wind, like falcons who beat
the air with their wings. His bodyguard with the kt(kt) is no better than
they. The king himself is like Month, a powerful one, unequaled by
any in his army. A knowing one is he, skilled in every task, a second
Thoth.

The king himself was in his chariot to inspire the running of his
army. He ran with them at the back of the desert of Memphis in the
hour "She Has Given Satisfaction." They reached Fayum in the hour
"Sunrise." They returned to the palace in the hour "She Defends Her
Master." He distinguished the first among them to arrive and arranged
for him to eat and drink with his bodyguard. [He] distinguished those
others who were just behind him and rewarded them with all manner
of things. For His Majesty loved the work of battle, for which they were
selected. His God loved [him in the water of creation], in the womb
where he was chosen before he was born. He gave him life in its
fullness and his appearance upon the throne of Eternal Horus. The
name of the desert area where the stela stands is "[Encampment]
Road."9

Perhaps a paraphrase can clarify the content: King Taharqa, named at the
beginning of the text with his complete title, has had a stone monument
erected to preserve the record of a memorable run.

The historical background of the run is as follows: The king had commit-
ted a select troop to daily training runs. In the diction of the traditional
royal dogma he praises the state of the world order established by the god
Amon and guaranteed by the king's superiority against harm from Egypt's
enemies. The function of this speech by the pharaoh can well be compared
to a parade-ground address to motivate his men.

One day, Taharqa inspects the camp of the men sent there for training in
running, and he finds them in splendid condition. The scene shifts: In
order to test the runners' form, a race has been organized from the capital
city of Memphis through the desert to Fayum. Pharaoh, who accompanies
the runners in his chariot, actually dismounts and joins the troops for part
of the distance, a hitherto unheard of event that may be attributable to
Nubian influence on the royal dogma. The first half of the distance is
covered in the coolness of night. After a two-hour pause—a unique occurrence in the history of running—the runners set out on the road back to
Memphis. The victor is singled out for special distinction, those who arrive
shortly after him are rewarded by a banquet in the company of the royal
bodyguards, whose equals they have proved themselves to be, and all

those who finish the run receive an unspecified prize. The conclusion contains language that once again sounds the theme of the parade-ground address: The glory and the destiny of the king.

This report requires a further commentary. If the naming of differentiated prizes is a surprise for Egypt of this period, surprise becomes astonishment when we consider the runners' performance. The distance from Memphis to the border of the oasis of Fayum is approximately fifty kilometers. If we translate the times given on the stela into our temporal measurements, the distance was covered in some four hours. Although it is not specifically said how long the runners took for the fifty-kilometer return to the capital after their two-hour rest, one can reasonably calculate a slowed pace because of the effects of the rising sun and increasing fatigue. If these effects together slowed the runners by 25 percent, their total running time for one hundred kilometers was nine hours.

If we compare the Egyptian results with today's, the time of the fastest runner seems quite credible. To offer a pair of comparisons: Today's record for fifty kilometers, set by Jeff Norman in 1980, is two hours, forty-eight minutes, and six seconds. No one has covered one hundred kilometers faster than the British runner Don Ritchie, who needed six hours, ten minutes, and thirty seconds for his 1978 record.[10] Of course, one should probably not compare the Egyptian runners with the record levels of performance attained by modern athletes who have emerged at the front of the international pack after years of carefully planned training on the basis of the latest scientific studies. Furthermore, the conditions of a modern asphalt highway are considerably more favorable than those of an ancient Egyptian desert road. Accordingly, it seems methodologically right to compare the achievements of Taharqa's troops with results over similar distances in the nineteenth century, when modern track and field was still in its infancy. In 1879, the thirty-two mile record for a professional runner, who splendidly continued the British tradition of the "running footman," was slightly under three hours and forty minutes, while the fastest time for 101 kilometers (just less than twice this distance), achieved in 1884, was exactly eight hours.[11] The Egyptian report also gains credibility in light of the fact that it is compatible with the few accounts we have of the achievements of the ancient Greek *hemerodromoi* (day runners) and *bematisten* (long-distance runners).[12]

Despite the uncertainties about exact distances and times, the latter measured in *wnwt* (hours) but not in briefer intervals, one has to marvel at the achievements of the Egyptian runners who were, after all, trained for military rather than sport performance.

We cannot say with absolute certainty who the runners were, but they were definitely not of Hamitic origin like the East African athletes who have in recent years made names for themselves through their successes in international track competition. Because Taharqa and his troops had been summoned from their homeland by his predecessor, his Nubian country- man Shebitku (698–690 B.C.), to fight against the Egyptians (whose throne soon became Taharqa's), we cannot rule out the possibility that these re- markable runners were Nubian soldiers. On the other hand, anthropologi- cal and other evidence tends to invalidate such a hypothesis. It is widely known that the stocky build of the Nubians predestined them not for distance running but for combat sports like wrestling and stick fighting (discussed later in this chapter). With this in mind we might better assume that the king wished to create a body of swift shock troops recruited from native Egyptian stock. Such a policy was also wise for domestic politics. For the Kushite dynasty (named from the Egyptian word for Nubia) to main- tain its domination, the initial preference given to its own peoples had to give way to a policy of integration of the two populations. In all probability, the stela commemorates such an integrating tactic on the part of a far- sighted king determined to win over the Egyptian element of the kingdom for his political ends.

It should be emphasized that the stela offers quantified results, a rare event in ancient Egyptian sport history.[13] The stela of Taharqa, which emerges like a rocky island in the otherwise unbroken surface of late Egyptian sport history, can be seen not only as our most important single source for ancient Egyptian running but also, generally, as a first-rate source for pharaonic sport history. It is not just that the stela documents a remark- able example of sport competition in the Nile Valley; it provides us for the first time with irrefutable evidence of an Egyptian running contest. The hint of daily training is worth noting even if there is no indication of its intensity. Finally, it is also worth reminding ourselves that the unusual pause in the middle of the race has not been recorded for the running contests of other cultures or periods. In modern sports, pauses of a similar sort are quite common, especially in team sports. Soccer, American foot- ball, team handball, basketball, and field hockey, for instance, are all inter- rupted by a halftime pause. Ice hockey is divided into three periods; water polo is divided into four, which calls for three pauses. In other disciplines pauses also occur regularly. Boxing and wrestling have their rounds, during which there are brief periods for recuperation. The decathlon is contested over two days, which allows for a long pause after the first five events. Long- distance bicycle races, like the Tour de France or the Giro d'Italia, continue for weeks and are quite unimaginable without pauses. In modern track, however, the contrary prevails; pauses are unknown no matter how lengthy the distance. It would certainly strike us as odd to introduce the Egyptian rule (the details of which, after all, remain unknown to us). We must, however, acknowledge that the rule is fair in that it corresponds to our principles of justice and equality of opportunity. Since the Egyptian text strongly suggests that all the runners began the second half of the race at the same time, those who finished ahead over the first half had a longer recovery time and did not lose their advantage. Although it is theoretically possible that each runner had a two-hour pause, this possibility is not hinted at in the text and would have been quite impractical. Accordingly, we can presume that the stretch from Memphis to Fayum was a preliminary event and that the final outcome was not decided until the end of the second half of the race.[14]

That this competition occurred for the benefit of the king, who wished to reassure himself about the condition of his soldiers, is fairly clear from the context of the stela and becomes even plainer when we recall that there were no spectators to observe the event. Their presence would have distracted attention from the process of integration of the event into the royal dogma and would also have given the race a profane coloration.

Centuries after Taharqa's reign, his stela may have reappeared in altered form in a report in the first century A.D. by the Greek writer Diodorus. In the Egyptian part of his universal history Diodorus introduces a certain King Sesoosis, who we now know was named Sesostris by other Greek authors. This imaginary figure, whose deeds united the feats of numerous pharaohs, was the prototype of the Greek-style hero.[15] Diodorus says of him that the careful education he received from his father created the basis for his heroic deeds. The son and all the other boys born on the same day were given a highly selective education that included physical exercise, often quite strenuous, and toughening. "None of them was allowed to take nourishment before he had run 180 stades [lengths of a stadium]."[16]

Undoubtedly, the report is exaggerated. It is difficult to believe that the young Egyptian elite regularly ran thirty kilometers before breakfast. Besides, one must consider that the twenty-fifth dynasty, to which Taharqa belonged, was one of foreign rule and was, therefore, hardly cherished by later Egyptian historians. It is unlikely that the stela exerted any direct influence on the Greeks. Nonetheless, it remains astonishing that centuries after the end of Egyptian sovereignty, which had occasionally been recovered after the twenty-fifth dynasty, memories survived of extraordinary long-distance races and of their precondition: daily training.

Jumping

Compared with the importance of jumping in modern track and field, where it occurs as long jump, high jump, triple jump, and pole vault,

jumping as a sports discipline occurred strikingly seldom in ancient Egypt.
The force of this observation is increased if one takes a look at ancient
Greece, where the long jump is encountered as an isolated discipline in
book 8 of the *Odyssey*, when Odysseus is among the Phaeacians. Later, one
finds the long jump as a part of the pentathlon, where it was contested as
the second event. Accompanied by flute music, the athlete had to make
five continuous jumps, one after another, without a running start (so that
all the jumps were two-legged). The total length of the jumps was what
mattered. During the jumps, the athlete carried hand weights, the so-called
halteres, which were supposed to increase the length of each jump and also
to stabilize the landing.[17] One can hardly err in assuming that a former
military necessity—the sure-footed leap of an attacking hoplite—was here
turned into a sport as, indeed, was the case for the entire ancient pentathlon, whose other disciplines—the discus, the javelin, running, and
wrestling—originated in the need to prove the citizen-soldier's many-
sided military preparedness. The halteres may possibly be explained as
relics of the lance and the shield.

From ancient Egypt have survived two representations in particular
which can be seen as practice jumps. Both follow the same pattern, and
both are found in the context of a series of children's games. They are
mentioned here, apart from their context, only for the sake of a systematic
approach. Both scenes come from the graves at Saqqara: one from that of
the vizier Ptahhotep (fig. 31) dating from the end of the fifth dynasty, the
other from the grave site of his colleague Mereruka, dating from approximately fifty years later. As represented by the ancient artist, the second
scene remained puzzling until a modern Egyptian archeologist was reminded, while studying it, of a game from his childhood.[18] He realized that
the boys who are portrayed in the relief, one above the other and looking
in the same direction, should be imagined as a pair facing one another and
forming a living hurdle over which the third boy will jump (fig. 32).[19] The
task was made progressively more difficult as the sitting boys raised their
spread hands, bit by bit. Since the sitters spread their legs as well, the game
obviously combined the long jump with the high jump. Mereruka's tomb
shows a series of three running jumpers, but the tomb of Ptahhotep shows
only one as he prepares to spring. To the right of this jumper stands a pair
of boys with their arms about each other's neck, but there is no need to
conclude that they complete the kind of triad depicted in the tomb of
Mereruka.[20] While the picture of the approaching jumper has a caption
that probably gives the Egyptian name of the game, "The Kid in the Field," a
separate inscription refers to the standing pair.[21] At any rate, the game
seems similar to the children's game of leapfrog. The inscription above the
jumping scene is a cry: "Hold tight, look, I'm coming, comrade."[22] This text

31 "Khazza lawizza": tomb of Ptahhotep, Saqqara (fifth dyn.)

can quite plausibly be understood as the call of the approaching jumper to the boys forming the hurdle. There is no reason to insist, as does Z. Saad, that this modest event was actually a competition between two teams like that observed today when those who miss a jump take the place of the "hurdle."[23] The name of the contemporary game, *khazza lawizza*, is possibly a distortion of the Arabic expression *katta al wizza*, "jumping over the goose."[24] The possibility should also be mentioned that jumping was an

32 "Khazza lawizza": right side redrawn from modern point of view

aspect of acrobatic dancing. The tomb of Senet, wife of a man named
Antefoqer (twelfth dynasty), also contains a scene in which a dancer standing between two clapping women makes an impressive vertical leap.[25] The
fact that the figure has left the base line justifies this interpretation. A similar
representation with a leaping male dancer has been preserved in the tomb
of Imenemhet (eighteenth dynasty; fig. 33).

Two graves at Beni Hasan also show the standing high jump, performed
in this instance by a woman whose legs are tucked behind her. The movement is divided into its individual phases so that one has the sense of a
cinematographic sequence (fig. 34).[26] Finally, it should be mentioned that
an obscure passage in the fairy tale "The Doomed Prince" leaves open the
possibility that a high jump competition took place.[27] Everything depends
on the meaning of a single word, p3j, which is completely uncertain because it occurs in no other place and its context does not allow an unambiguous interpretation. Some scholars think the word refers to jumping,
others opt for climbing.[28] If it is a high jump competition, then it is part of a
prenuptial contest, a struggle between Syrian princes and an Egyptian
prince for the hand of a Syrian princess. The challenge is to reach a window
seventy ells (about thirty-seven meters) above the ground, which, if accom-

33 Leaping dancer,
tomb of Imenemhet,
TT 82 (eighteenth dyn.)

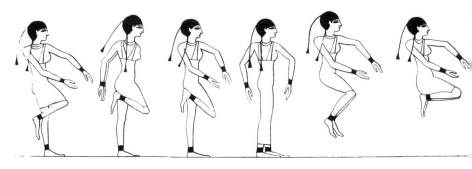

34 *Phases of buttocks kick, tomb of Baqti III, Beni Hasan, no. 15 (eleventh dyn.)*

---

plished, would certainly have been a fabulous high jump achievement. It is easy to guess the outcome of the contest: the Egyptian prince is the only suitor equal to the challenge.[29]

Combat Sports

In the early ages of human history, physical strength was an essential determinant of a man's social rank. Simplistically expressed, the establishment of social hierarchy was a process that took place by means of two-person contests that were, for the sake of group survival, ritualized and carried out under the rules of sport.[30] An echo of this reality can be detected in the high valuation of combat sports in many early civilizations. Thus it happened that the ancient Mesopotamian hero Gilgamesh had to wrestle against the undefeated Enkidu at a crucial moment in the Gilgamesh epic. Wrestling and boxing are both fairly often attested in the ancient Near East from the beginning of the third millennium. From Minoan Crete comes the famous rhyton (funnel vase) of Hagia Triada, upon which appear various phases of boxing among different age classes. While the rhyton expresses the earnestness of hard combat, one might better characterize as charming the famous fresco from the island of Thera (fifteenth century B.C.), with its face-to-face pair of "boxing princes."[31] The youthful grace of the figures seems to overlay a different, harsher reality that appears in the oldest Greek textual evidence for the sport. In book 23 of the *Iliad* Homer describes both the boxing and the wrestling that occurred during the funeral games in honor of Patroclus as bloody events with deadly consequences for the defeated boxer (lines 653–99 and 700–739). In their brutality, however, boxing and wrestling were exceeded in later times by the pancration, a favorite spectator sport.[32] This Greek inven-

70

tion, which allowed a fighter almost any move aimed at disabling his opponent, had no counterpart in ancient Egypt. Still, the sources from Egypt, many of which are extremely ancient, document the existence of three kinds of combat sports—wrestling, stick fighting, and boxing—that deserve further investigation.

Wrestling

Of all the Egyptian sports disciplines, wrestling has the best visual documentation. From the beginnings of Egyptian history in the early third millennium until the end of the New Kingdom in the eleventh century B.C., numerous representations of pairs of wrestlers have been preserved, a circumstance that suggests the high prestige of this discipline among the Egyptians. Written sources for wrestling do not, however, exist, if one discounts captions, which usually consist of a single sentence of challenge or boastfulness.[33] The Egyptian word for "wrestling" is unknown, and the optimistic hopes of C. E. DeVries that the discovery of a "wrestling papyrus" might solve the problem have not yet been fulfilled.[34]

The first depiction of wrestling occurs on the so-called cities palette from the time of the unification of the kingdoms. Here the wrestling pair is obviously utilized as a hieroglyph. They are shown at the beginning of a match, a static phase appropriate to their function as an ideogram. Perhaps they are Horus and Seth, the classic opponents of the Egyptian pantheon, confronting one another.[35]

The six "snapshots" of a wrestling match from the tomb of Ptahhotep (fifth dynasty) are completely free of any emblematic character (figs. 35 and 36). Ptahhotep's son Achethotep, who shares the tomb with his father, fights as a youth against a friend his own age. The age of the two naked wrestlers is signaled by their youthful locks of hair. The bold swings and throws are surprising for the period (Old Kingdom). We can already recognize two principles that will remain valid in later times. The rules permitted seizing any part of the body, which was also the case for Greek wrestling. There was, therefore, a close similarity to modern freestyle wrestling. None of the six scenes picture combat taking place on the ground, and such scenes occurred very infrequently. From the point of view of those familiar with the techniques of wrestling, it seems noteworthy that two phases of the combat follow immediately one upon the other. Wilsdorf, an expert on ancient Egyptian wrestling, speaks here of the effects of a "slow-motion shot."[36]

By far the greatest number of wrestling scenes come from the Middle Kingdom. Outstanding among these are the scenes from the tombs of the princes of the Antelope District in Middle Egypt. They are built into a rock

35 *Wrestling boys, tomb of Ptahhotep, Saqqara (fifth dyn.)*

formation, near the modern village of Beni Hasan, from whose height one can see far into the Valley of the Nile (fig. 37). Of the thirty or so graves, four are decorated with wrestling scenes: grave 29 (Baqti I) contains (like the tomb of Ptahhotep!) the six phases Wilsdorf sees as "practice holds."[37] He characterizes the fifty-nine pairs from grave 2 (Amenemhet) as the "small wrestling area" (figs. 38 and 39) and the 122 pairs from grave 17 (Kheti) as

36 *Wrestling boys, tomb of Ptahhotep, Saqqara (fifth dyn.)*

37 Beni Hasan, rock formation with tombs of Middle Kingdom nomarchs

the "middle-sized wrestling area" (fig. 40), while the 219 pairs that can be seen in grave 15 (Baqti III) are called the "large wrestling area" (fig. 41).

In the last-named grave, the wrestling scenes are painted across the east wall. The action of the wrestlers, nearly forty centimeters tall and distinguished one from the other by the color scheme (from dark brown to light brown), can be followed easily, especially now that an interfering layer of soot, which greatly darkened the frescoes, has been removed. Without the color code for the wrestlers' bodies, it would hardly have been possible to make sense of the very complicated grips and bodily entanglements (fig. 42). The fighters are stripped except for their belts. The sequence of the

38 Six wrestling pairs, tomb of Amenemhet, Beni Hasan no. 2 (twelfth dyn.)

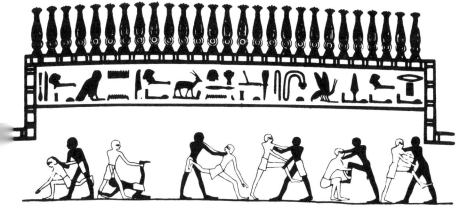

39 Wrestlers, tomb of Amenemhet,
Beni Hasan no. 2 (twelfth dyn.)

40 Wrestlers, tomb of Kheti, Beni
Hasan no. 17 (eleventh dyn.)

41 *Wrestling scene, tomb of Baqti III, Beni Hasan no. 15 (eleventh dyn.), east wall*

"large wrestling area" begins with the placement of this bit of equipment that often belongs to the sport of wrestling (as it does, for instance in Icelandic *glima*, Japanese sumo, or the belt wrestling of Alpine Europe). The next scenes picture the exploratory moves and the first attempts at a hold. Swings and throws follow in swift alternation with positions on the ground. The actual struggle on the mat is relatively unimportant, figuring in

42 *Wrestlers, tomb of Kheti, Ben Hasan no. 17 (eleventh dyn.)*

only 2 percent of the representations.[38] In the heat of the battle, belts become loose. All the Beni Hasan wrestling scenes demonstrate the agile motion of pairs of highly skilled opponents who resort to an astonishing repertory of holds and who display a remarkable ability to parry. At no time, however, was it the artist's intention to reproduce a bout in its entirety. The scenes, which follow swiftly one after the other, are like a cinematographic reproduction of a sequence of movements that can be divided into five individual phases. One might well consider them impressions of a wrestling match.

In the grave of Kheti (grave 17) are depictions of ten pairs of wrestlers, with captions that repeat the cries of the wrestlers; the captions, however, are very hard to understand (fig. 43).[39] Seldom is there the clear correspondence between text and picture that exists for group 36, where the sentence "I grab you on the leg" exactly corresponds to the visual representation. Another cry is widely applicable: "I cause your heart to weep and to fill with fear."[40]

Despite the number and variety of the Beni Hasan wrestling scenes, information on the rules continues to elude us. Specifically, we lack a clear indication of the rules for determining victory and defeat. There is no evidence to support the claim often made in the scholarly literature that the wrestlers were professionals. On the contrary, the iconographic con-

43 Inscriptions for wrestling scenes, tomb of Kheti, Beni Hasan no. *17* (*eleventh dyn.*)

text leads rather to the conclusion that wrestling was part of the soldiers' training program; in graves 15 and 17, wrestling scenes appear directly above scenes of military combat. The soldiers are involved in the battle for a fortress, and a number of them are engaged in hand-to-hand struggle (grave 15). The paramilitary use of wrestling is obvious.

The love of wrestling displayed by the princes of the Nome of the Antelopes was shared by their contemporaries, even if the scenes in their graves depicted only a few pairs of wrestlers. The most interesting of these scenes is that found in the grave of Neheri (el-Bersheh), where a referee stands between two combatants and speaks the sentence, "Do what you will."[41] Perhaps one wrestler, who is apparently on the verge of dominating his opponent, is receiving permission to exploit his advantage in whatever manner he can. Finally, it is worth mentioning that it is only from the Middle Kingdom that we have objets d'art with a wrestling motif. Statuettes of wrestlers can be seen in four museums and collections.[42]

The evidences of wrestling from the New Kingdom are considerably fewer, but they illuminate a new aspect of the sport. The theme of wrestling appears frequently on clay and limestone shards, where it takes the form of a hasty sketch in which the actors occasionally appear with their hair arranged in a manner reminiscent of the *cirrus in vertice* of Roman athletes.[43] The head is shaved except for a number of tufts and a lock that hangs from the part. During the New Kingdom, the custom of naked wrestling, the dominant mode at Beni Hasan, was abandoned. Except for those figures scratched upon shards, wrestlers were always clothed with a short skirt of the sort worn principally by soldiers. Thus it seems that the group identity of the wrestlers had not changed from that of the Middle Kingdom. Also new was the arrival on the scene of an ethnic group associated with wrestling even to the present. Nubian soldiers seemed simply predestined for this sport because of their commanding physiques. In the grave of Tjanuni (eighteenth dynasty) a group of Nubian wrestlers appears among the soldiers whose standard refers to their specialization. A placard attached to a pole is decorated with a pair of wrestlers (fig. 44). Their festively feathered legs could also indicate that the troop is on its way to a match. A pair of Nubian wrestlers also appears on a stone block from the reign of Amenophis IV, who named himself Akhenaten and moved the capital to Amarna (fig. 45).[44] The wrestlers on the Amarna stone wear skirts from the cords of which hang small, globular shapes. To this day the Nubian wrestlers, whose life Leni Riefenstahl documented in an impressive book of photographs, wear skirts to which they attach calabash gourds (fig. 46).

In the New Kingdom, wrestling matches were a part of the program for such ceremonies as the pharaoh's acceptance of tribute from the Sudan. At

44 Nubian wrestlers, tomb of Tjanuni, TT 74 (eighteenth dyn.)

any rate, four pairs of wrestlers are scattered among the colorful crowd of people who have gathered on this occasion before the throne of Akhenaten (shown in the tomb of Merire II). Two of the pairs have reached the end of their match. The victor raises his arms in a gesture of jubilation while the defeated man lies on the ground in a position of piety or exhaustion.[45]

A wrestling event that took place beneath the audience balcony of Ramesses III occurred with international flair.[46] The palace window opened upon the first courtyard of the royal funerary temple (fig. 47). The king is portrayed on both sides of the window in the pose of a victor

45 Wrestlers and fencers, block from the Amarna period (eighteenth dyn.)

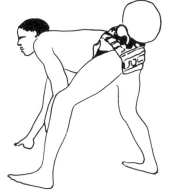

46 Modern Nuba wrestlers, Sudan

---

striking down the defeated enemy. The base of the window is composed of the sculpted heads of the same alien peoples who appear in the wall below the window in carved scenes of fencing and wrestling (fig. 48). Each pair is made up of an Egyptian and one of a number of different foreign opponents. Negroes, Libyans, and Syrians, the traditional enemies of Egypt, are each shown to have been defeated by their Egyptian opponents (fig. 49). Of the ten pairs, seven are engaged in wrestling (fig. 50). Among the spectators who flank the wrestlers are foreign ambassadors, as well as the princes and

---

47 Court with audience window, Medinet Habu, temple of Ramesses III (twentieth dyn.)

48 *Audience window of Ramesses III, Medinet Habu*

aristocracy of Egypt. Since the Egyptians are invariably victorious, the diplomatic officials must witness the defeat of their countrymen. The visual theme of the king victorious in war is thus replicated in the sport scenes, which also serve to buttress the royal dogma. The entire composition seems to imitate a representation from the Ramesseum, the funerary Temple of Ramesses II.[47] Aspects of the model are introduced into the later depiction, for example, the two central pairs demonstrating the proud stance of the winner and the impotence of the loser.

The captions refer to the presence of the pharaoh. The referee, who holds a trumpet, presumably to announce the beginning and the end of

49 *Contests beneath the audience window of Ramesses III, Medinet Habu, detail*

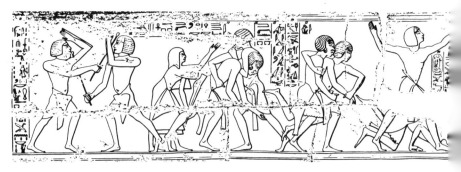

50 *Wrestlers beneath the audience window of Ramesses III, Medinet Habu*

the match, says, "Pay attention, you are in the presence of your lord, the pharaoh—long may he live, hale and hearty." Elsewhere, an Egyptian wrestler warns his opponent, "Watch out! I'm grabbing your leg and throwing you on your side in the presence of the pharaoh—long may he live, hale and hearty."

Another text may well shed further light on the whole representation. An Egyptian wrestler fighting against a Libyan, whom he seems to confuse with another opponent, speaks, "On guard, you hostile Syrian bragging at the mouth! My lord the pharaoh—long may he live, hale and hearty—is with me and against you."[48]

While there can be no doubt that wrestling matches in the presence of the reigning monarch were staged on festive occasions, we cannot exclude the possibility that wrestling and fencing matches also occurred to honor deceased royalty. In the tomb of Amenmose (nineteenth dynasty) these contests stand in close connection with the statue-shrine of the deified Tuthmosis III (fig. 51).[49] A pair of stick fighters and two pairs of wrestlers,

51 *Wrestlers and stick fighters before the statue of Tuthmosis III, tomb of Amenmose, TT 19 (nineteenth dyn.)*

who are clearly in the first and last phases of their matches, are separated by an inscription repeating the cries of the wrestlers. The right-hand wrestler of the group on the left says, "On guard, you miserable, boastful soldier!" His opponent replies, "I'll leave it to you to say what foolishness it is to lay a hand on one of His Majesty's soldiers!" The victorious wrestler announces, "Amun is the god who commands our ruler's victory over every land."[50]

A question now arises: have we an example here of the funeral games that were at a later period such a widespread event throughout Greece?[51] The Greek custom is attested as early as the late thirteenth century B.C., when it was pictured on a Mycenaean larnax (clay sarcophagus).[52] These games in honor of the dead could have been a part either of the actual burial rites or of a periodic ceremony in memory of the deceased. The unique Egyptian source from the time of the pharaohs should probably be classified as the latter, since Tuthmosis III was already dead for more than a century when the scene referred to above was placed in the tomb of Amenmose at the beginning of the nineteenth dynasty (around 1300 B.C.). If it were, on the other hand, a depiction of funeral games, it would be to the best of my knowledge the oldest evidence we have for this custom.[53]

Stick Fighting

During the New Kingdom, stick fighting, which the ancient Egyptians saw as closely related to wrestling, became quite popular. It has already been suggested above that the Egyptians liked to include both in their sport programs. In addition to their presence in the picture placed before the statue-shrine of Tuthmosis III (fig. 51), which may have been a depiction of funeral games, and in the representation of "international" competition beneath the audience balcony of Ramesses III (fig. 48), the two kinds of athletes appear together in the tribute ceremony at the feet of Amenophis IV. The first three persons in the above-mentioned wrestling group from the tomb of Tjanuni carry staves that hint at their twofold qualification (fig. 44).[54] Similarly, both disciplines are represented on the Amarna Stone, upon which the Nubian wrestlers and stick fighters are depicted (fig. 45). In a departure from convention, a shard pictures a stick fighter opposed to a wrestler.[55]

There are, moreover, representations in which stick fighters are the sole motif. In one case they stand in close contact with boxers. Whether or not stick fighting was imported from Asia, as some scholars suspect, cannot be determined.[56] At any rate, the staff as a weapon and symbol of majesty had a tradition that antedated the New Kingdom, and there is proof that it was used at least once for sport.

Some of the staves used for stick fighting have survived to our own times, among them a number from the tomb of Tutankhamon. They are approximately a meter in length and often branch at the lower end to provide a surer grip (fig. 52). The upper end is occasionally strengthened with a bit of metal (fig. 53).[57]

A comparative evaluation of the representations of stick fighting is made

---

52 *Fighting sticks, dagger, arrows, and bows from the tomb of Ramesses III, Thebes, Valley of the Kings no. 11*

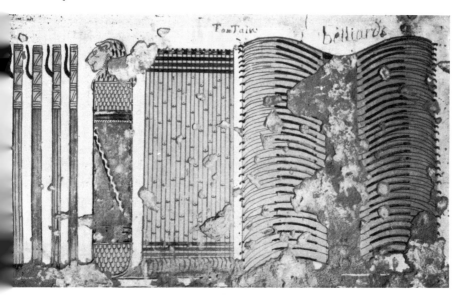

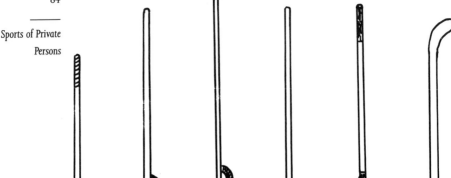

53 Fighting sticks of various types

possible not only by commentaries on variants of the discipline but also, to a certain degree, by modern reconstructions of the match. Before the combat, the fighters bowed to the public. To start the match, the weapons were crossed. After this ceremony, the striking, parrying, and feinting began. One can imagine the swiftly changing scene, with the staves used for hacking, not for thrusting. Of the types of modern fencing, saber matches are the closest equivalent.

To protect themselves against painful blows, the Egyptians thought of various devices. One such was a shieldlike board, fastened to the forearm and reaching to the fingertips. Another was a band, perhaps of leather, to cover the forehead and the chin, as is the case with the stick fighters represented in the scene under the balcony of Ramesses III in Medinet Habu (fig. 54). When not wearing such protective equipment, the fighters generally carry a weapon in each hand (fig. 55). Some staves were equipped with basketlike handguards to protect the fingers. Old-fashioned curved sticks were also used, some of which ended in a knob. Archeologists have found only one staff so long and heavy that it had to be wielded with two hands (as is customary with the staves used by twentieth-century Egyptian stick fighters).[58] Most of the stick fighters wore skirts like those of Egyptian soldiers, which naturally gives us a clue as to their origin. In addition to impromptu bouts, matches can be divided into those fought at ceremonial occasions in the presence of the king and those that were an aspect of religious cult. In the context of the third Sed Festival, pictured in the tomb of Kheruef, numerous pairs fight with papyrus stems while workers raise the Djed-pillar, symbol of the holy cult of Osiris (fig. 56).[59] The symbolism

54 Stick fighters, audience window of Ramesses III, Medinet Habu

55 Ostrakon with stick fighters, Deir el-Medina (twentieth dyn.), Louvre E 25304o

56 *Stick fighters with papyrus stems, tomb of Kheruef, TT 192 (eighteenth dyn.)*

was apparent because the purpose of this ceremony was the regeneration of the king, and the Egyptian ideogram for "green," "young," "fresh"—read as w3d—has the form of the papyrus plant. This scene forms a station in the "Dramatic Papyrus from the Ramesseum," an ancient ritual book followed during the eve of the jubilee ceremony for Sesostris I (twelfth dynasty).

In the tomb of Kheruef the antagonists are called the "people of Pe" and the "people of Dep," two cities which at an early date were merged into the city of Buto. These sites played an important part in the myth of Horus. Upon all the visible combatants, including the boxers, the words appear, "grab hold [in the sense of 'carry out combat sports'] for Horus Appearing in Truth [i.e., for Amenophis III]." From this one might conclude that a mythical battle for the god Horus was the model for the cultic scene.[60]

From the perspective of sports technique it should be noted that one group of three stick fighters departs from the customary pattern of paired combatants. A challenging question from one of the officials to a superfluous but eager athlete—"You (still) don't have an opponent?"—reminds one of the practice of Greek sports.[61] For tournaments carried out through the elimination system (wrestling, boxing, pancration), it was the Greek custom for opponents to be paired by lots. To draw a bye meant that one advanced without a match to the next round. Perhaps this scene from the tomb of Kheruef is the first to dramatize the plight of an *ephedros* (bystander) whose stage fright and impatience have flung him into unwanted motion.[62]

Thanks to the attentiveness of O. Keel we are aware of another stick fighting scene, which can be called not merely singular but positively spectacular.[63] Depicted in the tomb of Khons (nineteenth dynasty) is a processional bark of the god Month with rowboat in tow. The boat carries a baldachin upon the roof of which two stick fighters are engaged in combat (fig. 57). This is understandable in light of the fact that Month was the Egyptian god of war. The naturally defined surface upon which the combat occurs can easily be likened to a modern boxing ring.

We can also consider as a kind of stick fighting the duel carried out by two figures in a small papyrus boat. With unorthodox stances, they hold aloft their sticks or staves, which they grasp with both hands.[64] The Greek historian Herodotus, who journeyed through the Nile Valley in the middle of the fifth century B.C., was still able to witness stick fighting as a central part of a cult ceremony in the city of Papremis, in the delta of the Nile (II 63). Although the account given by Herodotus suggests a kind of riot, a sportlike cultic scene was presumably the intention, one with roots in the distant past. The "Dramatic Papyrus from the Ramesseum" was also possibly part of the tradition of this event, which may have had its origins in the age of the pyramids.[65]

Boxing

Boxing constituted the third combat sport, for which, however, the Egypt of the pharaohs has left us but a single source. This comes from the tomb of Kheruef, where pairs of boxers join the stick fighters associated with the ritual of erection of the Djed-pillar (fig. 58).[66] The erection of

---

57 Stick fighters atop a Cabin, tomb of Khons, TT *31* (eighteenth dyn.)

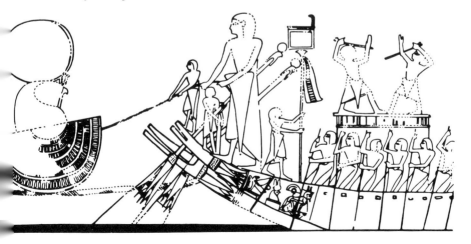

58 Boxing, tomb of Kheruef, TT *192* (eighteenth dyn.)

this cult symbol during the course of the third Sed Festival of Amenophis III was accompanied by dancing, music, and combat sports. Altogether, six groups of boxers are shown in various combat stances, some of which are repeated. Their fists are quite unprotected. Surprisingly, four boxers let one arm hang down while the other is bent and held above the head. These figures mirror rather exactly the poses of the dancers portrayed opposite them. The otherwise skillful Egyptian artist who fashioned these scenes seems not to have been familiar with boxing. Perhaps, as suggested by the paucity of sources, boxing occurred only occasionally in ancient Egypt. The boxer groups appear with inscriptions consisting of the words 'mnt and ndr, which occur only in this pugilistic context. DeVries, concluding from the stance of the boxers that ndr must refer to an aggressive action, has translated the term as "to strike." Since the other term, 'mnt, is clearly associated with a defensive position, DeVries has suggested "to protect" as its meaning.[67] Despite a lingering doubt, it does seem reasonable to see the pairs as boxers, not least because they are placed in such close proximity to the stick fighters whose participation in a sport cannot be questioned.

It should also be noted that DeVries classifies as boxers one of the pairs of athletes whose sporting performance enlivens the scene from tomb of Merire II, in which emissaries from the South offer tribute to Akhenaten. H. Wilsdorf, however, categorizes them decisively as wrestlers.[68] In my view, the unfortunate state of the fresco and the lack of an accompanying text prevent us from reaching a definite conclusion about the exact nature of the illustrated combat sport.

Aquatic Sports

Swimming

Swimming did not have the same place in ancient Egyptian education as it did in Plato's *Laws* (3.689d), where it is expressly named as something every educated person should learn. Egyptian sources nonetheless give the impression that those who had mastered the skill had reached a higher level of culture than those who had not. From the sixth dynasty comes the biography of Herchuf, who led many expeditions to Nubia and transported the precious goods of the South to the capital. He managed to persuade a pygmy to accompany him on the journey back to Egypt. Whether he bought him, coerced him with threats to board the ship, or persuaded him voluntarily to join the Egyptian troops is not explained. The pygmy, who is slated to gladden his majesty as a royal dancing dwarf, is carefully watched night and day during the voyage down the Nile. The guard is to check on him ten times during the night, and the officer in charge bears the responsibility for ensuring "that he doesn't fall into the water."[69] One hears the subliminal message: if he *did* fall overboard he would drown, and thus diminish the success of the expedition Herchuf has conducted.

In the Egyptian view, hostile peoples were unable to swim, and they proved themselves by this inadequacy to be inferior to the pharaoh. This was demonstrated in the famous Battle of Kadesh on the Orontes, where the Hittite troops set a trap for the Egyptians under Ramesses II, then in the fifth year of his reign.[70] The Egyptian report of the battle credits the Egyptians' escape to the superhuman bravery of the king. Directly relevant to our topic—the foreigners' inability to swim—is the experience of the Hittite prince. During the battle he fell into the water and was rescued by the time-honored technique of standing him on his head and, ignoring the indignity done to the reputation of their leader, shaking him dry of swallowed water.[71]

It is likely that the art of swimming was more widely known in the Nile

Valley than we might conclude from the relatively small body of evidence. It is probable that nearly all Egyptians, living as they did on the Nile or on one of the canals branching from the river, knew how to swim for utilitarian purposes. This was especially true for fishermen and boatmen, for whom the ability to swim was a life-or-death matter, but we are not justified in asserting that everyone involved in these water-related occupations knew how to swim. It would also be wrong to assume that knowing how to swim led automatically to swimming contests. If we compare the Greek situation with the Egyptian we can quickly establish the fact that swimming contests were extraordinary exceptions in both cultures.[72]

Unambiguous proof of an early knowledge of the art of swimming is contained in the form of crockery tops and hieroglyphics in the shape of swimmers (fig. 59), most of whom are portrayed doing what seems to be a version of the crawl. Propulsion by alternating arms is certainly a characteristic of these representations, but there is no reason to wonder at this fact because, even today, unpracticed swimmers are likely to use the "dog paddle." We must not, however, equate the ancient and the modern techniques, nor should we conclude that the Egyptians anticipated the invention of the modern crawl, the fastest of strokes, by Prince Kahanmoku of Hawaii in the early twentieth century.[73] Even older than these hieroglyph-form Old Kingdom swimmers are those of Libyan cave paintings. According to E. Mehl, the leading expert on the history of ancient swimming, these swimmers are doing the butterfly stroke,[74] but it seems to me that

59 *Swimming, hieroglyphics on a jug top (first dyn.)*

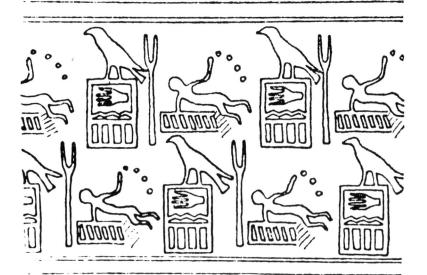

the room for individual interpretation is too great in the case of these
paintings to permit a definitive answer. Mehl was doubtless correct to
assert that the deserts of North Africa, familiar to us, had not yet come to
dominate the environment of the burgeoning ripine cultures that produced these pictures. In his original, overly ingenious view, Mehl classified the technique of these swimmers as midway between the crawl and
the breast stroke, but he revised his opinions after the introduction
of the butterfly stroke into modern sports, and he now thinks that the
swimmers of the Libyan wastes used this technique. The obvious counter
to his argument is that the discovery of a technique in the twentieth century A.D. proves nothing whatsoever about its existence in the fourth millennium B.C.

Fortunately, the rather vague archeological evidence is complemented
by written sources that transmit reliable information. The oldest of these
documents is also the fullest. It derives from Kheti, the prince of Siut, who
lived toward the end of the third millennium B.C. The biography found in
his tomb describes the prince as a clever organizer and a capable warrior.
The list of his accomplishments, which is very individualized in comparison to most of the tomb biographies, includes a passage emphasizing
that Kheti enjoyed the king's favor. Kheti claims, "He allowed me to take
swimming lessons (nbj) together with his own children."[75]

This distinction given to him in childhood, of which he was so proud
that he referred to it in his tomb for all posterity to read, reflects historical
reality because it is unique. It is, in other words, no meaningless com-
monplace of funerary rhetoric. The communication is even more informative than appears at first glance.[76] We see that the king takes a personal
interest in the education of his sons, which is conducted along with that of
the children of the high aristocracy. Swimming belongs in this educational
program. The lessons in question are given by a swimming instructor.
There is no need to imagine a special courtly official for this purpose. The
procedure was most likely that followed when the young Amenophis II
received archery lessons from the nomarch Min of This; a nobleman
who had proved himself an especially capable swimmer passed his knowledge on to his young charge. We can also be certain that the king too
learned swimming as a child, because the crown prince must have been
among the "children of the king."

A numerous and well-documented group of artifacts is composed of the
so-called spoons in the shape of a female swimmer (fig. 60).[77] These objects were used to dispense ointments, presumably such as those used
daily to anoint the statues of a cult. The handle was in the shape of a naked
girl with outstretched arms and legs. She holds the bowl of the spoon in
her hands and thus appears as if she were in the gliding phase of the breast

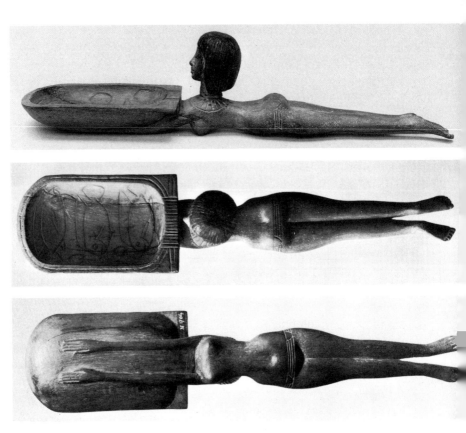

60 *Swimming girls as spoon handles (eighteenth dyn.), Louvre N. 1704*

stroke. Occasionally it looks as if the maiden were doing the kick part of the crawl. This impression that she is a swimmer is strengthened by the body of the spoon, which is often in the form of a fish or of a duck the wings of which can move together to seal the open bowl (fig. 61). That this type of spoon, which has come down to us in some quite lovely versions, really does represent a swimming girl cannot be proven, but, although a degree of skepticism seems in order, there is no reason to reject out of hand a characterization that has a long history in Egyptology.

In favor of the traditional interpretation is the fact that swimming maidens in postures like that of the spoon handles occur elsewhere in Egyptian art. The decor of a silver bowl of the twenty-second dynasty, for instance, is formed by a group of girls who are swimming, diving, and reaching for fish and waterfowl (fig. 62).[78] This motif of the swimming girl also appears on a shard (twentieth dynasty) now in Turin and on the handle of an ointment bowl (eighteenth dynasty) in Berlin (figs. 63 and 64).[79] The motif occurs in love poetry as well, where the maid pulls a fish from the water and hands it to her beloved.[80]

61 *Swimming girl as spoon handle (eighteenth dyn.), Louvre N. 1725 b.*

In the New Kingdom, especially during the Amarna period, the garden of a well-appointed upper-class home contained a rectangular artificial pond (fig. 65). Even without the evidence, one can assume that the basin, like that of a modern swimming pool, was filled with water and used for

62 *Bowl with swimming girls, tomb of Psusennes I (twenty-second dyn.), Tanis no. 775, Cairo JE 87 742*

Marcelle Baud

63 Ostrakon with swimming girl, Turin

swimming and diving. At least the size of the basin, which also served as a reservoir for watering the garden, makes such use a possibility. In addition, just as in the Near East, such pools functioned as natural air conditioners and beautified the garden, allowing those plants to thrive which need water to flourish.

As already indicated, competitive swimming is unmentioned in the Egyptian sources. Yet there exists in the literature a reference to an aquatic

64 Ointment bowl with swimming girl (eighteenth dyn.), Berlin *14 076*

65 *Artificial pond in garden, tomb of Sobkhotep, TT 63 (eighteenth dyn.)*

contest which presupposes the ability to swim. The gods Horus and Seth, engaged in a struggle for dominion over the universe, agree to settle their differences by means of a diving contest, the details of which will be discussed later.[81] At least once, moreover, diving was visually represented. In the tomb of Djar (eleventh dynasty) in Thebes we can see an upside-down diving fisherman whose head is touching the bottom of a draw-net attached to a boat (fig. 66).[82] He is adjusting the weights of the net, which have become disordered, or he is clearing a net that has been caught by water plants.

66 Diving, tomb of Djar,
Deir el-Bahri (eleventh dyn.)

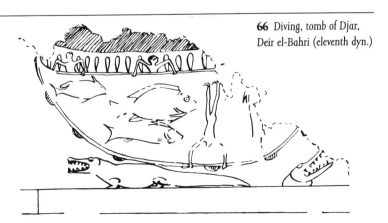

A number of those who have concerned themselves with the monument that Amenophis II consecrated in a temple lying across from the sphinx have interpreted a passage in the inscription as a description of the crown prince as an oarsman. As has already been mentioned, the theme of the Sphinx Stela is the king's athletic achievements which, according to the royal dogma of the period, join with the virtues of the warrior and the hunter to determine the picture of the ideal monarch. But the activity of rowing in the company of other oarsmen is in no way appropriate to the position of the pharaoh. Textual remains also require us to revise this notion of an oarsman prince. The "rowing episode" follows a mention of the prince's ability as a swift runner and his knowledge of horsemanship and archery. The text reads as follows:

> Strong were (his) two arms, so that he was not tired when he grasped the rudder and steered from the stern of the falcon ship and governed its two hundred men. They stopped after they had brought forth (an achievement of) one-half itrw (a good five kilometers), for they were weak and their limbs had grown tired, and they could no longer breathe. His Majesty, however, was powerful with his rudder of twenty ells' length. When he ceased and his falcon ship made land, he had brought forth (an achievement of) three itrw (around thirty-one kilometers) in steering, and without a pause in his hold on the rudder. The faces of those who beheld him as he did this were full of admiration.[83]

The philological grounds for this translation are given elsewhere.[84] The office of helmsman is appropriate for the king. He determines the direction of the voyage and the initiative of the oarsmen. (This conception led later to the metaphor of "the ship of state.") Steering a boat with two hundred oarsmen is moreover a physically strenuous activity. The power of the helmsman is exemplified by the "ship of the sun" of Cheops, discovered in a grave near his pyramid and reassembled from parts found in the vicinity.[85] It is worth mentioning that the Sphinx Stela refers to spectators who witness the king's marvelous deed. Whether the reference is to the oarsmen of the boat or to a public posted on the banks of the river, which seems more probable, is not clear in the text.

In yet another way, the king is connected to rowing. In the eighteenth dynasty a number of soldiers were singled out for promotion because they were conspicuous in serving the king as oarsmen. Interestingly, this evidence comes from the reign of Amenophis II.[86]

According to an ancient Egyptian fairy tale, King Cheops, the builder of the Great Pyramid, sought to banish boredom by listening to stories of marvelous events. In one of these stories, his predecessor Snofru seeks uncertainly for a way to cheer himself up. His wonder-producing head priest suggests that cheerfulness can be obtained through the aesthetic experience of rowing. The rowboat ride across the Lake of Pleasure is erotically stimulating because the crew consists of twenty shapely young maidens dressed only in nets, the garment of Hathor, the goddess of love.[87] "They rowed back and forth and the heart of His Majesty was glad to see them row." The idyll is disturbed by the mishap of one of the rowing maidens. She loses a bit of jewelry that can be recovered only by the magician who has arranged the boat ride, because only he can part the waters and bring the two halves together again.[88]

A regular regatta of rowboats is not to be found in the Egyptian sources, although it is not difficult to imagine that boats' crews held impromptu races and endurance contests. It is unclear whether or not a difficult passage in the myth of Horus and Seth refers to a race between the boats of the two quarreling gods. As claimants to the inheritance of the king of the gods, they want to settle their dispute by means of a diving contest, but circumstances prevent this (see p. 107). A further contest, involving boats, is agreed upon. The Egyptian word *trr*, which appears only in this passage, might mean "to ride for a wager." We can, however, with the same degree of probability conceive of the contest as a popular fishermen's sport in which each tried with a long pole to push the other from his boat into the water.[89]

Although we are not well informed about the sport of rowing in ancient Egypt, we can say something about the rowing technique involved because we have reconstructions based on visual representations of the numerous transport vessels that plied the Nile, its tributaries, and the Mediterranean coast. Since there is no indication that special boats were built for sports, we can assume that ordinary equipment was used for competition (fig. 67). Virgil's *Aeneid* (v 113–258) casts some light upon the darkness when the poet describes a fictional regatta that presumably resembles the reality of the first century B.C., when ordinary naval vessels were used for races.

The question of Egyptian rowing technique was first raised around 1930, when scholars from the famous expedition to Punt began to speculate on the different sorts of oar handling exhibited by the crews depicted in the funeral temple of Hatshepsut at Deir el Bahri.[90] The conclusion reached at that time, based on simulation of stroke phases that were not pictured, was that Egyptian rowing technique was characterized by a cyclical alternation of sitting and standing (fig. 68). It was also assumed that the blade remained in the water during the entire cycle. This surprising conclusion included the assumption that the stroke frequency reached forty per minute, which is what one expects today for an eight-oared racing shell. One's doubts are further aroused by the claim that the blade of the oar was "feathered," so

67 Rowers, temple of Hatshepsut (eighteenth dyn.), Deir el-Bahri

that the edge cut the water during the backstroke. This last claim was made with the help of a cinematographic device to reconstruct the four stroke phases shown in Egyptian representations, but there was no experiment to test the results of the technical reconstruction. Although skepticism was called for, almost fifty years passed before these early conclusions were challenged. Recent experiments, together with a wider evidential base and a more sophisticated awareness of the peculiarities of Egyptian artistic representation, have forced a revision.[91] The experiments involved two reconstructed Egyptian rowing stations upon a pontoon boat tied to the banks of the Rhine River. Egyptian equipment, including the oar itself, was duplicated as closely as possible, but the effort to row with the reconstructed equipment and techniques was a total failure.[92]

The actual characteristics of Egyptian rowing technique in the eighteenth dynasty were as follows: scholars were right to assume a cycle of alternating of sitting and standing; also correct was the notion that the oar was held in both hands. The stroke begins with the oarsman standing; during the pull, he sits on the knee-high board seat (figs. 69 and 70). At the

end of the pull, the hands push the oar downward so that the blade
emerges from the water. At the same time, the inner leg is drawn back so
that the oarsman can stand again. After the recovery, the legs are brought
together again. The tempo of the more or less circular movement is
damped. It is easy to see why the rowers' skirts had to be made of leather;
ordinary cloth would quickly have been worn through by the constant
sitting down and standing up (fig. 71).[93]

Fishermen's Jousting

When life in the swamps and canals of Egypt is represented on the
walls of the graves of the Old and Middle Kingdoms, scenes of fishing for
food with skeins, draw nets, and hand nets are complemented by a wide
variety of scenes with another theme—fishermen's jousting, which is also
known in the literature under the name of boat jousting. In the New
Kingdom, it disappears as a motif for tomb decorations. The artists seized
upon this realistic subject in such different ways that we can hardly general-
ize about the more than two dozen known representations.[94] Apparently
fishermen's jousting began as an impromptu contest that might have had
its origins in harmless horseplay on the way to work or home again, but it
often intensified to bloody seriousness. Fishermen's jousting involved

68 Rowers in the middle of their stroke, tomb of Sennefer, TT 96 (eighteenth dyn.)

69 Egyptian rowing stroke, initial phase, simulation   **70** Egyptian rowing stroke, final phase, simulation

71 Rowers with leather-reinforced skirts, temple of Hatshepsut (eighteenth dyn.), Deir el-Bahri

two, three, sometimes even four groups who happened to find themselves on shipboard at the same time. These quite maneuverable vessels, constructed of bundles of papyrus reeds, were manned by three, four, or in exceptional cases as many as six men, who performed their work naked or clothed with a short skirt. The long poles with which they maneuvered the boats served them as sporting weapons (fig. 72). Typically those standing on the bow of the boat sought to push their counterparts on the other boat into the water, while their mates stood at the stern, steering and keeping the boat on an even keel. Occasionally the fishermen standing in the middle of the boat entered the fray. When the struggle at a distance failed to bring a decisive result and the boats approached more closely, the poles ceased to be useful and the men engaged in pulling and shoving that sometimes resembled a regular wrestling match.[95] The swaying platform and the efforts of one's opponent were often enough to send one plunging into the water, which after all was the goal sought from the start (fig. 73). This tumble usually ended the contest—if the other members of the crew were not too caught up in the fury of the contest to stop their grappling.

In one example, a member of the team marks the fall of his opponent with a kind of victory gesture, which resembles the gesture of jubilation at the end of a wrestling match or stick fight.[96] The man who has fallen into the water is obviously concerned to reach safety, and there are hands stretched out to help him. From this, we can infer that he probably was

---

72 Fishermen's jousting, tomb of Ptahhotep, Saqqara (fifth dyn.)

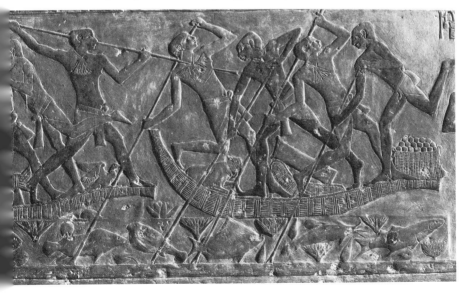

unable to swim. The real danger for anyone who fell from a boat into deep water is dramatically pictured in one scene, in which a lurking crocodile has seized an unfortunate man by the leg.[97] His comrades holding fast are his only hope. Danger also threatens from angry opponents when they consider the effects of the blows from their poles and give up the tacit understanding about limiting the force of their blows (fig. 74). Furiously, they lift their poles high above their heads and accompany the brutal attack with sharp words: "Open his box for him!" In less metaphoric English: "Break his skull open!"[98] Thus the challenge begun with playful intent often ended in bloody duels, and calmer souls were hard put to separate the hotheads. One scene is unique; a crew refuses to accept the challenge offered by the neighboring boat.[99] There were, presumably, no binding regulations for these sportlike encounters. The rules were probably revised from occasion to occasion, depending on the mood. L. Klebs believes that she has found one specially arranged fishermen's joust, viewed by the owner of the tomb, which took place under set rules, but she weakens her own argument when she refers to the unequal numbers in the two boats' crews.[100]

The oversubtle observation that the boats upon which the crews jousted

73 Fishermen's jousting, tomb of Nianchkhmun and Kknumhotep, Saqqara (fifth dyn.)

74 *Fishermen's jousting, tomb of Nefer, Saqqara (fifth dyn.)*

were involved in a contest to see which boat first reached its master ignores the spontaneous character of the duels.[101] The impromptu jousts allow an insight into the emergence of a discipline that doubtless has sport components but which has not yet taken on the seriousness often found in organized sports competition. It seems that the fishermen's joust is attested in no antique culture other than Egypt's, but the custom has been well documented for many of the rivers of central Europe; pictorial evidence exists from early modern times. Even today, in many cities in southern Germany—Ulm and Halle, for instance—there survives a relic of this riverboat sport, doubtless popular among spectators now as then.[102]

5   Competition

For many years scholars maintained that the Greeks were unique among the peoples of the ancient world because they alone had known sports competitions. This belief became an article of faith when it was evoked to explain the allegedly unequaled heights of Greek culture. It was said that the competitive element present in such an unexampled way as the essence of Greek culture had carried the Greeks to their lofty achievements and had created a society significantly superior to the other civilizations of antiquity. The seminal statement of this idea, which owes much to neo-Humanism, was that of the Swiss scholar Jakob Burckhardt. He coined the concept of the "agonistic," using an invented word, which allowed him to collect whatever the entranced historian envisioned as the driving force of Greek culture: rivalry, competition, achievement, ambition, and similar phenomena strikingly characterized by Homer: αἰὲν ἀριστεύειν καὶ ὑπείροχον ἔμμεναι ἄλλων (always to be the best and to excel beyond the others).[1] This idealistic perspective on the Greeks, which dominated the cultural histories of the nineteenth century, was understandable in a period when the archeological investigation of ancient cultures had barely begun. This view must, however, be characterized as one-sided when it either overlooks or denies the results of modern oriental studies. J. Juethner was a justly admired investigator of Greek sports, but his judgment that "sports competitions were not to be found in ancient Egypt"[2] is—like the similar statement by his English colleague E. Norman Gardiner—a formulation that was already outdated when he wrote it.[3] Today such views can be recognized as scholarly positions held as a result

of a long tradition of overvaluation of Greek gymnastics and agonistics. The

Greeks themselves contributed greatly to this evaluation of their sports as ethnically typical when they thought in terms of a Hellenes-Barbarians dichotomy or when they used the institution of the gymnasium as a class barrier, as they did in Hellenistic Egypt.[4]

A critical evaluation of the entire complex of ideas from a universalistic perspective comes inevitably to the conclusion that sport contests were in no sense a genuinely Greek invention. On the contrary, they play a role in nearly every human culture and might well be termed an anthropological constant. This observation is valid for cultures older than that of Greece— those of ancient Egypt and most Asian civilizations. This conclusion does not deny the great significance attributed to sports in Greece, nor the wide palette of contests that colored the sports landscape, nor the important political role played by Greek sports. One can also admit that the unusual breadth of the sources for Greek sports normally overshadows the surviving materials from other ancient cultures. I shall attempt, in what follows, simply to gather the most important sources for sport competitions of the pharaonic age and thus to correct the distorted claims of Greek uniqueness in this area of culture.[5]

Those interested in Egyptian competitions will be struck first of all by representations of wrestling. They survive from the first dynasty and appear most impressively in the form of the hundreds of pairs of wrestlers pictured on the walls of the graves of the nomarchs at Beni Hasan.[6] These remarkable documents of Middle Kingdom sport competition, which were already commented upon in standard nineteenth-century works on Greek sports, should in themselves have warned scholars away from an overvaluation of Greek contests.[7] Next to the representations of wrestling are those of other combat sports such as stick-fighting and boxing, but these are far fewer in number than representations of wrestling.[8] It is in the nature of things that combat sports should be practiced by soldiers, as can be concluded from the juxtaposition of combat sports and martial scenes in the pictures at Beni Hasan. If we compare these scenes with representations of Greek athletic competition, we can see that the latter too were unmistakably stamped by their military origin. Wrestling, boxing, the pancration, the race in armor, the pentathlon, and the chariot race constituted almost the entire program of the ancient Olympic Games. The close connection between sports and warfare is also illustrated in the Olympic dominance of the military state of Sparta, which in its heyday accounted for the majority of Olympic victors.

By 1932 at the latest, every scholar should have known that the ancient Egyptians regularly organized such competitions for a select public. In that year the wrestling and stick fighting scenes from the funerary temple of Ramesses III in Medinet Habu were published in an exemplary edition (fig.

48).[9] The striking thing about these scenes is that, in sharp contrast to the Greek sport practice that made Olympic participation an exclusively Greek privilege, they show sport contests between Egyptians and foreign athletes.

In addition to the enormous number of sources for combat sports derived from man-to-man struggle, one finds further Egyptian material displaying competitive behavior. Thus the frequent representations of fishermen's jousts demonstrate a struggle for team victory like that present in certain types of ball games or in a tug-of-war between two groups.[10]

Common to all the hitherto mentioned sources for Egyptian competitions is the fact that they are visual representations. This kind of evidence is supplemented by written documents that allow a more differentiated consideration of the Egyptian attitude toward competition and that qualitatively expand the conclusions based on the visual material.

The oldest written account of a military contest is preserved in one of the masterworks of Egyptian literature, the "Story of Sinuhe." One of the classics of Egyptian education, it has been transmitted to us in numerous manuscripts.[11] Stimulated by the form of the traditional autobiography and enriched by other genres of Egyptian literature, this tale from the early Middle Kingdom (twelfth dynasty) describes the trial of an Egyptian court official caught in a crisis with which, initially, he cannot cope. He flees to Syria to escape the struggle for the Egyptian throne. There, thanks to his physical and spiritual abilities, he rises to become the chieftain of a tribe. He arouses the envy of a certain "strong man from Retenu," who challenges him to a life-or-death duel.[12]

The description of the duel contains elements that are later to be found in sports. In this context they sound archetypical. Indeed, in order to increase the suspense, the Syrian hero is described as the favorite, but care is taken to keep the contest equal. On the eve of the fight Sinuhe checks his weapons and practices one last time. In the gray of dawn a crowd of excited spectators has already gathered. Married women are present but not maidens, which is precisely the opposite of the Olympic Games, from which married women were barred.[13] Sympathies are with the Egyptian because he seems to be the underdog. Calmness and courage prove to be superior to raw power. Sinuhe slays his opponent, triumphs, and wins the Syrian's estate. This dramatic episode, the high point of the action, evolved into a less bloody form of challenge and duel and had many parallels in other cultures.[14]

Agonistic virtues also characterize the young Egyptian in the fairy tale "Truth and Falsehood." The fairy tale simply follows the standards of the society when it is said of the youth that his skill at weapons surpasses that of his older comrades.[15] Myth, nourished by reality, reveals most clearly how deeply competition was rooted in Egyptian thought. Sport contests are often the means by which urgent questions of existential importance are decided. In the myth "The Quarrel between Horus and Seth" both gods claim to have inherited world dominion from the king of the gods.[16] The effort to settle the quarrel juridically comes to naught. The parties to the quarrel finally agree upon a diving competition to hurry the drawn-out affair to its conclusion. Both gods will submerge. Whichever of the claimants surfaces before three months have passed will be excluded from the inheritance. The divine rivals transform themselves into hippopotamuses, but the course of the competition is distorted by the unforeseen interference of the goddess Isis, who meddles in the event as a partisan. At this point there is a second episode of competition. The text is unclear, but it is probably a boat race for a wager. It is, however, also possible that a kind of fishermen's joust determined the final decision. In any event we see clearly, once again, that a contest is the proper way to decide a difficult legal question.

Since the story is transcribed upon a papyrus that has been dated from the twentieth dynasty, it seems initially to mirror the customs of the New Kingdom. The degree to which the story preserves the views of the Middle Kingdom, during which it was presumably written, can only be surmised. A glance at the duel in the "Story of Sinuhe," however, suggests the possibility that "The Quarrel between Horus and Seth" can also be dated from the Middle Kingdom.

The next item to appear in this chronologically organized summary of Egyptian competitions is the Running Stela of Taharqa (twenty-fifth dynasty). As indicated above, it concerns a long-distance run that was clearly competitive in nature. Pharaoh is not above inspiring the contestants with the proper motivation by running with them for a certain distance and by contributing prizes. Details have already been given.[17] Here, in connection with sources arranged thematically rather than by sporting disciplines, it should be noted only that this text from the seventh century B.C. speaks of competition as something self-evident. Performances of this sort are made possible by daily training. The best runners are honored by a banquet, which recalls the Greek custom.[18] The impression made by this newly discovered inscription, with a motif unexpected for late Egyptian times, can perhaps reduce somewhat the skepticism hitherto directed at a chapter of Herodotus (ii 91).[19] In his *Histories* the famed traveler to Egypt of the fifth century B.C. mentions a gymnastic competition he witnessed at the city of Chemmis. It has been maintained that the inhabitants of the city were merely carrying out a religious ritual that Herodotus, thinking of Greek sports, misunderstood, but a wider acquaintance with Egyptian sport history gives credence to Herodotus.

The reverse of this problem occurred when Egyptians who were not familiar with Greek sports translated Greek agonistic texts into hieroglyphics. One occasion for this terminological difficulty was the funeral games held for Antinoos, the youthful beloved of the Roman emperor Hadrian (second century A.D.), who drowned in the Nile.[20]

Although this survey of the relevant sources for competition documents common Egyptian practice and daily custom, qualifications must be made with regard to the pharaoh. It was not that the pharaoh took no part in sports. The exact opposite is true. As we know, it was a central tenet of the royal dogma that the pharaoh be a mighty warrior and, especially during the eighteenth dynasty, an outstanding athlete. In this regard, nothing stood in the way of his participation in competition. What *did* interfere with his participation was the possibility of comparison with other contestants. Direct competition was too risky because of the theoretical possibility that doubt might be cast upon the superiority required by the royal dogma. With this conception of royalty, it was unthinkable that anyone should question the king's position as guarantor of the world order and victor over the forces of chaos. It is, however, the essence of a sport competition that it identify the winner as the best of those who competed under neutral rules and equal conditions. In this sense, the idea of the agon totally contradicts the basic idea of the Egyptian royal dogma. It is a natural consequence of this dogma that the pharaoh could not be challenged to a sport contest.

Up to now, the only known exception to this tenet is the inscription from Medamud that narrates the story of the pharaoh's participation in an archery contest. This has already been discussed in full in a previous chapter, but it must be mentioned in the present context that Amenophis II, the unbeatable archer of the report, appears as the challenger after his masterful shot has set the standard.[21] The horror that might have occurred if a mortal had boldly acted upon the king's challenge is somewhat diminished by the presumed powerlessness of the other contestants to equal the king's performance. In the end, the requirements of the royal dogma are satisfied. Nonetheless, it is probable that the ideal and the actual coincided for Amenophis II, at least in the area of sport archery. This, at any rate, is a reasonable conclusion from a study of the relevant inscriptions.

Before we conclude our discussion of ancient Egyptian competition with a commentary on one last source, I should like to make an observation that has not, to the best of my knowledge, been made by earlier writers. For well-known reasons, the royal dogma acted to forbid the pharaoh's participation in sport contests. This ban acknowledged the exceptional status of the monarch. The king could not diminish his worth by competing as an equal against mere mortal men. To compete against an equal was impossible because there was only one person to hold the rank of king. In the eighteenth dynasty, however, one great exception to the rule against sports competition became thinkable when it was realized that the chains previously preventing competition might be struck off with the formula "extension of that which exists." The king might compete with his predecessors and his successors. The recorded sport achievements of a king could be surpassed by another king. In this way one remained with one's peers and nonetheless responded to the demands of the age, which called for achievement and, as proof of this virtue, for competition.

As has been indicated, one more document remains to conclude this chapter. Like the previous one, it touches upon the milieu of the king. The person in question is the king's son. The fairy tale "The Doomed Prince" breathes the spirit of the New Kingdom.[22] For the sake of adventure, an Egyptian prince undertakes a journey to the Middle East, to the valley of the Tigris and Euphrates. The ruler of Naharin has arranged for a contest to determine who will marry his only daughter. She dwells in a house whose window is some thirty-seven meters above the ground. The goal is to reach this window. The native princes have already tried and failed to meet the test when the Egyptian prince arrives incognito. He rides in a chariot with a driver and a hunting dog. The etiquette is well understood: the newly arrived guest receives a bath, his horse is given fodder, his companion is cared for. The sequence is informative. Only when all courtesies have been extended is the Egyptian prince queried about his origins, but he keeps his identity a secret.

> Many days afterward he said to the young princes, "What are you doing, young people?" They answered him, "It's already been three (?) full months that we've spent jumping because whoever reaches the window of the daughter of the prince of Naharin will have her as his bride." Then he said to them, "Ah, if my feet weren't injured, I'd go jump with you." Then they went jumping, as they did every day. The young man stood at a distance and watched. Then the face of the daughter of the prince of Naharin turned toward him. Several days later, the young man came to join the princes in their leaping. He jumped high and reached the window of the daughter of the prince of Naharin. She kissed him and embraced all his limbs.[23]

Despite the initial resistance of her father, the Egyptian prince married the princess.

The papyrus that has preserved for us this not-quite-finished story comes from the beginning of the nineteenth dynasty. Thus it is relatively close in time to the unique account of a pharaoh's participation in a contest, the inscription of Amenophis II from Medamud. Since the king's son is not under the sway of the royal dogma, the story "The Doomed Prince" is not a second exception to the rule. The fairy-tale competition for the bride, from which the Egyptian prince emerges as victor over the noble youth of Mesopotamia, mirrors the self-confidence of the New Kingdom.

In this Egyptian papyrus from the thirteenth century B.C. we have the first written version of a motif encountered in other parts of the world. Within the context of sport history, this motif became famous in connection with the myth of the founding of the Olympic Games by Pelops. A stranger from Asia Minor, Pelops had to defeat King Oinomaos of Pisa in a chariot race in order to win the hand of the king's daughter Hippodameia. Pelops won the kingdom as well, and a Mycenaean settlement near Pisa became the cultic site of the Olympic Games.[24]

This investigation of the Egyptian sources has shown that sport competitions occurred in many forms in the Nile Valley in the age of the pharaohs. Older opinions that maintained the opposite rested upon insufficient knowledge of the sources or were the result of an idealized view of the Greeks. They are no longer tenable. Under the influence of the athletic Amenophis II, even the royal dogma, diametrically opposed to the concept of sport competition, had to give way in the eighteenth dynasty to an exception: the king as contestant.

6   Games

Ball Games

In no ancient culture did ball games have the extensive and significant role that they play today. The Romans can be shown to have come the closest to a preference for this kind of sport.[1] It is striking that, in contrast to our own day, when almost every kind of ball game lays claim to its own field, court, or hall, no such artificial space exclusively for ball games has survived from antiquity. Even the *sphairisterion*, often cited in this context, was more probably a training room for boxers than a court for ballplayers.[2] Technological progress has contributed greatly to the later development of ball games. Improvements in the materials for balls seem to have contributed a great deal to the interest in ball games, as did the techniques for the production of hollow balls.[3] Our picture of ancient Egyptian ball games conforms closely to these general considerations.

The first thing to be noted is that we have quite a number of original balls made from a broad variety of materials but that all of them—with a single exception—are stuffed or solid, not filled with air. The best of them consist of leather strips, as many as twelve in number, sewn around a core of straw, reeds, hair, yarn, or chaff (fig. 75). In appearance they resemble the balls used for the German game of *Schlagball* (somewhat similar to baseball). Such balls are still used by today's children although they are much less common than they were (fig. 76). Simple coverless balls were fashioned from wood, clay, papyrus or palm leaves. The diameter of the extant balls ranges from three to nine centimeters.[4] The highly breakable hollow

75 Balls with leather covers, Cairo JE 43 981, 43 982

76 Balls with clay overlays and straw decorations, Hannover 1976, 58 a–d

faience balls with imitation leather segments could have been used only by real experts—if they did not serve exclusively as funerary objects with no actual sport use.

The material characteristics of the balls set natural bounds to their possible use in sports. Basically only two types of ball games can be seen in visual representations from daily life, and written texts have nothing to add to this body of evidence. Both types can be distinguished in two separate ways. The first group includes catching and juggling games. In both of the documents in which they appear, they are exclusively women's games. For the other type, a bat of some kind is necessary. This second type occurred in the eighteenth dynasty and then, after a pause of a millennium, in the Ptolemaic period. We have every reason to believe that it was already rigidly ritualized at the time of its first appearance.

If we turn to the first type, we discover ball games pictured in the tombs of two nomarchs of the early Middle Kingdom. Although the tombs contain the famous representations of wrestling, which I have mentioned several times already, the ball games appear in connection with exclusively female occupations.[5] The rows of pictures in which the ball games appear contain spinning and weaving as well as some further sports or sportlike activities (jumping, spinning about, forming a bridge by bending backward, and—perhaps—running on all fours).

The ballplay scenes under discussion can be differentiated with respect to various conceptions of play.[6] It is easy to recognize juggling. Skillful girls keep three balls in the air, a feat that, incidentally, Greek women also had in their repertory. When the catching is done with crossed arms, the level of skill is heightened to a point that is, after millennia, still breathtaking. The accompanying word jmḏ, which occurs nowhere else, presumably denotes the name of the game.[7]

There are also two parallel scenes for the second kind of game, a kind of rhythmic throwing and catching. Two small groups of three female players stand across from each other. The two outer members of each group clap their hands to a certain rhythm in accordance with which the girls posted in the middle throw the ball. Once again, we have an accompanying word, rwjt, that seems to name the game and that occurs nowhere else.[8] We cannot exclude the possibility that this was a team game. At least the fact that the two groups of players are numerically even allows for this interpretation. If we conjecture the rules from what is pictured of the game, we can imagine that the point of the game was for the players to take turns stepping forward from their row to throw and to catch the ball, but there is no way that we can guess from the materials we have what the consequences were for a badly thrown or dropped ball.

A kind of mounted ball game (fig. 77) that appears as a third variant was

77 Riding ball game, tomb of Kheti, Beni Hasan no. *17* (eleventh dyn.)

also known in Greek antiquity, under the name of *ephedrismos*, but there is no need to posit a connection between the Greek and the Egyptian games. Two girls, each carrying a girl on her back, stand across from each other while the sitting girls throw a ball back and forth. If the Egyptian rules were the same as the Greek, a missed ball meant an exchange of positions.[9]

The great twentieth-century German author Thomas Mann was inspired artistically by these ballplaying girls from Beni Hasan. In his novel *Joseph and His Brothers* ball games are a colorful event during the grape harvest: "There were ball games too, and the girls were skillful at keeping several balls in the air at once with their crossed arms or in setting themselves upon each other's hips."[10] The harmless character of these pastimes is emphasized in a passage of the pyramid texts where the dead enjoy a ball game.[11] This aspect is also stressed when ball games appear in animal fables.[12]

Distinguishable from true sports are two rituals that consist formally of elements of ball games but whose function is to destroy the enemies of the gods or to protect the god Osiris. The first ritual, bearing the title "Hitting the Ball," appears nineteen times from the eighteenth dynasty on, mostly in the temples of the Ptolemaic period.[13]

In the oldest depiction of a ball game, Tuthmosis III stands before the god Hathor. In his right hand he holds a bent stick of olive wood (fig. 78) and in his left a ball.[14] In other representations, the stick is either straight or—more often—clublike. Only in this depiction do we see the two priests who hand the king additional balls. It is said of them: "Catching (of the balls) by the servants of god after he (the king) has struck them away."[15] In texts from later temples we learn that the king's striking of the ball has symbolically damaged the eye of Apophis, the enemy of the gods, and thus has rendered him harmless. It is possible that the material used to make the ball was a certain wood mentioned in connection with this myth.[16] The theory that the balls were made of clay is not tenable.[17]

That the ritual origins of ball play had not been wholly forgotten is proven by a textual variant that alludes to the young king "who amused himself as a child."[18] Evidence of the earlier existence of a kind of bat-and-ball sport is preserved in this sacral context. Without wishing to claim the dependence upon Egyptian ball games of the ancient Persian game of gūy-u-čaugān (bat and ball), a game similar to modern polo, I believe it is worth noting the games' similarity in outward form and function.[19]

Elements of ball games appear in yet another ancient Egyptian ritual which is, however, known to us in only one representation.[20] While running, King Taharqa throws four balls in the four heavenly directions (fig. 79), a ritual that has its counterpart in the shooting of four arrows by "the divine wife of Amun" (a high priestess). The pharaoh, who holds a club-shaped object in his other hand, is shown with the three hemispheric bases characteristic of the ritual running scenes of the jubilee festival. The ceremony was considered as a seizure of possession until J. C. Goyon was able to prove that the ritual utterances preserved on a number of papyri serve to protect Osiris.[21] They refer to the throwing of clay balls to the four winds.[22]

Here, too, as is so often the case in Egypt, we encounter an interesting

78 Tuthmosis III as batter, before the Hathor, temple of Hatshepsut (eighteenth dyn.), Deir el-Bahri

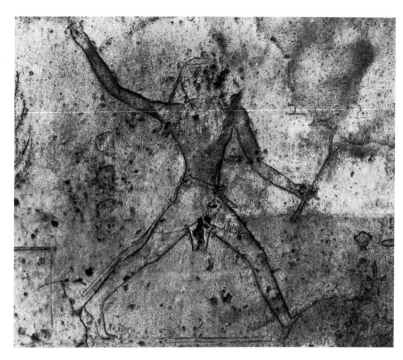

79 Ball ritual, kiosk of Taharqa (twenty-fifth dyn.), Karnak

effect of cult upon sport practice. The observance of rituals in ancient Egyptian cult that were once a part of ball games has led to the adventuresome thesis that all modern ball games derive from the games once played in the Nile Valley in the days of the pharaohs.[23] Today, however, this theory has been shown to be erroneous.[24]

To conclude this section on ball games, I must mention a game found only in very early tombs that displays similarities to bowling.[25] Numerous fragments of the original games have been discovered, but none of the samples was complete until one was found in a child's grave.[26] A set of pins was to be bowled over by balls rolled through a gate made of three stones. The game is nowhere pictured.

Children's Games

This section deals with all sorts of children's games except for ball games and board games, each of which has its own section. Because of systematic considerations, the game *khazza lawizza* is also excluded; it was discussed in the section on jumping in chapter 4. The rubric "children's games" was chosen despite the fact that not all the players shown in the relevant scenes are actually children. The character of the games was such that they were, in the overwhelming majority of cases, appropriate for children. A classification of the children's games pictured in some of the tombs of the Old and Middle Kingdoms (but not of the New Kingdom) is difficult to deal with because the point of the games is not always clear.[27] The accompanying texts are often of laconic brevity and our comprehension is often baffled by our inability to decipher the specialized vocabulary.[28] These types of games usually appear in a whole complex, as is the case at Saqqara in the tombs of the viziers Ptahhotep (fifth dynasty) and Mereruka (sixth dynasty), at Giza in the tomb of Idu (sixth dynasty), and at Beni Hasan in the tomb of the local princes Kheti and Baqti III (twelfth dynasty). The motifs of other tombs in the same places reveal that the games belonged to the same artistic tradition and may even have come from the same workshop.

As a rule, the children's games were played by two partners or by a larger group, while equal teams of opponents were the exception. Apart from ball games, where equal teams were usual, such parity certainly occurred in a contest that resembled a tug-of-war without a rope (fig. 80).[29] The game, once pictured as one played by foreigners, involved groups of up to seven persons.[30] Actually, this number was exceeded in two scenes from the tomb of Kheti in Beni Hasan; there eight and nine persons are shown involved in an activity that is not well understood.[31] The background of the scene, however, suggests that the activity was a children's game.[32]

There is only one departure from the rule that the games involved strict sex segregation. This occurs in a whirling game from the tomb of Baqti III, which lies not far from that of Kheti.[33] If one attempted to order the games into types, the following rough division might be suggested: balancing games, tests of strength, games of agility and dexterity, fighting games, resting games, and a residual category for otherwise unclassifiable games.

The group of balancing games is pictured in a variety of scenes in which one person attempts to maintain himself on the shoulders of a row of striding persons (fig. 80).[34] Similarly constructed pictures show a game the object of which was to bear someone to a goal.[35]

One scene from the tomb of Ptahhotep shows a boy creeping on the ground and carrying two children, one on each side, looking rather as a donkey might when its load is divided in two parts (fig. 81). The name suggested for the game, "Donkey Game," seems appropriate.[36] The difficulty lay less in carrying the relatively light load than in the small boys hanging on and not losing their balance, which required a great deal of effort.[37] For that reason, the game can also be classified among the tests of strength.

80 Children's games, tomb of Mereruka, Saqqara (sixth dyn.)

The most exciting member of the set of balancing games was the whirling game, for which we have three representations (fig. 82).[38] As mentioned above, boys and girls played the game together, at least in the version pictured in a scene from the Middle Kingdom (tomb of Baqti III),

81 Children's games, tomb of Ptahhotep, Saqqara (fifth dyn.)

where two girls are swung about by two boys standing with their feet planted in the middle of a circle. The velocity of the movement is indicated by the wide angle of the leaning bodies. It would be possible to categorize this game as a "gymnastic exercise" without doing violence to the description,[39] but the essential point is rather that all of us have played this game as children.[40] If the whirling is fast enough, one becomes quite dizzy. Once experienced, the sensation is not easily forgotten. Precisely this experience motivated the Egyptians to name the game "Setting up a Vineyard"—that too was a place for dizziness when the gifts of the god of the winepress, Shesmu, were too richly enjoyed. In the tomb of Ptahhotep, where each of two boys standing in the middle swings a playmate about, the inscription reads, "Whirl, four times."[41] The third occurrence of the motif, in the grave of Mereruka, depicts four girls at play (fig. 80).[42]

Tests of strength could consist of pulling or shoving contests between individuals who were either sitting (Kheti) or standing (Idu, Kheti, Mereruka) (fig. 83). The unique depiction of a tug-of-war from Mereruka's grave, in which two teams of three boys each participated, doubtless belongs to this type of game (fig. 80)[43] The two team leaders hold each other by the hands and lean backward, foot planted against foot, and each tries to pull the other to his side. Behind them stand the other players, two to a side, who form a chain by hanging on to the player in front of them. To the leader on the left it is said, "Your arm is stronger than his, don't give way!" The other side encourages itself with the cry, "My group is stronger than yours. Hang tight, comrade!"

Speed is a part of a uniquely represented exercise in the tomb of Baqti III, but one can also characterize the activity as weight lifting.[44] Three young men endeavor to hoist pear-shaped objects that might be seen as sacks of sand[45] but that can also be interpreted as wooden dumbbells.[46] One of the men has succeeded in a one-hand snatch and holds the object aloft. The "weight," however, is not an item of sports equipment, as was formerly suspected. The puzzle is solved in the nearby tomb of Kheti.[47] There one can see two men using the same objects to drive a boat's mooring post into the sand of the riverbank. One of them has raised his wooden mallet in a way similar to the successful weight lifter's. Like the ordinary commercial copper ingots that were transformed into sports equipment for archery contests, nautical implements can become, temporarily, sporting goods.

Games of agility and dexterity exist in essentially three types: a hoop game, a throwing game, and a foot-grabbing game. The first named, depicted only in the tomb of Kheti,[48] has been compared to field hockey, but wrongly, because it is not played with a ball nor is it a team game (fig. 83).[49] Two men clothed with belts and the hint of a skirt stand facing each other and leaning slightly forward. With their two hands, they hold sticks with

82 *Whirling about, tomb of Ptahhotep, Saqqara*

hooked ends and attempt to control the hoop that lies between them. We cannot determine the material from which the hoop, somewhat larger than a headband, is made.

From the tombs of Ptahhotep, Idu, and Baqti III three examples of a throwing game played with pointed sticks have come down to us (fig. 81). In two representations it seems that the target is a wooden disk lying on the ground, but it may be that it is only a marked field within which the stick must strike. In the grave of Ptahhotep we can see two crossed sticks already stuck in the target area while the two playing boys gather themselves for the next throws. Each holds a stick in both hands.[50] The caption, "Throwing for Shesmu," adds little to our understanding. Although the god Shesmu is the patron of the winepress, which is represented close by, a plausible connection eludes us. The game is also to be found in the tomb of Idu, where it is played by Idu's two sons.[51] Here, although no target area is visible, the boys each have a stick in each hand. It is striking that the two of them wear vegetation as a headdress. This finery reminds one of the lotus plants worn during the swamp hunt.[52] The depiction from the Middle Kingdom grave of Baqti III shows two simultaneous games.[53] To the right is the usual group of two boys, while a third boy approaches the pair on the left, perhaps to challenge the winner of the first round. Common to both scenes is the pulling out of the sticks. Might it have been the object of the Egyptian game to dislodge the stuck spear of one's opponent?

In the third type of game, the children must have been agile to touch and tease the one sitting in the middle, to nudge him with their feet; he, in turn, had to try to catch them and make them exchange places.[54] The name "foot-grabbing" seems appropriate (figs. 80 and 81). A caption from the grave of Mereruka hints of the requisite agility: "The team is made up of gazelles."[55] Another sentence accompanies a second view of the game from the tomb of Ptahhotep: "Who is it whom you've struck?"[56] What is presumably a version of the game played by only two boys was found in the tomb of Kheti at Beni Hasan.[57]

Under fighting games we can place two groups of playful activities that we can call "foreigner games" and "hut games."[58] The first type of game is known only from the Old Kingdom, when drawings of it decorated the

83 *Children's games, tomb of Kheti, Beni Hasan no. 17 (eleventh dyn.)*

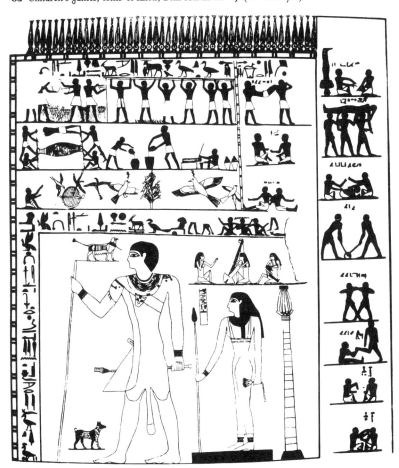

walls of the tombs of Ptahhotep, Mereruka, and Ichechi (fig. 80). Common to the three examples is a bound prisoner who is carried away by a group of running boys. The inscription from the tomb of Mereruka reads, "A foreigner comes. Hear his wish. Another sees [it] and is frightened."[59] Perhaps this act of intimidation is a way to express fears of a strange intruder and thus to neutralize them.[60] The degree to which the scene might refer to the dangers of the underworld, which thus accompany the deceased, is hard to determine. The prisoner is in the middle. All eyes are on him. The front runners turn their heads. The guards threaten the prisoner, whom they lead by a rope, with blows from the sticks or papyrus plants they hold in their hands. In the grave of Ptahhotep, six youths with neither weapons nor rope lead a prisoner who has his arms tied behind him.[61] The inscription is identical with the beginning of the one just quoted: "A foreigner comes. Hear his wish."

The scene from the grave of Ichechi survives in fragments, but it is possible to recognize the prisoner in the middle, this time with a restraining collar, and the guards, all of whom are holding the rope.[62] The caption indicates a difference from the stereotype of the other two scenes, but it is badly damaged. The end reads, "priest of the dead, comrade."[63] Today's children's game of "Cops and Robbers" is probably not all that different from this ancient Egyptian model.

For the second fighting game, for which we have suggested the name "Hut Game," the external characteristic is a hutlike place in and around which the game seems to have been played.[64] It is represented three times: in a fifth-dynasty relief now in the British Museum (inventory no. 994), in the tomb of Idu, and in the tomb of Baqti III.[65] Still, there is controversy about its meaning. The two representations from the Old Kingdom are nearly identical while the Middle Kingdom scene from Beni Hasan is recognizable on the basis of the inscription and the positions of the participants, although the hut itself is not visible.

The players who find themselves in the hut divide into a pair that is involved in some kind of action and two simultaneously depicted boys whose raised arms seem to refer to or to affect the action of the other pair. A fifth player stands outside the hut and takes part from there in the central action. The pair in the hut consists of one player who is lying on the ground and apparently trying to raise himself and a second player who is behind and bent over him, apparently touching him on the head and shoulders. One can also interpret the positions of the pair so that one holds the other to the ground while the player thus held stretches a hand out of the hut to get the attention of the player standing outside. The accompanying text, which is the same for all three examples, reads, "I'll rescue myself from here by myself, comrade." In all likelihood, this utterance refers to the call

of the player on the ground inside the hut; he is calming the outside player
who is presumably rushing to the rescue.

Because of the hut some scholars have wanted to relate this game to
initiation ceremonies like those recently documented for the African cultures of the Congo. On the occasion of circumcision, such huts are used
ritually.[66] We are unaware, however, that such a connection exists or existed in Egypt; the question of the meaning of the game must remain an
open one.

One more playful exercise must be mentioned. Two boys depicted in
the tomb of Ptahhotep are sitting in an extreme version of the tailor's
position, which is possible only when the legs are stretched to an extraordinary degree (fig. 81).[67] Finally, it may be that a wall painting from the
tomb of Mereruka concerns play of some sort, but part of the scene was
lost when a door was built in the wall. One can, however, still see a row of
boys before whom there was probably a runner. The incomplete inscription contains the Egyptian word for "team" (fig. 80).[68]

The resting or sitting games are our last category. They are integrated into
the depictions of more active games, which indicates the Egyptians' conception of where they belong. They appear only in the Middle Kingdom
graves of the nomarchs at Beni Hasan—a source that has already transmitted much of the material for this chapter. With a single exception the
games are for two people. Although all the scenes are accompanied by
brief inscriptions, the games are not easy to understand because the texts
are hard to interpret. The simplest caption is the cry "Say it!" The depicted
pair may be playing a game whose outcome depends on guessing the
number of outstretched fingers about to be shown (fig. 83).[69] In that case
the command would be a signal for opening the hand. If one studies the
representations from the tomb of Kheti, one follows a vertical sequence
that runs from the floor to the ceiling of the grave. The topmost scene,
which also appears in a neighboring tomb, involves little sticks. The figure
next to the pair with sticks is doing a headstand and has no role to play in
the stick game. Below a trio carrying a supine player above their heads
(already mentioned in connection with games of agility and dexterity) is
another group of three playing another guessing game. The player squatting on the ground must say, with his eyes closed, which of the others has
struck him. This simple game is another that has survived through millennia. The bottom two pairs in the vertical row of games have a counterpart in
the tomb of Baqti III.[70] The inscriptions might be translated as follows:
"Give one blow on the hand. Give one blow to the head."[71] Although the
gestures of the players would fit the inscriptions well, we remain unsure of
the exact point of the game.

The last game, played with pairs of pots, can also be seen in a group from the tomb of Baqti.[72] Klebs has suggested that the point was to guess what was hidden under the pots, but this interpretation is debatable.[73] It assumes that one player had simultaneous control over all the pots, which is not at all certain from the representation we have.

This brief survey of Egyptian children's games proves that the children and youths of the Nile Valley in the days of the pharaohs had lively imaginations, which is only to be expected. As the surviving documentation cannot possibly include the whole treasury of games, we have no right to assume that the young people of Egypt were any less imaginative than children of other cultures and other ages. Our documentation comes almost exclusively from five graves, and the tradition breaks off at the beginning of the Middle Kingdom. We cannot know why the motif of children's games is lacking in the sources from the New Kingdom. Still, even this restricted body of evidence provides us with some twenty games, not counting their variants. This number might seem negligible in comparison to the games catalogued in Johann Fischer's *Gargantua und Pantagruel* or in François Rabelais's more famous version of the same story, but, measured against what has been transmitted from other ancient cultures, the number is impressive.[74]

Our systematic survey was based on the contents of the games. One might also categorize them on the basis of equipment or number of players. The first category would then include throwing games, stick games, hoop games, and the game with four pots. If one categorized them on the basis of the number of players, one would see that, with the exception of the tug-of-war, there were no team games. Two-person and several-person games occurred in about the same number.[75]

Board Games

Senet Board Game

The extreme heat characteristic of the Egyptian summer leads us to assume that sitting and resting games were preferred during the hottest months rather than the games that required greater physical exertion. If this consideration was true for children, then it must have held even more strongly for adults (fig. 84). Grown-ups drove off boredom by playing board games in the airy shadowed halls of their dwelling places. Representations of these games are accompanied by inscriptions that capture the relaxed atmosphere: "You sit in the hall; you play the Senet board game; you have wine; you have beer."[76]

If we measure a game's popularity by the number of references to it

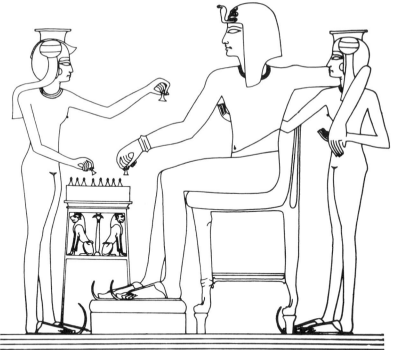

84 Ramesses III playing a board game, funerary temple of Ramesses III (twentieth dyn.), high gate, Medinet Habu

through the course of Egyptian history, then the one just referred to was clearly the favorite.[77] At any rate, we have many more examples of visual representation and original artifacts for this game than we do for any other social game played on a board or similar field. In the scholarly literature it is known as Senet (from its Egyptian name *snt*), but the game is also known as the "Thirty-Field Game," or simply as the "Game of Thirty". *Snt* means "to pass" or "to go by"; these refer to the main point of the game, which is to move while avoiding the dangerous squares in a field of thirty positions. It is not impossible that the game was originally a "separation game" that involved a blockade of the opponent's pieces.[78] The Senet game, which was a much loved leisure-time activity in all social classes through all periods of Egyptian culture, has come down to us in quite a number of originals.[79] The playing surfaces range from simple scratches in a flat stone to boards made of clay to artfully manufactured chests with two playable surfaces (figs. 85 and 86). Four boards from the tomb of Tutankhamon are among the best pieces. One of them rests on an apparatus that functions as a playing table.[80] The tops of the playing chests ordinarily have a field of thirty squares, while the bottoms customarily are set aside for the twenty-

85 Board game, scratched outlines, tomb of Nefersechemptah, Saqqara (fifth to sixth dyn.)

86 Senet game of Mrymaat (eighteenth dyn.), MMA *01.4.1A–P*

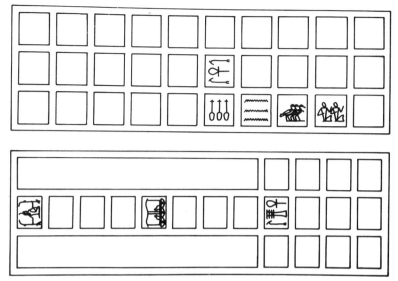

87 Playing surfaces for the thirty-square game and the twenty-square game, Tutankhamun's board game (eighteenth dyn.), Cairo JE 62 058 A

field game (fig. 87).[81] The narrow sides contain drawers for the equipment, which consists of a set of stone pieces and implements for determining the moves. One series of pieces, made mostly from faience stones, is spindle-shaped, while the counterpart pieces are formed like bowling pins, often with a rounded top. The outward appearance of such stone pieces is similar to that of pieces used in modern German games like Mensch, aergere Dich nicht (Man, Don't Get Upset) or Halma (akin to the American game Chinese Checkers). There are also very differently modeled pieces shaped like human or animal heads. Still other figures are crowned by demons' heads. Depending on the historical period, the complete set of stone pieces varies from five to seven per row, while the number five seems to be canonical for the New Kingdom.[82] The function of our dice was fulfilled in ancient Egypt by throwing four small sticks or two astragals, dice made from the bone of the rear legs of young lambs (figs. 88 and 89). The astragals allowed the same range of possibilities ("eyes") as the small sticks. The length of a given move was determined by the position of the sticks, which could be thrown so that they landed face up or face down. The number of spaces moved could similarly be set by the differently formed sides of the animal bones.[83]

The playing rules are known in their outlines, but the details escape us.[84] At the beginning of the game, the pieces were placed alternately on the first squares of the board. The field for play was divided into thirty squares in

88 *Senet game of Tya (eighteenth dyn.), MMA 12.182.72*

---

three adjacent rows of ten squares each. One snaked one's way through the three rows from square one to square thirty. Since the highest possible throw was a five, a player with five pieces in a row blocked his opponent from moving head.[85] Opposing pieces standing alone, with no contact to others, could be taken. Presumably such pieces had to start again from the beginning. Certain squares are inscribed. Ordinarily, these are squares fifteen, twenty-six through twenty-nine, and sometimes thirty. In exceptional cases, all thirty squares are inscribed. Square fifteen (House of Rebirth) and square twenty-six (The Beautiful House) had positive significance while square twenty-seven, a field of water, was to be avoided. Landing on that square sent the piece back to square fifteen, where the hieroglyphics frequently referred to rebirth. From the last three squares one had to throw the exact number needed to put one on the imaginary thirty-first square.

---

89 *Tutankhamun's astragals (dicing bones), Cairo JE 62 058 F, G*

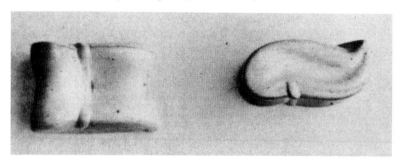

We can conjecture that the necessary numbers were written in the last squares. Presumably a match could last for quite some time. The player who first traversed all the squares with all his pieces was the winner. The Senet game was not simply a matter of luck, because the number of moves indicated by the thrown sticks or dice could be apportioned among the various pieces. In several features the game is somewhat comparable to our modern backgammon.

This game, well documented in Egypt, is also found in neighboring cultures so that similar game boards have been unearthed in the Sudan, in Cyprus,[86] and in Phoenicia (fig. 90).[87] The game is also mentioned in a Greek text by Plutarch (*De Iside* 12). A derivation of the game survives today in the Arabic game *al-ṭāb al-sīgah*.[88] Perhaps one should assume that the Senet board game was played by the Egyptians with the same enthusiasm displayed today for backgammon in the eastern Mediterranean (Greek: *tavli*, from the Latin *tabula*) and in the Near East (Persian: *nard*).

It must be added that the Senet board game had a religious significance in the New Kingdom in addition to its everyday function as a pastime. The game itself or its representation often appeared as a grave artifact (figs. 91 and 92) and symbolized the path of the dead through the underworld. A success at the game played against an imaginary opponent guaranteed the deceased spirit the rebirth that was a precondition of eternal life and happiness in the life beyond.[89]

90 *Ivory playing board, Phoenician, Kamid el-Loz, KL 78:534*

91 Board game scene, tomb of Nebenmaat, TT 219 (nineteenth to twentieth dyn.)

92 Board game scene, tomb of Nefertari, wife of Ramesses II (nineteenth dyn.), Valley of the Kings no. 66

Through the nineteenth dynasty it was customary in the New Kingdom for the chests that carried the Senet game to display the field of twenty squares on their bottoms.[90] In some periods the variant seems to have become the norm. This is presumably the case when the instructions written on the side of the chest can be read only when the twenty-square field is uppermost. It is possible that the chest's owner preferred the simpler game and banished the thirty-square game to the bottom. The twenty-square game was played on a field of three by four with an additional row of eight squares. The three parallel rows known to us from the thirty-square version are shrunk to four squares each and an eight-square row extends from the middle row so that it contains, in effect, twelve squares (fig. 90).[91] In this game too certain squares are inscribed, but the rules of the game are even less decipherable than those of the Senet game. This twenty-square version was replaced in the twentieth dynasty by another variant known to us in only three examples.[92] The field, drawn once upon papyrus and twice on the backside of a Senet board, reproduced the order of the twenty-square game but added a second set of three by four squares. The projecting row was then reduced from eight to seven squares, which left a board of thirty-one squares ($3 \times 4 \times 2 + 8 - 1 = 31$).[93]

One can also speak of a version of the twenty-square game with "folded symmetry." The Egyptians referred to it as the "Uniting of the Twenty Squares."[94] That this game too had a connection with the grave and with the further life of the deceased is clear from a papyrus text referring to a thirty-one-square game: "that I enter the hall of the thirty [and that I become god at square 31]."[95] Thus the game serves symbolically to assist the deceased before the thirty-judge tribunal at the trial of the dead.

The Snake Game

In use only in the Old Kingdom was a game played simultaneously by many persons on a circular surface with a trapezoidal base (fig. 93).[96] The Egyptian name mḥn (ring snake) is derived from the surface of the board upon which a snake was customarily represented. The body was so wound about the head that the tail projected outward (fig. 94). The body of the snake was divided into sections that can be understood as the field for the game. At Saqqara in a grave from the third dynasty containing the body of Hesy, a chest with the playing equipment was depicted next to the playing board (fig. 95).[97] Six lions are arranged next to six balls. Other representations permit us to suspect that the balls were held in the hand so that the move could be determined by means of guessing. The lions were then moved. We cannot, however, exclude the possibility that throwing sticks

93 Playing surface for snake game, chalk, early period,
Berlin *13 868*

94 Playing surface for snake game, chalk, Old Kingdom,
Leiden F *1968/3*, I

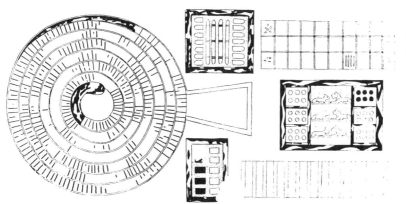

95 *Snake game and Senet game with accessories, representation from the tomb of Hesy, Saqqara (third dyn.)*

fulfilled this function in other versions of the game.[98] In that case, the role of the balls, which might in any event also have been represented in the spiraling, would be a puzzle.[99] In Egypt itself the game was no longer represented after the Old Kingdom, but it was still played in Cyprus in the second millennium B.C.[100]

In the Nile Valley, the coiled snake mḥn, which gave the snake game its name, was later associated with the Senet board game. According to a text, the dead person played against the snake. He won and threw the snake into a watery field. The sense of the game was probably that the deceased could protect himself in this manner against the bite of poisonous snakes. This conjecture is confirmed by spell 172 in the Book of the Dead.[101] On the other hand, in the nineteenth dynasty the mḥn snake became a kind of patron saint for the Senet game. In slightly altered form, the snake game is played today by the Arabs of Cordofan.[102]

The Marble Game

It seems likely that the marble game evolved from the snake game, for which, as has been mentioned, six balls were provided. The name of this game, ṯꜣw in Egyptian, has been erroneously applied up to now to the twenty-square game.[103] The game has been attested only twice. According to E. B. Pusch it was "a game combining dexterity and guessing," the point of which was to determine correctly the number of marbles one's opponent was quickly transfering from one hand to the other.[104] The player who correctly guessed the number received the marbles.[105]

There is one last game for which we have game boards but no visual representations.[106] The game has been named either the thirty-point game or, because of the similarity of the board to various forms of the defensive weapon, the "shield game" (fig. 96). The playing board has holes in which the playing pieces, the tops of which represent dogs' heads, are stuck. The holes are divided so that each half of the board has an inner row of ten and a roughly parallel outer row of nineteen to make a total of twenty-nine holes for each player. The field is completed by a centrally placed thirtieth hole. Unlike the players of the Senet game, each player of the shield game has his own field (except that they seem to have shared the thirtieth hole). Not only does the number of holes remind one strongly of the Egyptians' beloved thirty-square board game, but the set of five playing pieces is also identical to the number used during the New Kingdom for the thirty-square game. A further resemblance can be noted in that certain positions are provided with the hieroglyph nfr (good). For instance, an

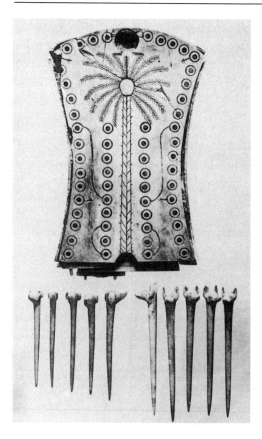

96 Shield game, Deir el-Bahri, pit tomb no. 25 (twelfth dyn.)

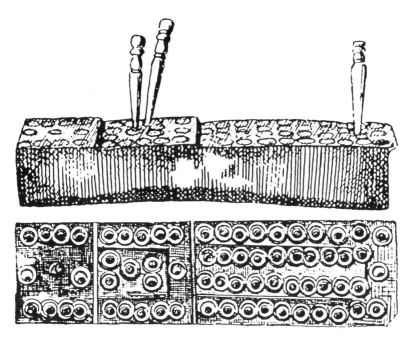

97 Coptic board game, Cairo JE 78 126

example of the game from the twelfth dynasty has this word next to the fifteenth hole, which corresponds exactly to what occurs in the Senet game, and also next to the twenty-fifth hole, which is close to the positively inscribed twenty-sixth square of the Senet game. It seems permissible to assume that both positions brought advantages to players who landed in them.

In addition to approximately a dozen specimens of playing boards,[107] there are extant at least four examples of a legitimate descendant of this ancient Egyptian game in the form of a game from the Coptic period—Egypt's Christian epoch.[108] The board resembles the elongated rectangle of the Senet game but has a steplike format and, like the shield game, has holes to contain the playing pieces (fig. 97). The new element is a kind of labyrinth, a field with a changing number of positions and a sort of middle terrace. Nonetheless, the number thirty continues to play a dominant role, just as was the case in the ancient Egyptian model. Interestingly, there is proof that this Coptic game served as a funerary object, just as the Senet board game customarily did.[109]

7 Acrobatics

A discussion of acrobatics might well be included in a presentation of Egyptian dance because both activities are to be reckoned among sports in the widest sense of the term.[1] Since, however, the present book is intended to provide nothing more than a brief survey of Egyptian sports, I have decided to restrict it to the essentials and thus to omit a treatment of dance, making an exception only for its spectacular element, dance as highly skilled performance.[2] That such dances are only "the tip of the iceberg" must be accepted. Next to such performances I shall discuss other feats of physical skill that do not derive from the milieu of dance.

Among the dance forms are some of a markedly acrobatic character. Already in the Old Kingdom there was one dance that fits this description (fig. 98). The most detailed representation of this dance is in the tomb of Anchmahor (sixth dynasty).[3] Here, next to the girl clapping time, we see five other girls holding their left legs in the air while leaning back to an almost horizontal position. Their arms are swung forward to maintain their balance. The girls, clad only in short skirts, wear their hair braided into little balls that can be seen as almost the insignia of the female acrobat.[4] An unusual dance of this epoch, which could be performed as part of the funeral procession, has similar elements.[5]

The judgement of E. Brunner-Traut, the best authority for Egyptian dance, is generally true for the Middle Kingdom: "Acrobatics have strongly influenced dance forms and have indeed intruded themselves into the dance, and they have even in one instance quite replaced the art of the dance."[6]

98 *Acrobatic dance, tomb of Kagemni, Saqqara (sixth dyn.)*

During this period the "acrobatic dance of divine cult" changed its form.[7] It is now characterized by a pose that requires an extremely flexible spine. A good illustration comes from the grave of Antefoqer. Supported by their outstretched arms, two girls lie with their hips on the ground and touch their heads, bent backward, with the soles of their feet (fig. 99).[8] Immediately next to them a Hathor leaping dance is represented. Three men are pictured, one of them leaping powerfully into the air while the other two clap their hands. This dance form, transmitted in other scenes as well, can also be called acrobatic (fig. 33).[9] A portion of another dance, performed during the procession of statues, we might consider to be a pirouette (fig. 100). Divided into three or four phases in the visual representations, it

99 *Dance with acrobatic elements, tomb of Antefoqer, TT 60 (twelfth dyn.)*

100 *Pirouette during dance, tomb of Baqti III, Beni Hasan no. 15 (eleventh dyn.)*

appears four times in the graves of Beni Hasan.[10] The artist has masterfully reproduced the dancer's swift whirling about in place with outstretched arms and an outstretched leg. The turning of the head also speaks an unambiguous language. We might also conceive of the scene as made up of four dancers who are shown in four different positions. Whether there was supposed to be a "gymnastic part" to the dance or such "dance movements" is unimportant for our present purposes.[11]

During the New Kingdom, a complicated acrobatic exercise became a standard part of the dance. Although it appears in some depictions to have been simply a bridge, it was probably a forward flip. A series of impressive representations are extant. Here, too, the various phases depicted enable us to surmise what the complete movement looked like. In scenes like the famous drawing inscribed upon a chalk shard (preserved now in the museum in Turin; fig 101), one is reminded of the bridge, the final phase of which is achieved by raising the body from a supine position or—difficult to perform—by bending the body backward and simultaneously stretching the arms backward.[12] We may have such a bridge twice represented at Beni Hasan, but if this is the case then the hands are in the wrong position and the angle of the head is astonishing.[13] In the bridge, the head must be within the semicircle formed by the body and the limbs. The scenes in Beni Hasan and a contemporary statuette made from the same scheme (fig. 102) can in a "literal" interpretation be better understood as a running on all fours with one's back to the ground.[14] But the intent of the New Kingdom representations, perhaps truer to the actual form of the exercise, seem to refer to handsprings, which, especially when performed in a continuous sequence, were surely appropriate to make a processing in honor of the gods attractive and festive. The integration of the exercise in such a procession is, moreover, a further argument for thinking of it as a forward directed movement. Its role in such a procession renders another

138

101 *Acrobat doing a flip, Ostrakon, New Kingdom, Turin 7052*

possible explanation—that the stunt was actually a backward flip—extremely implausible. Only dancers performed this exercise; the slim, well-trained bodies of the girls were normally clothed only with a skirt, and their full, wavy hair underlined the elegance of their movements. Their

102 *Statuette of an acrobat from Abydos, Brooklyn Museum 13.1024*

presence in processions is attested by carvings from the reign of Queen Hatshepsut on the marvelously lovely blocks from Karnak (figs. 103–105)[15] and also by pictures from the tomb of Tutankhamon (eighteenth dynasty) in the temple of Luxor.[16] At the latter site, the visit of the god Amon of Karnak to the temple of Luxor is represented. The statue of Amon is carried to the holy wedding on the shoulders of the priests. The sistrum players give the beat for the acrobatic dancers; other groups contribute with drums and noisemaking sticks to the festivities of the occasion. The relaxed and simultaneously festive character of the event is well captured by the artist. One can feel the exertions of the dancers as they perform their forward flips and handsprings. The continual pressure on the upper body is betrayed by signs of fatigue.[17]

From the various representations of the New Kingdom, one could in fact determine five phases of the stunt which, if ordered properly, might serve as a floor exercise illustration for a modern book of gymnastics (which today has become a very acrobatic sport; figs. 106 and 107).[18]

Upon one of the Hatshepsut blocks we can see not only three phases of the forward flip but also a fourth position that, if we judge by the placement of the arms, suggests a sideways flip. For that reason, some scholars have seen the exercise as a wheel (fig. 108).[19] Because, however, the feet are together, it seems rather to be a cartwheel. The position of two bending men on a relief of Osorkhon II at Bubastis could be one or the other.[20] Of course, both exercises—the sideways flip and the cartwheel—were in the

---

103 *Forward flip, block of Hatshepsut (eighteenth dyn.), Karnak*

104 Forward flip, block of Hatshepsut, Karnak

105 Forward flip, block of Hatshepsut, Karnak

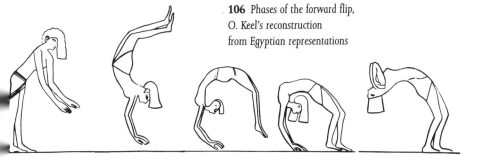

106 Phases of the forward flip,
O. Keel's reconstruction
from Egyptian representations

107 Preparation for the forward flip, tomb of Minnacht, TT *87* (eighteenth dyn.)

108 Preparation for the forward flip, cartwheel, block of Hatshepsut, Karnak

repertory of dancers who performed at private festivities, as proven by a scene from the grave of Amenemhet.[21]

One type of wheel performed under especially difficult conditions appeared as early as the Middle Kingdom. Best understood in connection with the dance, it is represented in a funeral procession before the statue of the deceased, entombed Amenemhet in Beni Hasan (fig. 109).[22] Once again, as was repeatedly the case for the pirouette, four phases are shown. First the arms raised preparatory to the run-up; then the turning phase with the help of the arms; then the most difficult part of the exercise, the spring to the back of a bent partner so that the outstretched arms of the leaping acrobat enable him to maintain his balance while standing on his partner's back; and, finally, the continuation of the ecstatic dance after the leap to the ground.

In the grave of the nomarch Khnumhotep (eleventh dynasty) in the same place, we encounter a mimetic dance connected with the cult of the statue of the dead. It too has acrobatic characteristics, including a unique danced representation of a tree shaken by the wind.[23] One of the three girls shown bends backward until her hands touch the ground.[24] Here one can surely speak of a backward bridge. The mimetic offering can be related to the "Song of the Four Winds," which appears in two books of religious sayings useful to the deceased: the coffin texts (spell 162) and the Book of the Dead (chapter 70).

To these examples of acrobatic elements in Egyptian dances more of the same sort could easily be added. From them, I include only the most

---

109 *Flip with stand upon partner's back, tomb of Amenemhet, Beni Hasan no. 2 (twelfth dyn.)*

striking. The physical feats demanded of the dancers are possible only on the basis of serious training. Otherwise, there is no explanation for the depicted control of the body and ease in performing difficult movements. This suspicion becomes even more likely when we consider the dance instructions that have occasionally come to light; through them the pupils were schooled in the necessary technical information and rhythmic awareness.[25]

Yet another acrobatic exercise can be classified as a flip: the flip with a partner (fig. 110). In Middle Kingdom art, in the tombs of Kheti and Baqti III, girls are twice shown performing the stunt.[26] The whirling bodies of the acrobats, holding themselves belly to belly and forming a single shape, must have created a powerful impression upon the spectators although the movement is actually easier than it appears. The three phases pictured show the exercise with such astonishing accuracy that the pictures could well illustrate a modern book of acrobatic instruction. In fact, even the scenes divided into two phases are enough to understand the artist's intention. These flips with partners were performed outside of the context of the cult occurrences with their processions of statues or of gods, and they were not regular parts of dances. They were, however, close to another exercise that consisted of leaping in the air and touching the buttocks with the heels (fig. 34).[27]

A skill that requires absolute control of the body is the headstand, which appears in stark immediacy in the tomb of Kheti (eleventh dynasty).[28] Next to the acrobat standing on his head crouch two others on the ground, busy with little sticks. We have no explanation for their game or for the presence of the acrobat, who is shown standing on his head without the support of his hands—an impossibly difficult balancing act. It is conceivable that such a position might be held for fractions of a second, but in this case, the

110 *Flip with a partner, tomb of Kheti, Beni Hasan no. 17 (eleventh dyn.)*

111 Pole climbing for
the god Min, temple
pylon, Luxor
(nineteenth dyn.)

Egyptian artist would probably have sketched the hands ready if necessary
to maintain the acrobat's position. The bent arms in the picture do not give
the impression that they are ready at the right moment to intervene and
prevent a loss of balance. Nor are they placed to help the acrobat in his
headstand with supporting elbows, as in Indian yoga. Still, an exercise
other than the headstand can scarcely have been meant. Despite the diffi-
culties, then, one must assume that the headstand may have been unique,
but it was unquestionably among the artistic feats of Egyptian acrobats.

Somewhat apart from all the hitherto mentioned acrobatic exercises was
a scene that we encounter repeatedly in Egyptian reliefs. It stood in close
connection with the cult of Min (fig. 111) and occurred first in the time of
the late Old Kingdom. The message of the picture was this: Four posts lean
against a sturdy middle post, up which a number of feather-bedecked men
seem to be climbing.[29] Their ornamental dress identifies them as Nubians.[30] The presence of other persons who hold in their hands ropes
attached to the posts has been interpreted as a complication; some
scholars opine that their pulling the posts one way and then the other set
them in lively motion.[31] The art of the climbers was, then, mainly to hang

on. Preferable to this rather ingenious theory is the explanation that the posts and ropes were the framework for a sacred tent built for the god as a cult symbol.[32] Within the context of cult behavior, climbing scenes might have displayed traits not only of athleticism but also, because of the height of the poles, of acrobatic aspects. In the event that this scene is identical with one described by Herodotus, we can see it as a competitive climb.[33] The Greek historian gave an eyewitness account of the cult practices and constructions in the city of Chemmis (ii 91), which the Greeks later named Panopolis on the theory that their god Pan corresponded to the Egyptian Min.[34] Herodotus was most intrigued by the fact that the inhabitants of the city conducted an athletic agon, that is, a Greek sports festival, something he thought was most un-Egyptian. The competition, for which cattle, coats, and skins were offered as prizes, was staged in honor of Perseus. Behind the name of the Greek hero we can glimpse an epithet of the Egyptian god Min, p3wrš, which sounded to Greek ears like their Perseus. It is quite possible that Herodotus watched the cult ceremony of post climbing, which accompanied the erection of a hut for Min. The ceremony dimly reminded Herodotus of the widespread sports competitions of his homeland. The later contests that sprang up on the site had Egyptian roots but assumed Greek forms and, as an agon, were known as the Paneia—competitions for Pan (or Min). They continued at least into the third century A.D.[35]

8   Hunting

Because one of the basic preconditions for the advanced civilizations of antiquity was the settled existence necessary for the regulated development of agriculture, it can easily be forgotten that the hunting and gathering period of human history lasted for millennia and that hunting was the more important activity. The acquisition of food and a defense against the threats of wild animals were hunters' motives; the life of their tribe depended on their success. It was only the domestication of animals and the beginnings of animal husbandry that diminished the once essential food-supplying function of hunting. As hunting lost significance as a primary source of food, its substitute function as a means of recreation—sport hunting—gained in importance. The disappearance of hunting as a necessity was balanced by its increasing importance as an outlet for energy in the form of a sport.

Our consideration of hunting in ancient Egypt will be restricted to its sport aspect and will not examine the role of hunting as a means of obtaining food (although this function continued even in the historical period). Of course, the two components are not always sharply distinguishable. Edible game was eaten even when the primary stimulus for the hunt was a sportsman's pleasure.[1] An initial look at the sources suggests a division of the materials into those relating to big-game hunting and those relating to swamp hunting. The king was involved first kind of hunt, while the second kind seems to have been devised especially for the nobility, but this somewhat arbitrary division of the hunting field does not preclude considerable overlap.

As a big-game hunter the pharaoh followed in the footsteps of the prehistoric chieftains, for whom the slaying of dangerous animals was the fulfillment of their role as protectors of the group under their care. In ancient civilizations, a leader's courage and dexterity, prowess and strength, vision and coldbloodedness were never more vividly on display than during the hunt.[2] In the Egyptian royal dogma, the successful hunter is interchangeable with the unconquerable warrior.[3] The merger of the two aspects was especially perceptible in the eighteenth dynasty. In the riparian thickets of the Nile Valley, crocodiles, hippopotamuses, and wild bulls could be threatening; in the desert, lions or a wandering rhinoceros were great dangers; and the elephant, which began to retreat from the land of Egypt as early as the beginning of the third millennium, was especially prized by royal hunters because of its size.

It is striking that the hunt for crocodiles was no longer attested for historical times, although the god Horus continued to spear the giant reptiles as a part of his ritual. The hunt for hippopotamuses was quite a different story (fig. 112).[4] Evidence for it appeared as early as the first dynasty, with an imprint from a cylinder seal of King Dewen that demonstrates how he harpooned a hippopotamus.[5] His small boat, made from

112 *Hippopotamus hunt, linen cloth, Gebelein, early period, Turin*

papyrus sheaves tied together, is easily maneuvered in his hideaway in the papyrus thicket. He can closely approach the hippopotamus. Escape is impossible because the line of the harpoon that the king draws back for the deadly thrust gives him power over the animal. Next to this harpooning scene is another that proves the king's unmatched courage: weaponless, he approaches the hippopotamus and wrestles it to the ground, in reality an impossible feat.

The killing of the hippopotamus was a splendid testimony to the king's fulfillment of his duty to care for his people, because the hungry animal's invasion of planted fields could do enormous damage. In a New Kingdom papyrus that extols the advantages of the scribe's vocation, this danger is strikingly evoked: "Do you think about the fate of the farmer when it's time to register the harvest? Snakes bore half of it away and hippopotamuses gobbled up the rest."[6] On the walls of the funerary temples of the kings Sahura (fifth dynasty) and Pepy II (sixth dynasty), the hippopotamus is depicted in larger-than-life dimensions; here, too, the principal human actor in each case is the king, who later appears many times as hippopotamus hunter.[7] Unique among these documents is the three-dimensional representation of the theme from the tomb of Tutankhamon, where two statues of the king represent him in a hunting skirt, standing in a boat and drawing the harpoon back for his thrust (fig. 113).[8] Bits of the harpoon line can be seen in his left hand. As if striding, he balances himself on the rocking boat. That he is wearing the crown of Lower Egypt gives the scene a highly official touch. By his victory over the hippopotamus, who has emerged from chaos, pharaoh re-creates the world's order. The animal is the incarnation of the god Seth, the opponent of the "good" gods Osiris and Horus. The latter god had revenged his father's death by harpooning the perpetrator, who had assumed the shape of a hippopotamus. For this reason, the king slips into the role of Horus whenever he kills the animal. It is an idealization of this deed to portray the king alone slaying the hippopotamus because, in reality, an entire hunting party cooperated for such hazardous work. The hippopotamus was a frightening animal capable of dismembering a crocodile with a single bite, as was often shown in Egyptian hunting scenes. Against such an animal only a large number of simultaneously engaged harpooners had any prospect of success. The representations of hippopotamus hunting in the Old Kingdom tombs of private persons correspond to this reality. In the grave of Ti (sixth dynasty), the deceased appears as an attentive spectator who has preferred to let his people undertake the dangerous but exciting work.[9]

Conventions changed during the New Kingdom. Sharing in the privilege formerly reserved for the monarch, the nobleman now allows himself to

113 *Statue of Tutankhamon as a hippopotamus hunter, Cairo JE 60 709*

be pictured as an active hippopotamus hunter (fig. 114). Like the king, he dominates the event in a sovereign manner.[10]

The environment of the papyrus thicket also provided a habitat for the wild bulls that the king alone, during the New Kingdom, had the right to hunt. The king proved emphatically his overwhelming power by slaying this animal, the strength of which gave rise to a metaphoric royal epithet: among the pharaoh's many titles was "powerful bull." Tuthmosis III, "in a single hour, brought in a herd of twelve wild bulls as booty."[11] The prize tails of the captured animals became part of the king's bodily ornamentation, a relic of the time when hunters still clothed themselves as animals. Amenophis III had himself immortalized in many copies of a commemorative scarab that impressively recaptured a wild-bull hunt (fig. 115),

114 Imenemheb as a hippopotamus hunter, TT *85* (eighteenth dyn.)

115 *Wild bull hunt scarab of Amenophis III (eighteenth dyn.)*

maintaining a custom that has been transformed into today's striking of commemorative coins. The text is important enough to transcribe:

> Year Two under His Majesty Amenophis III, gifted with life. The great royal consort Tiye, gifted with life like Re. A wonder that occurred for the sake of His Majesty.
>
> A man came to say to His Majesty, "There are wild bulls in the desert in the area of Fayum. His Majesty traveled north at eventide in the royal ship (named "To Appear in Truth." (His Majesty) set off on a good path. He arrived with satisfaction in the morning in the area of Fayum. His Majesty appeared on his chariot; the entire army accompanied him. (His Majesty) commanded the great ones and all the soldiers and the recruits to observe the wild bulls. His Majesty commanded that these wild bulls be confined by fences and ditches. Then His Majesty set out against all these wild bulls. A list thereof: 170 wild bulls. A list of those bagged by His Majesty on this day: fifty-six wild bulls. His Majesty spent four days without giving rest to his horses. His Majesty appeared on his chariot. List of wild bulls which he brought in from the hunt: forty wild bulls. In sum: ninety-six wild bulls.[12]

Hunting techniques changed with the introduction of light, two-wheeled, single-axled chariots at the beginning of the New Kingdom.[13] The swift vehicle was put in service for the hunt and made possible the pursuit of animals so fast in flight that they had hitherto been able to escape the beaters (fig. 116). Chariots and horses could easily be transported by

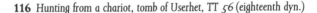

116 Hunting from a chariot, tomb of Userhet, TT 56 (eighteenth dyn.)

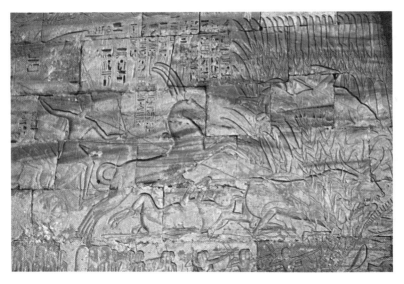

117 *Wild bull hunt, temple of Ramesses III (twentieth dyn.), Medinet Habu*

ship, as we see in many visual representations.[14] The fencing in of the wild-game area mentioned in the inscription was a hunting technique already known during the Old Kingdom. Interestingly, we have proof that such a hunting park actually existed for Amenophis III. In Soleb in Nubia the postholes of a hunting park six hundred by three hundred meters have been found.[15] This sort of hunter's paradise was also known in the ancient Near East. The worth of such methods from a sportsman's point of view is small, but Egypt was an indubitable world power and the success of and the pleasure in the hunt reached a level appropriate to the age's need for royal prestige.

The hunt for wild bulls has been preserved in a splendid representation on the first pylon of the funerary temple of Ramesses III at Medinet Habu (fig. 117). The chariot-borne king, accompanied by his foot soldiers, who serve as beaters, pursues a powerful wild bull that seeks, with its last strength, to find refuge in a papyrus thicket. The wounded animal seeks the cool wetness of the Nile water. Escape seems impossible. In his excitement, the king has flung his leg over the front of the chariot, has stepped upon the shaft, and is about to give the collapsing animal the coup de grâce with his lance. Another animal, wounded in the belly, rolls on its back beneath the galloping horses, and in the thicket lies a third wild bull struck by a fatal arrow. This sort of chariot-borne hunt demands physical dexterity and skill with weapons on the part of the royal Nimrod. The inscription links pharaoh with his booty: "He is like Month (the god of war), the powerful bull, when he rages, who strikes the lands of the Asians and annihilates their progeny. He causes the strong (the wild bulls) to shrink away so that they turn their faces up to the trees and their backs cover the land and they bend down before him"[16]

Capturing wild animals with the lasso, a technique that goes back to prehistoric times, is the subject of an impressive scene that decorates a wall of the temple of Sethos I (fig. 118). Ramesses II and a young prince make use of this ancient hunting technique for the first stage of a ritual sacrifice.[17]

An early palette, known because of its subject as the "lion-hunt palette," summons various provinces to a lion hunt, but the lion hunt of later periods was reserved for the king, to whom was ascribed the courage and strength of the "king of the beasts." The New Kingdom was the great age of the royal lion hunters (fig. 119). Tuthmosis III was able to display an impressive array of game: "In a single second I killed seven lions with arrow shots."[18] A gem depicting Amenophis II begins the representation of a new type of royal lion hunt: the king approaches the lion on foot. The way he fells the animal with a club is reminiscent of the deeds of the Greek hero Herakles, whose characteristic weapon was also the club. The killing of the Nemean lion counted as one of his twelve labors. The weapons of the king's companions could be spears or bow and arrows. Amenophis III, known as a great big-game hunter, issued a series of commemorative scarabs with arrays of the lions he had bagged in the first decade of his reign (fig. 120): "Lists of lions which His Majesty slew with his own arrow shots from Year 1 to Year 10: 102 wild lions."[19] For a passionate hunter, the alleged average achievement, a lion a month, is quite believable.

---

118 *Lassoing a bull, temple of Sethos I (nineteenth dyn.), Abydos*

119 Pharaoh killing a lion with a spear, Ostrakon, MMA 26.7.1453

On the same edifice, already known for its oversized wild-bull hunt, there is also an imposing scene of the royal lion hunt (figs. 121 and 122). In its organization, this representation on the first pylon of the funerary temple of Ramesses III in Medinet Habu is similar to the other large hunting picture: pharaoh finds himself alone in his chariot. His driver is—as dictated by the artistic conventions for chariot-borne kings—not visible. It looks as if the king is guiding the span of horses with reins wound about his hips and simultaneously employing his weapons. Once again he is accompanied by his soldiers, who fulfill the role of beaters. The lion, which lies on its back under the span of leaping horses, is already a part of the array of booty. A second lion, bristling with arrows and spears, flees into a papyrus thicket. A third is identifiable only by his paws; he appears behind the king's back and forces him to turn around. With his lance the king wards off the attacking animal. From the unique pose of the twisting king some have wanted to conclude that the struggle of man against lion took place on the razor's edge, that the threat to the ruler was in the realm of the thinkable.[20] The positioning, however, can just as persuasively be interpreted as a sign of royal sovereignty in that the turning about testifies to the king's flexibility

120 Lion hunt scarab of Amenophis III (eighteenth dyn.), Brussels E *2368*

121 Lion hunt, temple of Ramesses III, Medinet Habu

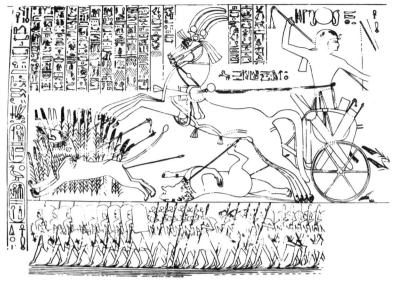

122 Lion hunt of Ramesses III, drawing

and dexterity. In any event, it is telling that many New Kingdom monarchs kept a tame lion whose place near the throne was an emblem of strength and power. In case of military conflict, however, he was a "battle lion," a symbolic figure that charged into the fray and raged against the enemy.

Only during the eighteenth dynasty, when Egypt extended its sphere of power toward Asia Minor and preempted a repetition of the invasion of the Hyksos, were there reports of elephant hunts. Although elephants were no longer to be found in the Nile Valley, a considerable number of them survived in the vicinity of the Syrian river Orontes. For the kings of that period, who passed through this area on their many Near Eastern campaigns, it was fashionable to lighten the routine of mundane military life with the pleasures of a hunt. Tuthmosis III seems to have caught a real hunting fever. Three sources agree in referring to his bag of 120 animals. Thus the elephant hunt is plucked from the sphere of the royal dogma (or—if you will—from the world of mere official court reports) and firmly ensconced in reality. We are all the more convinced of the story's historicity because the two official inscriptions are confirmed by the text of a private person. Significantly, the king reckons the elephant hunt in Niy among his heroic deeds, next to his successes in war and his athletic achievements. They are part of divine providence.

On his stela at Gebel Barkal we read, "He (the god Re) repeated for me a very brave deed by Lake Niy. He let me spy herds of elephants. My Majesty hunted them, a herd of 120 heads."[21] This elephant hunt is also mentioned in another text that relates the great hunting feats this ruler achieved in his first twenty-two years.[22] The hunt receives its particular charm from the tomb obituary of the official Amenemheb: "Again I [saw] another wonderful feat accomplished in Niy by the Lord of Both Lands. He hunted 120 elephants for their teeth. I positioned myself against the largest of them, the one that fought against His Majesty. I cut off his trunk while he stood [before] His Majesty and I found myself between two rocks. Therefore, my Lord rewarded me with gold."[23]

The eyewitness testimony by a participant in the hunt, his ruler's rescuer, should be accepted as a highly credible source because it, in contrast to the usual formulaic grave inscriptions, is a unique report of an actual elephant hunt. There can be no doubt about the extraordinary personal engagement of the pharaoh in this episode, even if the count of slain animals is seen as the booty of the entire army rather than—as the Egyptian conception had it—solely attributable to the successful ruler. A further hint of the historicity of this elephant hunt is the fact that with Egypt's diminishing political influence in the Near East the hunts apparently died out. The zenith of Egypt's political power in this area was reached during the reign of Tuthmosis III. Neither his successor Amenophis II, whose athletic abilities have been well documented, nor Amenophis III, who made a point of displaying his hunting successes, mentioned elephant hunts, which were so dazzling to those who observed them.

If we were already persuaded that Tuthmosis III was the greatest of the pharaoh-hunters, our impression would be deepened by a unique report of a rhinoceros hunt among the the Egyptian sources: the Stela of Erment,[24] also located outside of the Egyptian motherland, this time in Nubia. The king's challenge must have been enormous. Filled with pride, he not only had the animal pictured on a pylon of the Temple of Erment, but also gave the animal's physical dimensions.[25]

Swamp Hunts

Big-game hunting impresses us as a royal privilege, certain exceptions (hippopotamus hunting, elephant hunting) notwithstanding, but swamp hunts were first and foremost an aristocratic pastime, highly valued by the nobility through all periods of Egyptian history. Under the rubric of swamp hunting we gather together two elements—fish spearing and bird hunting with a throwing stick—that in Egyptian art constitute an inseparable unity (fig. 123). This follows from the nature of the activity. The papyrus thickets of the Nile Valley and Fayum, the preferred hunting grounds, invited the hunter to catch the fish that swarmed through the waters and to bring down the birds native to the place.

123 *Swamp hunt, tomb of Suenmut, TT 92 (eighteenth dyn.)*

We can conclude from two badly damaged scenes from the funerary temples of the first two kings of the fifth dynasty, Userkaf and Sahura, that the swamp hunt was also initially the prerogative of the pharaoh.[26] Only later did the motif appear in a private grave, and, remarkably, when it did the deceased was shown dressed in a royal loin cloth, obsessed with a passion for the hunt that was worthy of royalty. On the other hand, with few exceptions, swamp hunts with royal participation cease to occur in the art of later times.[27] The exact reasons for this state of affairs are unknown, but it seems probable that a profound transformation of the conception of the king occurred in the course of the fifth dynasty. In the wake of a social revolution there was a change in the canon of values that was responsible for the fact that every deceased person was now allowed to have himself portrayed at royal activities and to share magically in the king's power over death. Just as the royal hunter annihilated animals as symbols of his enemies, so the entombed private person defended himself in the beyond against the dangers that threatened from the underworld.

Subordinated to the tomb representation of the swamp hunt was a second, derivative meaning which was related to the rebirth of the deceased. The grave as site of eternal life was functionally related through its   159 decoration to Egyptian notions of the afterlife. A resurrection of the deceased was only possible through his rebirth, and that in turn necessitated that he first be conceived.[28] This conception, say the proponents of the thesis of a twofold meaning for the bird-hunting pictures, is expressed in disguised form. "Throwing stick" and the term "to sling a throwing stick" are both expressed by the Egyptian word qm3, which also means "to conceive." Only in this sense can we explain the presence of the festively adorned wife who appears as the attractive beloved in an erotic milieu. Similarly, the appearance of the children of the deceased is appropriate when seen in this context, because they are also the products of human conception. In this way, so goes the argument, the central concern of the Egyptians, the continuation of life after death, is magically secured by means of the bird hunt. Through its representation, the entombed person receives eternal life.

Without wishing simply to dismiss this interpretation as an impossibility, I must emphasize that the swamp hunt was a social event in which an entire hunting society, including women and children, participated (fig. 124).[29] This is, at any rate, the impression one receives from reading two stories, unfortunately preserved only in fragmentary form, that have been edited by R. A. Caminos under the titles "The Pleasures of Fishing and Fowling" and "The Sporting King."[30] These narratives of hunting in the marshes of Lake Fayum have an immediacy that enlivens their fine insights into the recreational sports of the Egyptian upper class. We see the passion with which the town dwellers enjoy the simple open-air life of the hunt. The first narrative, which begins with an evocation of the goddess of the hunt, Sekhet, reports in great detail on the preparations for the hunt and on the hunt itself.[31] The local god Sobk is promised a rich sacrifice in return for a successful hunt. A friendly hunting company gathers. All go off on the bird hunt and they catch an abundance of fish:

> I prepare my protective apron of juniper and cover it with pine wood . . . [at the] entrance to the marshes so that I can observe the children of Hwt-ihyt as they sling the throwing sticks at the wi3yt birds while every woman drives her wild birds forward before they can submerge. I camp at the water's edge, [ready] my cover and fasten my bait. I am in the shadows while my fish are in sunlight. The (fish) sitting (in the water) suspects nothing. I see him, but he can not see me. A fish is transfixed by my spear. I kill with every thrust and there is no stopping for [my] spear. I make a bundle of the white bulti-fish.[32]

There are detailed reports of bird catching with draw-nets, which require the hunter to pull the drawstring at the right moment in order to close them. Because of the weight of the netflaps and the necessary quick-

124 *Boat model with hunting party, tomb of Meketre, TT 280 (eleventh dyn.), MMA 20.3.6*

ness of execution in closing them, the cooperation of a number of persons is needed. Since they must wait under cover and cannot see the pond or the net-covered water, they must rely upon a lookout who gives them a signal with a cloth when it pays to draw the net (fig. 125).[33]

The fact that this hunting technique is mentioned in "The Pleasures of Fishing and Fowling" shows its sporting connotation in the eyes of the Egyptians. In fact, dexterity and a kind of team spirit were both called for in order to outsmart the quick, shy birds. The cooperation between the lookout and the netters had to be close, and the technique of the draw-net in particular had to function smoothly. When these factors failed to be optimally related to one another, the water birds had an excellent chance to escape. Since this kind of bird catching with a draw-net, which is frequently represented in Egyptian tomb art, was almost always carried out by the deceased man's servants, one hesitates to think of him as the sportsman. Normally, this group is also engaged in utilitarian labor on his behalf; they usually pluck and pickle the captured birds. Unlike the texts accompanying scenes of fish spearing and bird hunting with the throwing stick, the captions do not speak of the sporting pleasure of the bird catchers. Thus one hesitates to call the activity sport even when the lord has a hand in it.[34] It seems incredible that a single man could successfully execute a procedure that as a rule required five or six persons. Here we have another example of reality reworked to enhance the prestige of the entombed 161

125 Bird catching with a draw net, tomb of Nefer, Saqqara (fifth dyn.)

aristocrat. These considerations stand in the way of a fully satisfactory discussion of bird catching with a draw-net.

At one point the story, to which we now return, takes on a melancholy tone. The narrator, obviously a high official serving in the royal residence, wishes passionately that the bucolic idyll he has experienced during a few days of leisure might become his everyday lot. He feels the painful contrast between overly refined urban culture and the simple life in the country, from which he has come. His almost modern longing for a natural life can be easily understood in our own day. The complaint of the Egyptian nobleman reminds one in its central theme of Jean-Jacques Rousseau's cry "Back to nature!"

The story of "The Sporting King" is less clear in its structure because the papyrus version that survives is even more steeped in pathos than the tale "The Pleasures of Fishing and Fowling." Its contents consist of a swamp hunt undertaken by King Amenemhet II (twelfth dynasty) after an eloquent courtier painted it in glowing colors. The royal hunting party journeys to a recreational lake in Fayum. The women of the harem and the king's children are a part of the group. We cannot tell from the damaged text whether the king plays an active role in the fish spearing and the bird hunting with the throwing stick, or whether he merely enjoys the success of his hunters. It is significant that the pharaoh himself thrusts the fishing spear and flings the throwing stick with his own hand.[35] We see this with exemplary clarity in an inscription of one Sobkhotep, who was responsible for the swamp hunt of Tuthmosis IV in Fayum: "[I] accompanied [His Maj-

esty] and had the confidence of the Lord of the Two Lands when His
Majesty went upon his hunting excursion and enjoyed himself in his boat.
He crisscrossed the marshes of Fayum and went through the papyrus
thickets; as he did so, he killed [birds] with the throwing stick and speared
fish in great numbers, he, the image of a king, the beloved of Sekhet,
one . . . of the beloved of Sobk, the fish- and bird-catcher of the two ladies,
who acts with both arms, while I was in [his company]."[36]

That this was no isolated instance can be seen from the relatively frequent appearance of titles given to those whose task it was to organize the
royal hunts: "Overseer of the Two Bird Ponds of Pleasure" or "Overseer of
Every Lovely Pleasure of the King," whereby the reference is to hunting in
the papyrus thickets.[37]

From the many representations of this sport of the nobility we can
discern what this beloved upper-class recreation of swamp hunting must
have looked like.[38] The pictures of the hunt often charm us with their
tasteful composition, acute observation of nature, and lively colors. As has
already been mentioned, fish spearing and bird hunting with the curved
throwing stick constitute an artistic unity, usually against the background
scene of the hunt, namely the papyrus thickct (fig. 126). On one side we see
the deceased as bird hunter (fig. 127); on the other he spears the fish
swimming toward him (fig. 128). For both activities he stands astride a
small boat made from papyrus sheaves, with an elevated prow and stern,
that in reality must have been a very uncertain platform.

---

126 Bird hunting and fish spearing, tomb of Nacht, TT 52 (eighteenth dyn.)

127 Bird hunting with throwing stick, tomb of Khnumhotep, Beni Hasan no. *3* (twelfth dyn.)

128 Fish spearing, tomb of Khnumhotep, Beni Hasan no. *3* (twelfth dyn.)

The boats are sometimes artfully decorated and fit well with the festively adorned persons: mostly the hunter and his wife and children. The latter, of course, play a subordinate role, which is emphasized by the proportions. Occasionally, their activity consists of handing things over; they replace a poorly aimed throwing stick or extend a spear. The bird hunter raises the throwing stick to hurl it and, with his other hand, holds one or more birds by their legs (fig. 129). They are sometimes identified as booty. In that case they must be dead, which is hard to reconcile with the fact that they are restlessly fluttering. It is more likely then that they are decoy birds who are supposed to call their species-mates into the hunter's field of vision.[39] In the ideal case, which is often depicted, the whizzing throwing stick can break the neck of a flying bird (fig. 130). No doubt the whirling implement struck effective blows in the midst of a thick swarm of birds. Whether or not it returned after a bad throw, as is the case with the Australian boomerang, is a disputed question.[40] At any rate, among the types the bird hunters hold in their hands are some that are strikingly similar to the Australian throwing sticks (fig. 131). The same can be said of the surviving implements, a number of which were discovered in the tomb of Tutankhamon.[41]

It was a precondition for a successful hunt that the birds leave the cover of the thicket. In addition to the decoy calls of their tamed species-mates,

164

129 Bird hunter with throwing stick, tomb of Menna, TT 69 (eighteenth dyn.)

wildcats could be used to put them to flight.[42] The struggles about the nest set off by the incursion of these animals have been well observed. Another method, often pictured in the graves of private citizens of the Old Kingdom, was the vigorous shaking of a papyrus stem.[43] Presumably these scenes correspond to an earlier reality, when the nobleman, before he moved on to organize his own hunting excursions, still felt honored to be

130 Birds swarming, from a hunting scene, tomb of Menna, TT 69 (eighteenth dyn.)

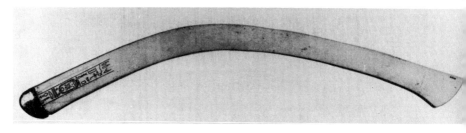

131 Throwing stick of Tutankhamon (eighteenth dyn.), Cairo JE *61 614*

allowed to undertake this auxiliary function during the king's swamp hunt.

A vision of the successful bird hunter sways before the eyes of the author of spell 62 of the coffin texts: "Water birds by the thousands will come to you, which lie on your way. You hurl your throwing stick at them, and they are thousands that drop with the sound of its path through the air, namely sr-geese, greenbreast birds, ṯrp-geese and male sṯ-geese."[44]

While traversing the papyrus thickets the swamp hunter had other things in mind in addition to the bird hunt. He carried with him a two-pronged spear that he employed, when conditions were favorable, for catching fish. The trick was to bring his little papyrus boat quietly and cautiously as near as possible to the prey, and then, at just the right moment, to thrust with the spear. One hand was used simply to guide the device while the other, holding the end of the shaft, propelled it. This technique was presumably more reliable than actually hurling the spear. If the fish spearer was especially lucky, each of the two prongs stuck a victim. This rare event is, however, repeatedly shown in the visual representations (figs. 123 and 128). Since the slightly bent position advisable for stalking the prey was incompatible with the dignity of a nobleman, artists tried to square the circle with a trick. They pictured so high a water level that the deceased nobleman whom they portrayed could stand upright to do his spearing. This peculiar manipulation of the water level is known in Egyptological literature as the "water mountain." It is more prominent in scenes from the Old Kingdom than in those from the New. In contrast to the chin-high water of the earlier scenes, the "water mountain" in later times sinks to the height of the hunter's knees.[45]

There is no doubt that this method of spear fishing gave the fish a real chance to escape. Only the skilled and practiced swamp hunter could reckon with a worthwhile catch. Thus the sporting character of spear fishing in the swamps, like that of bird hunting with a throwing stick, was quite pronounced.

The motif of the swamp hunt took a new shape under Tutankhamon. In a relief carved upon an ivory chest, the young king sits on a chair and

132 Bird hunting with bow and arrow, shrine of Tutankhamon, Cairo JE 62 481

shoots with bow and arrow into an artificial lake swarming with fish.[46] They are the same fish that appear in the "water mountains" of fish-spearing scenes in private graves. The pond is surrounded by bushes in which birds perch. They too are a target for the royal hunter, at whose feet the queen crouches, handing him an arrow. The results of the hunt are indicated by a servant who comes by with a fish and a bird, each transfixed by an arrow.

Shooting birds with bow and arrow is also the motif of the side of a gilded statue shrine from the grave of the same king (fig. 132).[47] It shares space with a traditional scene of bird hunting with the throwing stick. The unerring royal arrows have already found their victims in the swarm of birds fluttering above a papyrus bush. In this scene, too, the queen crouches on the ground before the sitting archer and hands him an arrow with one hand, while she points with the other to a bird's nest in the papyrus thicket.

9   The History of Research

In the age of Humanism, the conscious turning back toward classical antiquity led to an extensive Renaissance strongly influenced by the spiritual and material culture of Greek and Roman civilization. The more or less simultaneous invention in the fifteenth century of movable-block printing allowed the vigorous propagation of the ideas of the age—abetted by the generally favorable reception for Humanistic thought. During the sixteenth century philologists published a rapidly increasing number of critical editions of ancient authors, especially the Greeks, which made ancient conditions known in all their complexity. The pronounced importance of agonistics and gymnastics in Greek society made the sports of antiquity automatically salient for the burgeoning world of scholarship. Humanistic scholars seized upon this theme and it was not long before the first standard works began to appear in this field. For example, *De Arte Gymnastica*, the famous work of the Italian doctor and scholar Hieronymus Mercurialis, appeared first in Venice in 1569 and continued to be published in numerous editions for the next hundred years. In 1841 the German philologist Johann Heinrich Krause gathered together the preliminary studies that had been done up to his day and also included in his account of Greek sports the results of early archaeological research.[1] Krause also mentioned what was then known about ancient Egyptian sports.

Concentrated research into the sports of ancient Egypt scarcely began until the mid-twentieth century. Of course, scholars were aware soon after the birth of archeology, when, in 1822, the ingenious Frenchman J.-F. Champollion deciphered the hieroglyphics of the Rosetta Stone, that

Egyptian sources mentioned wrestling, hunting, and dancing; but the
young science of Egyptology had more important problems to attend to
than a domain of culture that many people even today regard as trivial. The
initially tiny band of Egyptologists devoted themselves first of all to philology in order to perfect their knowledge of the language that was the key to
further research into Egyptian culture. In the age of historicism political
history took priority. Chronology and genealogy were the favored approaches; the proverbial religiosity of the inhabitants of the Nile Valley was
worth tracking through the extensive mortuary texts; art and literature
were further themes attractive to nineteenth-century scholars.

When at the turn of the century a period of excavations began and new
archaeological material came to light, sport motifs still lacked the prestige
that might have engendered a serious discussion. The first visible results of
a systematic attempt at documentation in this connection were the collection of materials for cultural history edited by Klebs,[2] and the Egyptian
cultural history published by A. Erman[3] in 1885 and reworked by H. Ranke
in 1923 to bring it up to date with respect to the latest available research.
The latter work found a large number of readers. The First World War and
the crises that followed had a palpably negative effect on the young science
of Egyptology. It is, therefore, hardly an accident that it was not until 1930
that the serious consideration of Egyptian sports began. The trend toward
greater interest was presumably stimulated by the increasingly important
role played by sports in the public's consciousness, especially after Pierre
de Coubertin's 1896 effort to revive the interrupted tradition of the ancient
Olympic Games. Quite aside from the revival of the Olympics, sports had
clearly, by 1930, won a place in society, functioning as a counterweight to
the lack of physical fitness in our industrial age.

Be that as it may, the decade just before the Second World War was an
extremely fruitful one for the study of Egyptian sports history. H. Schaefer
published numerous essays on the topic of target archery.[4] J. A. Wilson
dedicated a splendid study to the ceremonial contests of the New Kingdom and researched the interesting captions in Medinet Habu, with their
scenes of wrestling and stick-fighting tournaments.[5]

The discovery of the great Sphinx Stela of Amenophis II by the Egyptian
scholar S. Hassan on 10 October 1936 meant to the study of sport history in
the age of the pharaohs approximately what the excavation of Olympia
meant for our knowledge of Greek relationships. The text of the stela, a song
of praise for the athletic ability of the young king, was extensively published
by its discoverer.[6] It stimulated numerous studies of the sporting kings,
especially after B. van de Walle's classic article "Les rois sportifs dans l'ancienne Egypte," an exemplary collection of comparative materials.[7]

A promising method for interpreting incomprehensible (or, better, not yet comprehended) scenes from pharaonic Egypt was demonstrated by the Egyptian archeologist Saad at the end of the 1930s when he convincingly explained, with the help of ethnological and ethnographic methods, that a hitherto misunderstood children's game from the Old Kingdom was a kind of combined long and high jump (in Arabic, *khazza lawizza*).[8] It was a great advantage to him that he himself had played the game as a child. It is striking that three extensive studies of the dance were published just before the Second World War, of which Brunner-Traut's is still considered standard for this area of ancient Egyptian cultural history.[9] Unfortunately, H. Wild's studies of the dance were never published in their entirety.[10] Originally a dissertation, the research into ancient Egyptian wrestling by Wilsdorf, published in 1939, is also still standard.[11] With the addition of J. Vandier-d'Abbadie's compendious 1940 study of stick fighting, research was complete enough for the combat sports of ancient Egypt to be fairly well known.[12]

These fruitful research initiatives of the 1930s were interrupted by the Second World War, and it was some time before the topic of sport was once again given the attention it deserved.

In 1957, at the same time as H. Brunner's attempt to investigate the role of physical education,[13] Hornung published the first of a still-unfinished series of thematically related articles addressing the Egyptian conception of history and of the king's role.[14] These studies form the indispensable framework for any investigation of the sports of the pharaohs. My own fairly extensive research into this area is greatly indebted to the paradigm established by Hornung.[15]

New paths in the field of ancient Egyptian sports historiography were marked by Caminos in 1958, when he masterfully edited two papyri belonging to the genre of the hunting tale: "The Pleasures of Fishing and Fowling" and "The Sporting King."[16] The same can be said of DeVries, whose 1960 publication provided a comprehensive view of the sports of the Nile Valley in the age of the pharaohs.[17] His themes went beyond a statement of the known facts; the objects of his research included the attitudes of the ancient Egyptians toward physical leisure-time activities. When A. D. Touny and Steffan Wenig decided in 1969 to bring ancient Egyptian sports to a wider readership,[18] they could build upon DeVries' unpublished book and upon valuable preliminary work by J. Vandier, who provided detailed documentation for certain areas of Egyptian physical exercises.[19] Accompanying their systematic presentation of the data is a carefully selected set of plates providing the core of the ancient Egyptians' visual representation of their sports.

In the 1970s, when sport historians began to pay more attention to the

early history of Egyptian culture, these efforts at systematization were continued in a variety of ways. Before the end of the decade there appeared in
German translation a collection of sources for the history of Egyptian
sports and then, with the discovery of new materials, a supplement to the
collection.[20] It was doubtless surprising that a bibliographical analysis of
Egyptian sports came to more than 700 titles.[21] This bibliography, which
first appeared in 1978, has been continually supplemented by new
entries—some 350 by the early 1990s.[22]

The many articles of the *Lexikon der Aegyptologie*, more than a hundred of
which discuss or touch upon sports, provide a solid base for further research into Egyptian sports. This nearly completed enterprise, edited by
Helck and W. Westendorf, is especially admirable because it appeared
without long delays between volumes—which means that the various
entries build upon a more or less identical body of research.[23]

Happily, the scholarly work on the tomb of Tutankhamon, discovered in
almost perfect condition in 1922, has recently made great progress. The
highly successful show that toured the world in the 1980s exhibited a
selection of objects among which those related to sports were—as one
might expect for a pharaoh of the eighteenth dynasty—well represented.[24]
The scholarly project "Tut'ankhamūn's Tomb Series," well designed to replace H. Carter's preliminary report on the contents of the tomb, contains
exemplary treatments of the tomb's numerous and various bows and other
archery equipment by W. McLeod[25] as well as excellent treatment of its
board games by W. J. Tait.[26] Recently, good work has also been done on the
royal chariot.[27]

In regard to the last decade, it should also be emphasized that works
have appeared that are dedicated to individual games and sport disciplines,
including Wiedemann's dissertation on running[28] and that of Pusch on
board games.[29] Recent attempts, like the very successful one by Ingomar
Weiler, to present Egyptian sport history in a cross-cultural, comparative
context should not be overlooked.[30]

Finally, I must mention the numerous essays that have recently focused
on smaller areas and finer details; they too provide bits of stone for the
larger mosaic of ancient Egyptian sport history. Contributions like that of
H. Altenmueller and A. M. Mousa on the Running Stela of Taharqa,[31] with
the long-distance race, its prerequisite training, the runners' achievements
and victory celebration, and the brief participation of the pharaoh, prove
that we can count upon new discoveries as long as the archeological investigation of the Nile Valley continues.

After this short survey of the history of research, it should be easy to
understand that a brief overview of ancient Egyptian sports and related
fields, which was the goal of this present book, was feasible. To write the

real history of this topic over the course of three thousand years of ancient Egyptian history, with its high points and low points, one must follow the pattern of the historical representation of cultural phenomena from the better researched cultures of antiquity; and that task requires even more intensive preliminary work.

Appendix: The
Egyptian Dynasties

The following list is based on Hornung's *Grundzüge der ägyptischen Geschichte*, 2d ed. (Darmstadt, 1978), 159–65. Only those pharaohs who are mentioned in the text are listed. All of them appear in a sporting context. Among them are the most famous of the Egyptian kings.

Earliest Period

First dynasty: *ca. 2950–2770* B.C.
  Dewen
Second dynasty: *ca. 2770–2640*

Old Kingdom

Third dynasty: *ca. 2640–2575*
  Djoser ca. 2624–2605
Fourth dynasty: *ca. 2575–2465*
  Snofru ca. 2575–2551
  Cheops ca. 2551–2528
  Kheruef ca. 2520–2494
Fifth dynasty: *ca. 2465–2325*
  Userkaf ca. 2465–2458
  Sahura ca. 2458–2446
  Niusserre ca. 2420–2396
Sixth dynasty: *ca. 2325–2155*
  Pepy II ca. 2254–2160
Seventh and eighth dynasties: *ca. 2155–2134*

First Intermediate Period

Ninth and tenth dynasties: *ca. 2134–2040*

Middle Kingdom

Eleventh dynasty: *ca. 2134–1991*
Twelfth dynasty: *ca. 1991–1785*
  Sesostris I ca. 1971–1926
  Amenemhet II ca. 1929–1892
Thirteenth dynasty: *ca. 1785–1650*
  (Upper Egypt)
Fourteenth dynasty: *ca. 1720–1650*
  (Delta)

Second Intermediate Period

Fifteenth and sixteenth dynasties: *ca. 1650–1540* (Hyksos)
Seventeenth dynasty: *ca. 1650–1551* (in Thebes)
  Seqenenre ca. 1570
  Kamose ca. 1555–1551

Eighteenth dynasty: ca. *1552–1306*
　Ahmose ca. 1552–1527
　Tuthmosis I ca. 1506–1494
　Hatshepsut ca. 1490–1468
　Tuthmosis III ca. 1490–1436
　Amenophis II ca. 1438–1412
　Tuthmosis IV ca. 1412–1402
　Amenophis III ca. 1402–1364
　Amenophis IV ca. 1364–1347
　(Akheneten)
　Tutankhamon ca. 1347–1338
　Ay ca. 1337–1333
Nineteenth dynasty: ca. *1306–1186*
　Sethos I ca. 1304–1290
　Ramesses II ca. 1290–1224
Twentieth dynasty: ca. *1186–1070*
　Ramesses III ca. 1184–1153

Third Intermediate Period

Twenty-first dynasty: ca. *1070–945*
Twenty-second dynasty: ca. *945–722*
　(Bubastids)
　Osorkhon II ca. 862–833
Twenty-third dynasty: ca. *808–715*
Twenty-fourth dynasty: ca. *725–712*

Late Period

Twenty-fifth dynasty: ca. *712–664*
　(Ethiopian rule)
　Piankhi ca. 740–713
　Shebitku ca. 698–690
　Taharqa ca. 690–664
Twenty-sixth dynasty: ca. *664–525*
　(Saits)
Twenty-seventh dynasty: ca. *525–404*
　(Persian domination)
Twenty-eighth dynasty: ca. *404–399*
Twenty-ninth dynasty: ca. *399–380*
Thirtieth dynasty: ca. *380–343*
Thirty-first dynasty: *343–332* (second
　Persian domination)
Macedonian rule: *332–305*
　Alexander the Great
Ptolemaic dynasty: *305–30*
Roman rule: *30* B.C.–A.D. *385*
Byzantine rule: *395–641*
Arab rule: *641–present*

Abbreviations

AcOr	Acta Orientalia, Copenhagen
AH	Aegyptiaca Helvetica, Basel and Geneva
AM	Mitteilungen des Deutschen Archäologischen Instituts, Bureau of Athenian Studies, Berlin
AnOr	Analecta Orientalia, Rome
AOAT	Alter Orient und Altes Testament, Kevelaer and Neukirchen-Vluyn
ASAE	Annales du service des antiquités de l'Egypte, Cairo
ASAW	Abhandlungen der Sächsischen Akademie der Wissenschaften zu Leipzig, Philological and historical section, Berlin
ASE	Archaeological Survey of Egypt, London
AV	Archäologische Veröffentlichungen, Deutsches Archäologisches Institut, Cairo Department, Mainz
ÄA	Ägyptologische Abhandlungen, Wiesbaden
ÄF	Ägyptologische Forschungen, Glückstadt, Hamburg, and New York
BCH	Bulletin de correspondance hellénique, Paris
BdE	Bibliothèque d'étude, Cairo
BEFAR	Bibliothèque des Ecoles françaises d'Athènes et de Rome
Beni Hasan II	P. E. Newberry, Beni Hasan II (ASE 2). London, 1894
BIE	Bulletin de l'Institut d'Egypte, Cairo
BIFAO	Bulletin de l'Institut français d'archéologie orientale, Cairo
BJB	Bonner Jahrbücher, Cologne and Kevelaer

BLFS	Beiträge zur Lehre und Forschung im Sport, Schorndorf
BMFA	Bulletin of the Museum of Fine Arts, Boston
BMMA	Bulletin of the Metropolitan Museum of Art, New York
Brunner-Traut, Tanz	E. Brunner-Traut, Der Tanz im alten Ägypten (ÄF 6). 2d ed. Glückstadt, Hamburg, and New York
BSAC	Bulletin de la société d'archéologie copte, Cairo
BSFE	Bulletin de la société française d'égyptologie, Paris
CdE	Chronique d'Egypte, Brussels
CW	Classical World, Bethlehem, Pa.
Decker, Leistung	W. Decker, Die physische Leistung Pharaos. Cologne, 1971
De Vries, Attitudes	C. E. De Vries, Attitudes of the Ancient Egyptians toward Physical-Recreative Activities. Diss., Chicago, 1960
EEF	Egypt Exploration Fund, London
ERA	Egypt Research Account, London
GM	Göttinger Miszellen, Göttingen
HÄB	Hildesheimer Ägyptologische Beiträge, Hildesheim
HdO	Handbuch der Orientalistik, Leiden and Cologne
JARCE	Journal of the American Research Center in Egypt, Boston
JEA	Journal of Egyptian Archaeology, London
KBSW	Kölner Beiträge zur Sportwissenschaft, Schorndorf (from vol. 6 St. Augustin)
Keel, Weisheit	O. Keel, Die Weisheit spielt vor Gott. Freiburg and Göttingen, 1974
LÄ	W. Helck, E. Otto, and W. Westendorf, eds., Lexikon der Ägyptologie. Wiesbaden, 1975–
MÄS	Münchner Ägyptologische Studien, Berlin and Munich
McLeod, Composite Bows	W. McLeod, Composite Bows from the Tomb of Tutʿankhamūn (TTS III). Oxford, 1970
McLeod, Self Bows	W. McLeod, Self Bows and Other Archery Tackle from the Tomb of Tutʿankhamūn (TTS IV). Oxford, 1982
MDAIK	Mitteilungen des Deutschen Archäologischen Instituts, Cairo Department, Berlin and Wiesbaden; Mainz
MIO	Mitteilungen des Instituts für Orientforschung, Berlin
OIP	Oriental Institute Publications, Chicago

OLP	Orientalia Lovaniensia Periodica, Louvain
OLZ	Orientalistische Literaturzeitung, Berlin and Leipzig
Or	Orientalia, Rome
PMMA	Publications of the Metropolitan Museum of Art, Egyptian Expedition, New York
Pusch, Senet-Brettspiel	E. B. Pusch, Das Senet-Brettspiel im Alten Ägypten, vol. 1 (MÄS 38). Berlin and Munich, 1979
QT	W. Decker, Quellentexte zu Sport und Körperkultur im alten Ägypten. St. Augustin, 1975
RAPH	Recherches d'archéologie, de philologie et d'histoire, Cairo
RdE	Revue d'égyptologie, Paris
RE	Realencyclopädie der classischen Altertumswissenschaft. Stuttgart, 1894–
SAK	Studien zur Altägyptischen Kultur, Hamburg
SAOC	Studies in Ancient Oriental Civilizations, Chicago
SHAW	Sitzungsberichte der Heidelberger Akademie der Wissenschaften, Philological and historical section, Heidelberg
SÖAW	Sitzungsberichte der Österreichischen Akademie der Wissenschaften, Philological and historical section, Vienna
SPAW	Sitzungsberichte der Preußischen Akademie der Wissenschaften, Philological and historical section, Berlin
TAPA	Transactions of the American Philosophical Society, Philadelphia
TÄB	Tübinger Ägyptologische Beiträge, Bonn
Touny and Wenig, Sport	A. D. Touny and S. Wenig, Der Sport im alten Ägypten. Leipzig, 1969
TTS	Tutʿankhamūn's Tomb Series, Oxford
Vandier, Manuel, vols. 4–5	J. Vandier, Manual d'archéologie égyptienne, vols. 4–5. Paris 1964–69
WdO	Die Welt des Orients, Wuppertal, Stuttgart, and Göttingen
Weiler, Sport	I. Weiler, Der Sport bei den Völkern der Alten Welt. Darmstadt, 1981
Wilsdorf, Ringkampf	H. Wilsdorf, Ringkampf im alten Ägypten. Würzburg, 1939
WZKM	Wiener Zeitschrift für die Kunde des Morgenlandes, Vienna

ZÄS Zeitschrift für ägyptische Sprache und
     Altertumskunde, Leipzig and Berlin

ZDPV Zeitschrift des Deutschen Palästina-Vereins, Leipzig
      and Wiesbaden

Notes

Chapter 2. The Sources for Ancient Egyptian Sports

1 Z. Saad, "Khazza lawizza," ASAE 37 (1937): 212–18; see also E. S. Eaton, "An Egyptian High Jump," BMFA 35 (1937): 54f.

2 E. B. Pusch, *Das Senet-Brettspiel im Alten Ägypten*, vol. 1, *Das inschriftliche und archäologische Material*, MÄS 38 (Munich and Berlin, 1979), slightly expanded by documents mentioned in a review by P. A. Piccione, JEA 70 (1984): 172–80.

3 H. Ranke, *Das altägyptische Schlangenspiel*, SHAW 1920, 4 (Heidelberg, 1920).

4 This topic will not be discussed in this book; see E. Brunner-Traut, "Spielzeug," LÄ 5 (1984): 1152–56.

5 M. A. Littauer and J. H. Crouwel, *Chariots and Related Equipment from the Tomb of Tut'ankhamūn*, TTS 8 (Oxford, 1985).

6 W. McLeod, *Composite Bows from the Tomb of Tut'ankhamūn*, TTS 4 (Oxford, 1970); W. McLeod, *Self Bows and Other Archery Tackle from the Tomb of Tut'ankhamūn*, TTS 4 (Oxford, 1982).

7 N. Jenkins, *The Boat beneath the Pyramid: King Cheops' Royal Ship* (London, 1980).

8 See E. Brunner-Traut, *Die altägyptischen Scherbenbilder (Bildostraka) der deutschen Museen und Sammlungen* (Wiesbaden, 1956).

9 I. Wallert, *Der verzierte Löffel*, ÄA 16 (Wiesbaden, 1967).

10 E. Hornung and E. Staehelin, *Skarabäen und andere Siegelamulette aus Basler Sammlungen Ägyptische Denkmäler in der Schweiz*, vol. 1 (Mainz, 1976); E. Staehelin, *Ägyptens heilige Pillendreher* (Basel, 1982).

11 For collected documents see W. Decker, *Quellentexte zu Sport und Körperkultur im alten Ägypten* (St. Augustin, 1975).

12 QT, document 32.

13 For the most recent revision, with a German translation by T. von der Way, see *Die Textüberlieferung Ramses' II zur Qadeš-Schlacht*, HÄB 22 (Hildesheim, 1984).

14 QT, document 3.

15 QT, document 14.

16 QT, document 15.

17 QT, document 17.

18 W. Decker, "Die Lauf-Stele des Königs Taharka," KBSW 13 (1984): 7–37.

19 QT, document 4.

20 QT, documents 23–24.

21 QT, document 39.

22 R. A. Caminos, *Literary Fragments in the Hieratic Script* (Oxford, 1956); see also QT, documents 8–9.

23 QT, document 1.

24 QT, document 6.

25 QT, document 29.

26 QT, document 36.

27 See B. W. Körbs, "Gymnasiale Mitteilungen in hellenistischen Papyri der frühen Ptolemäerzeit," *Carl Diem: Festschrift zur Vollendung seines 80. Lebensjahres am 24. Juni 1962*, ed. W. Körbs et al. (Frankfurt am Main and Vienna, 1962), 88–99; see also the collection of texts by M. Vandoni, *Feste pubbliche e private nei documenti greci* (Milan and Varese, 1964). P. Frisch has prepared a new selection of documents, *Zehn Agonistische Papyri* (Opladen, 1986).

28 On the gymnasium see J. Delorme's excellent *Gymnasion: Etude sur les monuments consacrés à l'éducation en Grèce*, BEFAR 296 (Paris, 1960). On the stadium see F. Krinzinger's dissertation "Untersuchungen zur Entwicklungsgeschichte des griechischen Stadions" (University of Innsbruck, 1968); and D. G. Romano, "The Stadia of the Peloponnesos" (diss., University of Pennsylvania, 1981). On both facilities see W. Zschietzschmann, *Wettkampf- und Übungsstätten in Griechenland*, vol. 1, *Das Stadion*; vol. 2, *Palästra-Gymnasion* (Schorndorf, 1960–61). There has not yet been a comprehensive study of the hippodrome.

29 A. Hönle and A. Henze, *Römische Amphitheater und Stadien: Gladiatorienkämpfe und Circusspiele* (Feldmeilen, 1981); J. H. Humphrey, *Roman Circuses: Arenas for Chariot Racing* (London, 1986).

30 The Sphinx Stela of Amenophis II mentions a "northern shooting place"; see QT, 59.

31 QT, document 16.

32 J. Leclant, "Un parc de chasse de la Nubie pharaonique," *Le sol, la parole et l'écrit: 2000 ans d'histoire africaine: Mélanges en hommage à R. Manny*, Bibliothèque d'histoire d'outre-mer, n.s., nos. 5–6 (Paris, 1981), 727–34.

33 A. Kammenhuber, *Hippologia hethitica* (Wiesbaden, 1961).

34 A. J. Knudtzon, ed., *Die El-Amarna-Tafeln*, 2 vols. (Leipzig, 1915; repr. Aalen, 1965).

35 See the excellent introduction by I. Weiler, *Der Sport bei den Völkern der Alten Welt*, 2d ed. (Darmstadt, 1988), 64–73.

36 G. F. Bass, *Cape Gelidonya: A Bronze Age Shipwreck*, TAPA, n.s., 57, 8 (Philadelphia, 1968).

37 W. Decker and J. Klauck, "Königliche Bogenschießleistungen in der 18. ägyptischen Dynastie: Historische Dokumente und Aspekte für eine experimentelle Überprüfung," KBSW 3 (1974): 23–55.

38 See W. Burkert, "Von Amenophis II zur Bogenprobe des Odysseus," *Grazer Beiträge* 1 (1973): 69–78; W. Decker, "Zur Bogenprobe des Odysseus," KBSW 6 (1977): 149–53.

39 QT, document 43.

40 QT, document 44.

41 QT, document 41; see also W. Decker, "La délégation des Eléens en Egypte sous la 26e dynastie," CdE xlix (1974): 31–42.

42 QT, document 40.

Chapter 3. The Athletic Kings

1 The following discussion of the Egyptian conception of history and of royal dogma is greatly indebted to the work of Hornung, who for many fruitful years has researched the different aspects of the topic. The brief bibliography of Hornung's writings that follows is chronological: "Zur geschichtliche Rolle des Königs in der 18. Dynastie," MDAIK 15 (1957): 120–33; *Geschichte als Fest* (Darmstadt, 1966), 9–29, 53–65 (for critical remarks on Hornung's views of the ancient Egyptian conception of history see W. Kaiser, OLZ 66 [1971]: 454–58); "Politische Planung und Realität im alten Ägypten," *Saeculum* 22 (1971): 48–58; "Von zweierlei Grenzen im alten Ägypten," *Eranos-Jahrbuch* 49 (1980): 393–427; "Pharao ludens," *Eranos-Jahrbuch* 51 (1982): 479–516; "Zum altägyptischen Geschichtsbewußtsein," *Archäologie und Geschichtsbewußtsein, Kolloquien zur Allgemeinen und Vergleichenden Archäologie*, vol. 3 (Munich, 1982), 13–30. For J. Assmann's directly opposing view of the role of Ramesses II see his "Krieg und Frieden im Alten Ägypten: Ramses II und die Schlacht bei Kadesch," *Mannheimer Forum* 1983–84, 175–231.

2 Hornung, *Geschichte*, 9f.

3 Ibid., 14f.

4 Hornung, "Pharao ludens," 479–516.

5 Hornung, "Politische Planung," 54–56.

6 C. M. Bowra, *Heroic Poetry*, 2d ed. (London, 1961).

7 W. Wolf, *Die Kunst Ägyptens* (Stuttgart, 1957), pl. 575.

8 H. Schäfer, "Das Niederschlagen der Feinde," WZKM 54 (1957): 168–76.

9 In a somewhat different context see P. Derchain, "Perpetuum mobile," *Miscellanea in honorem J. Vergote*, OLP 6–7, ed. P. Naster et al. (Louvain, 1976), 153–67.

10 W. Decker, *Die physische Leistung Pharaos: Untersuchungen zu Heldentum, Jagd und Leibesübungen der ägyptischen Könige* (Cologne, 1971), 152.

11 See W. C. Hayes, "The Sporting Tradition," *The Cambridge Ancient History*, 3d ed., ed. E. S. Edwards et al. (Cambridge, 1973), 2: 333–38. Also important is

the first treatment of this topic by B. van de Walle, "Les rois sportifs de l'ancienne Egypte," CdE 13 (1938): 234–57.

12 On the question of the Hyksos see M. Bietak, "Hyksos," LÄ 3 (1980): 93–103.

13 See M. A. Littauer and J. H. Crouwel, *Wheeled Vehicles and Ridden Animals in the Ancient Near East*, HdO I 2 B 1 (Leiden and Cologne, 1979); and J. Wiesner, *Fahren und Reiten*, Archaeologia Homerica F (Göttingen, 1968).

14 McLeod, "Composite Bows."

15 Decker, *Leistung*, 4–32.

16 M. Bietak and E. Strouhal, "Die Todesumstände des Pharaos Seqenenre' (17. Dynastie)," *Annalen des Naturhistorischen Museums in Wien* 78 (1974): 29–52.

17 E. Hornung has argued against the theory of Egyptian imperialism in "Von Zweierlei Grenzen."

18 See the extensive study by J. Delorme, *Gymnasion: Etude sur les monuments consacrés à l'éducation en Grèce*, BEFAR 296 (Paris, 1960).

19 QT, document 10. Textual lacunae are in the original.

20 QT, document 13.

21 QT, document 14.

22 QT, document 18.

23 QT, document 21.

24 K. Martin has treated this in LÄ 5 (1984): 782–90.

25 Thus named in E. Hornung and E. Staehelin, *Studien zum Sedfest*, AH 1 (Geneva, 1974).

26 W. Barta prefers this concept in *Untersuchungen zur Göttlichkeit des regierenden Königs*, MÄS 32 (Munich and Berlin, 1975), 62ff.

27 K. Martin in LÄ 5 (1984): 783.

28 E. Hornung and E. Staehelin, *Studien zum Sedfest*.

29 See W. Barta, "Die Sedfest-Darstellung Osorkons II. im Tempel von Bubastis," SAK 6 (1978): 25–42.

30 H. Kees, *Der Opfertanz des ägyptischen Königs* (Leipzig, 1912), 187.

31 W. Helck, "Bemerkungen zum Ritual des Dramatischen Ramesseumspapyrus," Or 23 (1954): 383–411, esp. 410.

32 P. Munro, "Bemerkungen zu einem Sedfest-Relief in der Stadtmauer von Kairo," ZÄS 86 (1961): 66.

33 E. Hornung and E. Staehelin, *Studien zum Sedfest*, 43.

34 J. Brinks, CdE lvi (1981): 13.

35 W. Helck, "Die Herkunft des abydenischen Osirisrituals," *Archiv orientální* 20 (1952): 72–85, esp. 81.

36 V. Vikentiev, "Les rites de la réinvestiture royale en tant que champ de recherches sur la période archaïque égypto-lybienne," BIE 37 (1956): 271–316, esp. 279–82.

37 B. H. Stricker, *De oorsprong van het Romeinse circus*, Mededelingen der Koninklijke Nederlandse Akademie van Wetenschappen, Afd. Letterkunde, n.s., vol. 33, no. 6 (Amsterdam and London, 1970).

38 A. J. Spencer, "Two Enigmatic Hieroglyphs and Their Relation to the Sed-

Festival," JEA 64 (1978): 52–55. On the problem of the meaning of the bases
see the wise judgment of D. Wiedemann in his dissertation, "Der Sinn des
Laufes im alten Ägypten" (Vienna, 1975), 64 and n. 2.

39 J.-P. Lauer, "Remarques sur les monuments du roi Zoser à Saqqarah," BI-
FAO 30 (1931): 333–60, esp. 356; C. M. Firth, J. E. Quibell, and J.-P. Lauer, The
Step Pyramid (Excavations at Saqqarah), 1 (Cairo, 1935): 115; vol. 2 (Cairo, 1935),
fig. 72. 1; J.-P. Lauer, La pyramide à degrés, 1 (Paris, 1936): 179; J.-P. Lauer, Histoire
monumentale des pyramides d'Egypte, vol. 1, Les pyramides d'Egypte, pt. 1, Les pyramides à degrés (IIIe dynastie) (Cairo, 1962), 115–17.

40 J.-P. Lauer, La pyramide à degrés, 1: 168; J.-P. Lauer, vol. 1, Les pyramides d'Egypte,
pt. 1, Les pyramides à degrés, 153f. On the bases see also Lauer's contribution to
ASAE 39 (1939): 452f.

41 W. Helck, "Herkunft und Deutung einiger Züge des frühägyptischen
Königsbildes," Anthropos 49 (1954): 961–91, esp. 986f.

42 Kees, Opfertanz; Stricker, Circus, 10f.

43 Wiedemann, "Der Sinn," 80 and passim.

44 D. Wiedemann, ". . . an diesem schönen Tage des Laufens," GM 83 (1984):
91–93.

45 W. Barta, "Königskrönung," LÄ 3 (1980): 531–33.

46 Ibid., 532.

47 W. Decker, "Sportliche Rituale im altägyptischen Krönungsritual," SAK 5
(1977): 1–20. In agreement, K. van Dam, Het Sed-feest, Onderwerpen uit de
Egyptologie 2 (Amsterdam, 1982), 23f; in disagreement, C. M. Zivie, "La
stèle d'Aménophis II à Giza," SAK 8 (1980): 269–84.

48 W. Helck, "Jubiläumsfest," Wörterbuch der Mythologie, vol. 1, Die alten Kultur-
völker, pt. 3, Ägypten: Die Mythologie der alten Ägypter, ed. H. W. Haussig (Stuttgart,
n.d.), 324; see also Wiedemann, "Der Sinn," 62.

49 V. Vikentiev, BIE 37 (1956): 304f.

50 E. Naville, The Festival Hall of Osorkon II in the Great Temple of Bubastis, EEF 10
(London, 1892), pl. 15.6.

51 Pausanias (V.1, 4); see also I. Weiler, Der Agon im Mythos: Zur Einstellung der
Griechen zum Wettkampf, Impulse der Forschung 16 (Darmstadt, 1974), 198f.

52 Ibid., 256–58, with references and examples drawn from non-Greek cultures.

53 QT, document 29; see also 117f.

54 Wiedemann, "Der Sinn," 83.

55 H. Goedicke, Re-used Blocks from the Pyramid of Amenemhet at Lisht, PMMA 20
(New York, 1971), no. 85.

56 An especially impressive example is given by McLeod in "Composite
Bows," pl. 14H.

57 W. Wolf, Die Bewaffnung des altägyptischen Heeres (Leipzig, 1926; repr. 1977), 14.

58 McLeod, "Composite Bows."

59 Ibid., no. 1.

60 Ibid., no. 20.

61 QT, document 10.

62 QT, document 14; the translation at the beginning is altered according to E. Edel, SAK 7 (1979): 31–33.

63 H. Brunner, *Altägyptische Erziehung* (Wiesbaden, 1957), fig. 2, source 33, and pp. 25, 104.

64 QT, document 16; see also H. Schäfer, OLZ 34 (1931); 91f.

65 The passage is not entirely clear, and the following translation is also possible: "However, as he returned from this deed to which I have directed your attention, he trod upon. . ." Because his discussion flows smoothly, I have been guided here by C. M. Zivie, *Giza au deuxième millénaire*, BdE lxx (Cairo, 1976), 72.

66 Ibid., NE 6; QT, document 17.

67 Decker, *Leistung*.

68 See n. 47 above.

69 W. Burkert, "Von Amenophis II zur Bogenprobe des Odysseus," *Grazer Beiträge* 1 (1973): 69–78; see also W. Decker, "Zur Bogenprobe des Odysseus," KBSW 6 (1977): 149–53.

70 QT, 58. The pharaoh's testing of three hundred bows makes the parallel even closer (QT, 59).

71 *Odyssey* xix 572–87; see also xxi.

72 O. Keel also adheres to this school of thought; see "Der Bogen als Herrschaftssymbol," ZDPV 93 (1977): 141–77.

73 The block is presently in the museum in Luxor; see *Musée d'art égyptien ancien de Louxor*, BdE xcv (Cairo, 1985), no. 88, fig. 53.

74 QT, document 19; for a correct reading of an important sentence, see E. Edel, SAK 7 (1979): 33.

75 In a much earlier period the target seems also to have been a post; see Goedicke, *Blocks*, no. 85.

76 QT, document 19; in OLZ 32 (1929): 236, H. Schäfer translates "pleasure" as "sports performance."

77 QT, document 20.

78 McLeod, "Composite Bows"; he discusses the bow of Amenophis II on p. 29 (F).

79 QT, document 21.

80 W. Decker, "Ein Amarnablock mit sportlichem Motiv," GM 20 (1976): 9–16.

81 Ibid., 175.

82 N. de G. Davies, BMMA (November 1935), sec. 2, p. 51, fig. 6; see also W. Decker, KBSW 3 (1974): 31f.

83 On the lion hunt see N. de G. Davies and A. H. Gardiner, *Tut'ankhamūn's Painted Box* (Oxford, 1962), pl. 4, also reproduced in W. Wreszinski, *Löwenjagd im alten Ägypten*, Morgenland 23 (Leipzig, 1932), pl. 13. On the ostrich hunt see the catalogue edited by J. Settgast, *Tutanchamun* (Mainz, 1980–81), no. 8; and W. Decker, KBSW 8–9 (1979–80), 90–94, figs. 11 and following.

84 QT, document 18.

85 McLeod, "Composite Bows," pl. 4, provides a good overview of the variations in the form of the arrowheads.

86 Ibid., 26–28, 44–49, pl. vi–xvi.

87 Ibid., 38–40, pl. xvii and following.

88 Ibid., 43, pl. xxix; KBSW 3 (1974): 29, fig. 3.

89 In addition to Bass's examples in *Cape Gelidonya* see representations of Ay (fig. 18) and Ramesses (fig. 19) as archers; see also BIFAO 69 (1971): 86, fig. 11 (= GM 20 [1976]: 16, fig. 1).

90 See Bass's documentation in *Cape Gelidonya*, 52–60.

91 Ibid., 78–81.

92 W. Decker, "Zum Ursprung des Diskuswerfens," *Stadion* 2 (1976): 196–212.

93 Letter from G. F. Bass to author, 13 October 1980.

94 W. Decker and J. Klauck, "Königliche Bogenschießleistungen in der 18. ägyptischen Dynastie," KBSW 3 (1977): 23–55, esp. 36–50.

95 On chariots in the ancient Near East and their environment see Littauer and Crouwel, *Wheeled Vehicles*, and Wiesner, *Fahren und Reiten*.

96 E. Hornung, *Grundzüge der ägyptischen Geschichte*, 2d ed. (Darmstadt, 1978), 67–71.

97 Relevant work by W. Helck is presented in SAK 11 (1984): 477 n. 1.

98 Knudtzon, *El-Amarna-Tafeln*, nos. 3, 7; see also C. Kühne, *Die Chronologie der internationalen Korrespondenz von El-Amarna*, AOAT 17 (Kevelaer and Neukirchen-Vluyn, 1973).

99 QT, document 29.

100 There is to date no monograph on ancient chariot races; see Weiler, *Sport*, 142f.

101 K. Kilian, "Zur Darstellung eines Wagenrennens aus spätmykenischer Zeit," AM 95 (1980): 21–31.

102 Weiler, *Sport*, 245–50.

103 A. Kammenhuber, *Hippologia hethitica* (Wiesbaden, 1961).

104 E. Ebeling, *Bruchstücke einer mittelassyrischen Vorschriftensammlung für die Akklimatisierung und Trainierung von Wagenpferden* (Berlin, 1951).

105 QT, document 17, p. 58.

106 QT, document 17, pp. 60f.

107 QT, document 33.

108 QT, document 31.

109 Von der Way, *Qadeš-Schlacht*, p. 325, paragraphs 270 and following.

110 C. Aldred, *Die Juwelen der Pharaonen* (Munich, Vienna, and Zurich, 1972), fig. 144.

111 QT, document 21.

112 G. Botti, "Il carro del sogno," *Aegyptus* 31 (1951): 192–98.

113 M. J. E. Quibell, *Tomb of Yuaa and Thuiu* (Cairo, 1908), pp. 65ff and 77, and pl. li–lvi.

114 Littauer and Crouwel, *Chariots*.

115 Discussed in W. Decker, "Der Wagen im Alten Ägypten," *Achse, Rad und Wagen*, 2d ed., ed. W. Treue (Göttingen, 1986), 36ff.

116 W. Decker, "Bemerkungen zur Konstruktion des ägyptischen Rades in der 18. Dynastie," SAK 11 (1984): 477–88.

117 For another interpretation of the construction see A. C. Western, "A Wheel Hub from the Tomb of Amenophis II," JEA 59 (1973): 91–94.

118 A successful experiment was conducted in which a reconstructed chariot with a driver weighing seventy kilograms was pulled by an automobile over a kilometer of level ground at a speed of thirty-eight kilometers an hour; see J. Spruytte, *Etudes expérimentales sur l'attelage: Contribution à l'histoire du cheval* (Paris, 1977), 39.

119 A. Guttmann, *From Ritual to Record* (New York, 1978).

120 One should, however, note Guttmann's insightful comment on ancient Egyptian hunting as a sport in *Ritual*, 42.

121 E. Hornung, "Zur geschichtlichen Rolle des Königs in der 18. Dynastie," MDAIK 15 (1957): 120–33, 125f.

122 The royal graves of the New Kingdom were dug increasingly deeply into the rocks; see E. Hornung, "Von zweierlei Grenzen im Alten Ägypten," *Eranos-Jahrbuch* 49 (1980): 393–427, esp. 408; on the number of entrances to the graves, which increased from five to thirteen, see E. Hornung, "Politische Planung und Realität im alten Ägypten," *Saeculum* 22 (1971): 48–58, esp. 56f.

123 A. Linfert, "Certamen principum," BJB 179 (1979): 177–86.

124 R. D. Mandell, "The Invention of the Sport Record," *Stadion* 2 (1976): 250–64.

125 See H. Eichberg, "Der Beginn des modernen Leistens," *Sportwissenschaft* 4 (1974): 21–48; H. Eichberg, "'Auf Zoll und Quintlein': Sport und Quantifizierungsprozeß in der frühen Neuzeit," *Archiv fur Kulturgeschichte* 56 (1974): 141–76; and H. Eichberg, *Leistung-Spannung-Geschwindigkeit* (Stuttgart, 1978).

126 For a modern definition of the sports record see K. Weis, "Rekord," *Sportwissenschaftliches Lexikon*, BLFS 49–50, 5th ed., ed. P. Röthig (Schorndorf, 1983), 300f.

127 QT, document 19; see also pp. 47f.

128 Guttmann, *Ritual*, 51–52.

129 E. Edel suggests that the record was equaled; see SAK 7 (1979): 38.

130 Ibid., 48–50.

131 QT, document 17, p. 60.

132 QT, document 29.

133 Ibid., 70ff.

134 QT, documents 12, 14–15.

135 QT, document 14.

136 QT, document 24.

137 QT, document 23.

138 QT, document 14 and n. 8.

139 QT, document 26; KBSW 8–9 (1979–80), 89–94, figs. 9–12. Ostrich hunts were certainly common among private persons; see J. Vandier, *Manuel d'archéologie égyptienne*, 4 (Paris, 1964): 829.

1 E. Eheloff, "Wettlauf und szenisches Spiel im hethitischen Ritual," SPAW 21 (1925): 267–74.

2 Weiler, Sport, 110, 146f.

3 A. R. Schulman, JARCE 2 (1963): 89f.

4 Z. B. Vandier, Manuel, vol. 4, figs. 365, 394.

5 R. Krauss, "Reisegeschwindigkeit," LÄ 5 (1984); 222f.

6 J. Jüthner, Die athletischen Leibesübungen der Griechen, vol. 2, Einzelne Sportarten, pt. 1, SÖAW 249, 2 (Vienna, 1968), pl. i–vi, viii–xi, xv–xvii, xxiii–xxxii.

7 A. M. Moussa, "A Stela of Taharqa from the Desert Road at Dahshur," MDAIK 37 (1981): 331–37; H. Altenmüller and A. M. Moussa, "Die Inschriften auf der Taharkastele von der Dahschurstrasse," SAK 9 (1981): 57–84.

8 For a sport-historical commentary, see W. Decker, "Die Lauf-Stele des Königs Taharka," KBSW 13 (1984): 7–37.

9 Ibid., 9f.

10 A. Milroy, The Long Distance Record Book (n.p., 1982), 25.

11 Ibid., 22.

12 H. Bengston, "Aus der Lebensgeschichte eines griechischen Distanzläufers," Symbolae Osloenses 32 (1956): 35–39; J. Matthews, "The Hemerodromoi: Ultra Long-Distance Running in Antiquity," CW 68 (1974): 161–69.

13 Ibid., 67.

14 J. Ebert has raised the question, in a letter to the author, whether winners might have been named for each half of the race. The "victors" (plural!) can perhaps be explained, he thinks, if the separate stages of the run were separately evaluated in order to arrive at a number of winners. Furthermore, if one follows his view, there might have been a contest of section versus section in which military units were evaluated.

15 M. Malaise, "Sésostris: Pharaon de légende et d'histoire," CdE xli (1966): 244–72.

16 QT, document 40 [= Diodorus I 53].

17 J. Ebert, Zum Pentathlon der Antike, ASAW 56, 1 (Berlin, 1963), esp. 44ff; Weiler, Sport, 157–61. On the last point see J.-P. Thuillier, Les jeux athlétiques dans la civilisation étrusque, BEFAR 256 (Rome, 1985), 287–94.

18 Z. Saad, "Khazza lawizza," ASAE 37 (1937): 212–18; see also E. S. Eaton, "An Egyptian High Jump," BMFA, August 1937, 54f.

19 For a reconstitution of the picture into a form expected by the modern observer see H. Schäfer, Von ägyptischer Kunst, 4th ed. (Wiesbaden, 1963), fig. 135b.

20 For a similar view see A. D. Touny and S. Wenig, Sport im alten Ägypten (Leipzig, 1969), 35, 37; for a different view see Vandier, Manuel, 4: 514.

21 On the whole question see C. E. DeVries's dissertation "Attitudes of the Ancient Egyptians toward Physical-Recreative Activities" (University of Chicago, 1960), 335–49.

22 See also Touny and Wenig, *Sport*, 34; Vandier, *Manuel*, 4: 514.

23 Z. Saad, ASAE 37 (1937): 216.

24 Ibid., 213.

25 Vandier, *Manuel*, vol. 4, fig. 231.

26 Ibid., 513. The movement can well be compared to the Greek *bibasis*; see Jüthner, *Leibesübungen* II 1, pp. 160f.

27 QT, document 29.

28 G. Lefèbvre, *Romans et contes égyptiens de l'époque pharaonique* (Paris, 1949), 120 n. 16, prefers "jumping."

29 See chapter 5.

30 K. Wiemann, "Die Phylogenese des menschlichen Verhaltens im Hinblick auf die Entwicklung sportlicher Betätigung," *Geschichte der Leibesübungen*, vol. 1, ed. H. Ueberhorst (Berlin, Frankfurt am Main, and Munich, 1972), 48–63, esp. 55–59.

31 For a survey of early testimony of wrestling and boxing in the ancient Near East and Crete see Thuillier, *Jeux athlétiques*, 17–24; and Weiler, *Sport*, 64f, 75.

32 See Weiler, *Sport*, 183–89, including references.

33 J. A. Wilson, "Ceremonial Games in the New Kingdom," JEA 17 (1931): 211–20; H. Wilsdorf, *Ringkampf im alten Ägypten*, Körperliche Erziehung und Sport: Beiträge zur Sportwissenschaft 3 (Würzburg, 1939), 53–67.

34 DeVries, "Attitudes," 372.

35 W. Decker, "Neue Dokumente zum Ringkampf im alten Ägypten," KBSW 5 (1976): 7–24, esp. 8–10 with fig. 1.

36 Wilsdorf, *Ringkampf*, 17; see also Touny and Wenig, *Sport*, pl. 3.

37 Wilsdorf, *Ringkampf*, p. 30; see also Touny and Wenig, *Sport*, p. 21.

38 Wilsdorf, *Ringkampf*, 32–40.

39 Wilsdorf is the only scholar to have discussed this; see ibid., 55–59.

40 On group 43 see ibid., 57.

41 Ibid., 27.

42 J. H. Breasted, Jr., *Egyptian Servant Statues* (Washington, 1948), 91f and fig. 86.

43 B. Gassowska, "Cirrus in vertice: One of the Problems in Roman Athlete Iconography," *Mélanges offerts à K. Michałowski* (Warsaw, 1966), 421–27.

44 W. Decker, KBSW 5 (1976): 10–13, with references.

45 Wilsdorf, *Ringkampf*, fig. 27 (p. 43); O. Keel, *Die Weisheit spielt vor Gott* (Freiburg and Göttingen, 1974), fig. 5.

46 H. H. Nelson et al., eds., *Medinet Habu II*, OIP ix (Chicago, 1932), pl. 111 and following.

47 J. A. Wilson, JEA 17 (1931): 212; C. F. Nims, Ramesseum Sources of Medinet Habu Reliefs," *Studies in Honor of George R. Hughes*, SAOC 39 (Chicago, 1976), 169–76.

48 For the text see QT, document 32.

49 J. A. Wilson, JEA 17 (1931): 211.

50 See also Wilsdorf, *Ringkampf*, 22.

51 See L. Roller's dissertation "Funeral Games in Greek Literature, Art and Life" (University of Pennsylvania, 1977).

52 W. Decker, "Die mykenische Herkunft des griechischen Totenagons," *Stadion* 7–9 (1982–83): 1–24.

53 This question will be discussed elsewhere. It is touched on by J. A. Wilson in JEA 17 (1931): 21, where Wilson indicates that he is seeking an explanation of this sort.

54 In this context it should be pointed out that Greek combat sports were often contested in various disciplines. Thus the athlete Theagenes of Thasos, who won thirteen hundred victories, a record, was supreme over a period of two decades not only in his specialty, boxing, but also in the pancration. On Theagenes see esp. J. Ebert, *Griechische Epigramme auf Sieger an gymnischen und hippischen Agonen*, ASAW 63, 2 (Berlin, 1972), no. 37. Similar feats were reported of other Greek participants in combat sports.

55 KBSW 5 (1976): 18, fig. 6.

56 J. Vandier d'Abbadie, "Deux nouveaux ostraca figurés," ASAE 40 (1940): 467–88, esp. 473f; Touny and Wenig, *Sport*, 25.

57 H. Carter, *Tut-ench-Amun* III (Leipzig, 1934), 161f; W. Wolf, ZÄS 61 (1926): 101–04.

58 W. Decker, KBSW 5 (1976): 10–13; on stick-fighting in today's Egypt see the photograph in Touny and Wenig, *Sport*, pl. 15, and the description in C. Diem, "Nabbût (Stockfechten)," *Olympische Rundschau* (1938), 3, 12–15 (repr. in *Olympische Flamme*, vol. 2 [Berlin, 1942], 636–39).

59 C. F. Nims et al., *The Tomb of Kheruef: Theban Tomb 192*, OIP 102 (Chicago, 1980), pl. 47, 60–63; see also the excellent photograph in Touny and Wenig, *Sport*, pl. 15.

60 W. Decker, KBSW 5 (1976): 9f; W. Decker, "Sportliche Rituale beim ägyptischen Jubiläumsfest," *Proceedings of the IX International HISPA Congress* (Lisbon, 1981), 103–12, esp. 108–10.

61 DeVries, "Attitudes," 229f. Since the inscription does not occur next to the "third man," it seems to be erroneously placed.

62 On this see Ebert, *Epigramme*, 228f.

63 Keel, *Weisheit*, 35 and fig. 8. (Both fighters stand naturally on the roof of the cabin.)

64 J. Vandier, *Manuel d'archéologie égyptienne*, vol. 5 (Paris, 1969): 513, 525, and fig. 223 (Deir el Gebrawi).

65 See also QT, document 44.

66 Nims et al., *Tomb of Kheruef*, pl. 47, 60–63; see also the excellent photographs in Touny and Wenig, *Sport*, pl. 12.

67 DeVries, "Attitudes," 222–28. The translation in the publication of material from the grave by Nims et al. indicates that DeVries's arguments have been adopted; see Nims et al., *Tomb of Kheruef*, 63–64.

68 DeVries, "Attitudes," 239 n. 1; Wilsdorf, *Ringkampf*, 44.

69 A. H. Gardiner gives the citation and a German translation of most of the inscription in *Geschichte des Alten Ägypten* (Stuttgart, 1965), 61.

70 On this see G. Fecht, "Das 'poème' über die Qadeš-Schlacht," SAK 11 (1984): 281–333; J. Assmann, "Krieg und Frieden im alten Ägypten: Ramses II. und die Schlacht bei Kadesch," *Mannheimer Forum* 1983–84, 175–231.

71 Touny and Wenig, Sport, pl. 24.

72 E. Mehl, Antike Schwimmkunst (Munich, 1927), 21.

73 W. Pahncke, Schwimmen in Vergangenheit und Gegenwart, 1 (Berlin, 1979): 74.

74 E. Mehl, "Die älteste Schwimmdarstellung der Welt," Leibesübungen und körperliche Erziehung 58 (1939): 274f.

75 QT, document 3.

76 W. Decker, "'Sportlehrer' im alten Ägypten," KBSW 1 (1972): 29–37.

77 Wallert, Löffel, 18–23, 38–41.

78 For bibliography see ibid., 19 n. 45.

79 A. Hermann, Altägyptische Liebesdichtung (Wiesbaden, 1959), pl. xa, ixa.

80 Ibid., 90, 145.

81 QT, document 36.

82 Wolf, Kunst, fig. 223.

83 QT, document 17, p. 59.

84 Decker, Leistung, 74–77.

85 Jenkins, Boat.

86 Decker, Leistung, 79.

87 R. Hall, GM 42 (1981): 37–43; P. Derchain, "Snéfrou et les rameuses," RdE 21 (1969): 19–25; E. Staehelin, ZÄS 105 (1978): 76–84.

88 QT, document 1.

89 QT, document 36, p. 90 n. 9.

90 C. D. Jarrett-Bell, "Rowing in the XVIIIth Dynasty," Ancient Egypt 15 (1930): 11–19.

91 L. Weber, "Rekonstruktionsversuch der ägyptischen Rudertechnik" (diploma essay, Deutsche Sporthochschule, Cologne, 1978).

92 Ibid., 34ff, 52, 60.

93 T. Säve-Söderberg, The Navy of the Eighteenth Egyptian Dynasty (Uppsala and Leipzig, 1946), 75–78; for an original (from the grave of Mai-her-peri) see 77, fig. 14.

94 Vandier gives the documentation in Manuel, 5: 510–31.

95 Ibid., fig. 225, 3, p. 529.

96 Ibid., fig. 224 [= P. E. Newberry, Beni Hasan I, ASE 1 (London, 1893), pl. xxxiv].

97 Vandier, Manuel, vol. 5, fig. 221, p. 523.

98 W. Guglielmi, LÄ, 2 (1977): 243.

99 Vandier, Manuel, 5:520.

100 L. Klebs, Die Reliefs und Malereien des mittleren Reiches, AHAW 6 (Heidelberg, 1922), 153f.

101 W. Guglielmi, LÄ 2 (1977): 243.

102 H. G. John, Zur Geschichte der Leibesübungen in Halle an der Saale von den Anfängen der Stadt bis zum Anfang des 19. Jahrhunderts (n.p., n.d.), 38–42; Touny and Wenig, Sport, pl. 49.

1 For critical commentary see I. Weiler, "Aien aristeyein," *Stadion* 1 (1975): 199–227; see also his *Agon*.

2 J. Jüthner, *Die athletischen Leibesübungen der Griechen* I, SÖAW 249, 1 (Vienna, 1965), p. 54.

3 E. N. Gardiner, *Athletics of the Ancient World* (Oxford, 1930; repr. 1955), 8: "Among such a people athletics are not likely to flourish."

4 M. Drew-Bear has forcefully summarized this thoughts in "Les conseillers municipaux des métropoles au IIIe siècle après J.-C.," CdE lix (1984) 315–32, esp. 317–21.

5 I base this on my essay "Das sogenannte Agonale und der altägyptische Sport," *Festschrift E. Edel 12. März 1979*, ed. M. Görg and E. Pusch, Studien zu Geschichte, Kultur und Religion Ägyptens und des Alten Testaments 1 (Bamberg, 1979), 90–104. Weiler has also referred to some examples in *Agon*, 7 n. 20, 303–05.

6 See pp. 71–82.

7 J. H. Krause evaluated these findings more than a century ago; see *Die Gymnastik und Agonistik der Hellenen*, Hellenika I 1–2, 2 vols. (Leipzig, 1841; repr. Niederwalluf, 1971), 237 n. 12, 934–35, 940, 945 and pl. xxv–xxviii.

8 See pp. 82–89.

9 Nelson et al., *Medinet Habu* II, pl. 111f.

10 On fishermen's jousting see chapter 4; on ball games see chapter 6; on tug-of-war see chapter 6.

11 QT, document 6.

12 See P. Behrens, "Sinuhe B 134ff. oder die Psychologie eines Zweikampfes," GM 44 (1981): 7–11.

13 E. Blumenthal, *Altägyptische Reiseerzählungen* (Leipzig, 1984), B 132, pp. 14, 45. For the relationships in Olympia see H.-V. Herrmann, *Olympia: Heiligtum und Wettkampfstätte* (Munich, 1972), n. 10.

14 See Weiler, *Agon*, esp. 247ff (and index, p. 337).

15 QT, document 28.

16 QT, document 36; for the diving episode discussed below see 103, 114f.

17 See the detailed discussion of the source on pp. 62–66.

18 H. Buhmann, *Der Sieg der Olympia und in den anderen panhellenischen Spielen*, 2d ed. (Munich, 1975), 55f, 111f.

19 QT, document 43.

20 W. Decker, "Bemerkungen zum Agon für Antinoos in Antinoupolis (Antinoeia)," KBSW 2 (1973): 38–56.

21 See pp. 41–42.

22 On this train of thought see also pp. 33–34.

23 QT, document 29

24 Weiler, *Agon*, 209–17; Herrmann, *Olympia*, 38–48.

1 Weiler, *Sport*, 265–68.

2 Delorme, *Gymnasion*, 281–86; for a contrary view see G. Roux, "A propos des gymnases de Delphes et de Délos: Le site du Damatrion de Delphes et le sens du mot sphairistérion," BCH 104 (1980): 1327–49; for the response see Delorme, "Sphairistérion et gymnase à Delphes, à Delos et d'ailleurs," BCH 106 (1982): 53–73.

3 M. Dolch, "Vom Ursprung des luftgefüllten Lederballs," *Stadion* 7 (1981): 53–92.

4 W. Decker, "Ball," *LÄ* 1 (1975): 608.

5 P. E. Newberry, *Beni Hasan II*, ASE 2 (London, 1894), pl. iv, xiii.

6 Discussed in context by Touny and Wenig, *Sport*, 49–52.

7 DeVries, "Attitudes," 358.

8 Ibid., 357.

9 The best reproduction is *Beni Hasan II*, pl. viiia. On Greek games see J. Jüthner, REV (1905), 2747; Gardiner, *Athletics*, 6. See also DeVries, "Attitudes," 361f. Klebs, *Reliefs und Malereien des mittleren Reiches*, 148 n. 1, refers to an Abysinnian variant.

10 T. Mann, *Josef und seine Brüder*, 1 (Stockholm, 1948): 167f.

11 Pyramidentext 279d: "Schlag den Ball auf der Wiese des Hapj." K. Sethe, *Übersetzung und Kommentar zu den altägyptischen Pyramidentexten*, 1 (Glückstadt and Hamburg, 1935): 298.

12 E. Brunner-Traut, *Altägyptische Tiergeschichte und Fabel*, 2d ed. (Darmstadt, 1968), 12 and fig. 35.

13 J. F. Borghouts, "The Evil Eye of Apopis," JEA 59 (1973): 114–15.

14 This is the view of C. E. DeVries in "A Ritual Ball Game?" *Studies in Honor of J. A. Wilson*, SAOC 35 (Chicago, 1969), 25–35, esp. 32 n. 21.

15 See J. Borghouts, JEA 59 (1973): 123; but he translates ḥnp as "rich."

16 Ibid., 138–40.

17 DeVries, *Studies*, 33.

18 J. F. Bourghouts, JEA 59 (1973): 129, text no. 8c (Ptolemaios vii).

19 B. H. Stricker, JEA 59 (1973): 148.

20 J. Leclant, R. A. Parker, and C. Goyon, *The Edifice of Taharqa by the Sacred Lake of Karnak* (Providence and London, 1979), 61–65, pl. 25. See also J. F. Borghouts, JEA 59 (1973): 138 n. 6; J.-C. Goyon, BIFAO 75 (1975): 352.

21 J.-C. Goyon, "Textes mythologiques, II: 'Les révélations du mystère des quatre boules,'" BIFAO 75 (1975): 349–99.

22 E. Otto, "Schlagen des Balles," LÄ 1 (1975): 608f, speaks of throwing the ball while Bourghouts and Goyon imagine striking it.

23 R. W. Henderson, *Ball, Bat and Bishop: The Origin of Ball Games* (New York, 1947), esp. 4.

24 E. Mehl, "Stammen die modernen Ballspiele von einem altägyptischen Fruchtbarkeits-Brauch ab?" *Die Leibeserziehung* 2 (1953): 6, 8–12; H. Gillmeister, "The Origin of European Ball Games: A Re-Evaluation and Linguistic Analysis," *Stadion* 7 (1981): 19–52.

25 DeVries, "Attitudes," 351, with references.

26 W. M. F. Petrie and J. E. Quibell, *Naqada and Ballas*, ERA 1 (London, 1896), 35 and pl. vii.

27 A first attempt was L. Klebs, *Die Reliefs des alten Reiches*, AHAW 3 (Heidelberg, 1915), 112–14; see also L. Klebs, *Reliefs und Malereien des mittleren Reiches*, 146–50; L. Klebs, *Die Reliefs und Malereien des neuen Reiches*, AHAW 9 (Heidelberg, 1934), 223–30. Vandier's suggestion in *Manuel*, 4: 509–27, is supported by Touny and Wenig in *Sport*, 47–64, and by Decker, "Spiel," LÄ 5 (1984): 1150–52.

28 On some of these inscriptions see A. Erman, *Reden, Rufe und Lieder auf Gräberbildern des Alten Reiches*, APAW 1918, 5 (Berlin, 1919), 59f.

29 P. Duell, *The Mastaba of Mereruka II*, OIP 39 (Chicago, 1938), pl. 162 and following; Touny and Wenig, *Sport*, pl. 30 (upper).

30 Touny and Wenig, *Sport*, pl. 30 (upper) and p. 61 ("Bringing in a Prisoner"); Vandier, *Manuel*, 4: 521, refers to it as a "little war (?)."

31 *Beni Hasan II*, pl. vii [= Klebs, *Reliefs und Malereien des mittleren Reiches*, 154, fig. 112 = Vandier, *Manuel*, vol. 4, fig. 278].

32 Klebs, *Reliefs und Malereien des mittleren Reiches*, 154, sees it as a "quarreling scene"; cf. Vandier, *Manuel*, 4: 524.

33 *Beni Hasan II*, pl. iv.

34 Vandier, *Manuel*, 4: 516f; Touny and Wenig, *Sport*, 52f.

35 Touny and Wenig, *Sport*, pl. 36 and fig. 31.

36 Vandier, *Manuel*, 4: 518.

37 Touny and Wenig, *Sport*, pl. 35.

38 Vandier, *Manuel*, 4: 518: "Jeux de la 'treille'"; Touny and Wenig, *Sport*, 58f; Klebs, *Die Reliefs des alten Reiches*, 113, sees it as a "circling run."

39 Touny and Wenig, *Sport*, 58f.

40 Vandier, *Manuel*, 4: 518.

41 Touny and Wenig, *Sport*, pl. 32, 37.

42 Ibid., pl. 31; Duell, *Mereruka II*, pl. 164 and following.

43 Duell, *Mereruka II*, pl. 162 and following; Touny and Wenig, *Sport*, pl. 30 (upper).

44 Touny and Wenig, *Sport*, 36 and fig. 12; *Beni Hasan II*, pl. vii.

45 C. Diem, "Körperkultur im alten Ägypten," *Olympische Flamme* II (Berlin, 1942), 612–36, esp. 617.

46 Touny and Wenig, *Sport*, 36.

47 *Beni Hasan II*, pl. xii.

48 Ibid., pl. xvi; Touny and Wenig, *Sport*, pl. 43.

49 C. Diem, "Körperkultur," 616.

50 N. de G. Davies, *The Mastaba of Ptahhetep and Akhethetep at Saqqareh I*, ASE 8 (London, 1990), pl. xxi; Touny and Wenig, *Sport*, pl. 33.

51 W. K. Simpson, *The Mastabas of Qar and Idu G 7101 and G 7102*, Giza Mastabas 2 (Boston, 1976), pl. 38 and p. 25; Touny and Wenig, *Sport*, pl. 41.

52 E. E. Kerrn, "The Development of the Ornamental 'Boatsman's Fillet' in Old and Middle Kingdom Egypt," AnOr 24 (1959): 161–88; E. E. Kerrn, "Addendum to 'Boatsman's Fillet,'" AnOr 26 (1961); 93–95.

53 *Beni Hasan II*, pl. vii.

54 Vandier, *Manuel*, 2: 522, considers the whole a continuation of the foreigner game, but he fails to notice that it occurs in another visual context in the grave of Ptahhotep; for a correct view see C. Sourdive, *La main dans l'Egypte pharaonique* (Bern, 1984), 103–06.

55 Duell, *Mereruka II*, pl. 162 and following; Touny and Wenig, *Sport*, 30.

56 Klebs, *Die Reliefs des alten Reiches*, fig. 91; Touny and Wenig, *Sport*, 56; Sourdive, *La main*, pl. xxvii, 1.

57 *Beni Hasan II*, pl. xvi, 3 (lower pair).

58 Vandier, *Manuel*, 4: 521–27.

59 Touny and Wenig, *Sport*, 30, 61; for a different view see Vandier, *Manuel*, 4: 522.

60 Ibid.

61 Touny and Wenig, *Sport*, pl. 42; Sourdive, *La main*, pl. xxvi, 1.

62 Sourdive, *La main*, pl. xxvi, 2, and pp. 101f; Vandier, *Manuel*, vol. 2, fig. 285.

63 Or: "and the priests of death all together." See Sourdive, *La Main*, 101.

64 Vandier, *Manuel*, 4: 524–27, speaks of a "game with racquets (?)" and discusses the evidence. Sourdive, *La Main*, 106–10, rejects the view that a hut is pictured.

65 See the three scenes in Sourdive, *La Main*, pl. xxviii.

66 Ibid.; see also Vandier, *Manuel*, 4: 526f, with references.

67 Vandier, *Manuel*, 4: 522; Touny and Wenig, *Sport*, pl. 33. It is not necessary to think here of yoga.

68 Ibid., pl. 31 (right); Vandier, *Manuel*, 4: 511, speaks of a "puzzle."

69 *Beni Hasasn II*, pl. xvi (middle left); Vandier, *Manuel*, 4: 509f.

70 *Beni Hasan II*, pl. xvi, 7 and 8 from the top (Cheti), and pl. vii (Baqti).

71 Vandier, *Manuel*, 4: 511, uses the question mark.

72 *Beni Hasan II*, pl. vii; Vandier, *Manuel*, fig. 278.

73 Klebs, *Reliefs und Malereien des mittleren Reiches*, 151.

74 On this point see C. Diem *Weltgeschichte des Sports und der Leibeserziehung*, 3d ed. (Stuttgart, 1971), 554, 576.

75 On the playing equipment not discussed here see the article by E. Brunner-Traut in LÄ 5 (1984): 1152–56.

76 Pusch, *Senet-Brettspiel*, 87.

77 The most important book on the topic is Pusch's *Senet-Brettspiel*; there is also a collection of documents, now somewhat outdated, by E. Meissenburg, "Altägyptische, griechische und römische Brettspiele," *Živa Antika* 22 (1972): 171–82.

78 Pusch, LÄ 5 (1984): 851.

79 Pusch, *Senet-Brettspiel*, 149–383; this account should be supplemented by some boards mentioned by P. A. Piccione in JEA 70 (1984): 172–80.

80 W. J. Tait, *Game-Boxes and Accessories from the Tomb of Tutʿankhamūn*, TTS 7 (Oxford, 1982).

81 This is well illustrated in ibid., p. 13, fig. 1, and pl. vii, viii (below).

82 Pusch, *Senet-Brettspiel*, board 36; the game chest was found with two sets of

five pieces each in a closed drawer. There is, however, no reason to imagine that this find excludes other possibilities.

83 T. Kendall, *Passing through the Netherworld: The Meaning and Play of Senet, an Ancient Egyptian Funerary Game* (Belmont, Mass., 1978).

84 E. B. Pusch, LÄ 5 (1984): 852, speaks of "principles of play"; Kendall, *Passing*, 59ff, boldly reconstructs the rules.

85 Even in a game with five pieces there can be a temporary blockade.

86 Evidence is presented in E. B. Pusch, LÄ 5 (1984): 854 n. 20.

87 J.-W. Meyer, *Frühe Phöniker im Libanon* (Mainz, 1983), ed. R. Hachmann, 101–05, catalogue nos. 17–19, 24–29.

88 Tait, *Box-Games*, 50f.

89 New reasoning is set forth in E. B. Pusch, LÄ 5 (1984): 852. One expects important new findings for this game to appear in the second part of Pusch's *Senet-Brettspiel*.

90 E. B. Pusch, "Eine unbeachtete Brettspielart," SAK 5 (1977): 199–212, esp. 208.

91 Sketches appear in ibid., 199, and in Tait, *Game-Boxes*, 13, fig. 2, and 25, fig. 2.

92 Pusch, SAK 5 (1977): 199–212.

93 For a sketch see ibid., 202.

94 Ibid., 209–211.

95 Ibid., 212; Pusch, *Senet-Brettspiel*, 383 (supplemented by pKairo 58 037).

96 For literature on the "snake game" see T. Kendall, "Schlangenspiel," LÄ 5 (1984): 653–55; Ranke, "Schlangenspiel"; E. B. Pusch, ASAE (forthcoming); E. B. Pusch, "Tjau-Spiel," LÄ 5 (1984): 608 n. 4.

97 J. E. Quibell, *Excavations at Saqqara* (1911–12): *The Tomb of Hesy* (Cairo, 1913), 18–21, pl. xi; W. B. Emery, *Ägypten: Geschichte und Kultur der Frühzeit 3200–2800 v. Chr.* (Munich, 1961), 270f and fig. 150.

98 T. Kendall, LÄ 5 (1984): 653f.

99 Two reliefs from the twenty-sixth dynasty that represent it imitate the archaic style and are thus excluded as evidence. See T. Kendall, LÄ 5 (1984): 654 n. 12; in reference to the grave of Ibj see also W. Kuhlmann and W. Schenkel, *Das Grab des Ibj: Theben Nr. 36*, AV 15, 1 (Mainz, 1983): 82f, pl. 28.

100 T. Kendall, LÄ 5 (1984): 654 n. 9.

101 Ranke, "Schlangenspiel," 24; E. Hornung, *Das Totenbuch der Ägypter* (Zurich and Munich, 1979), saying 172, pp. 57f.

102 R. Davies, *Sudan Notes and Records* 8 (1925): 145f.

103 See also Vandier, *Manuel*, 4: 505f; there is also a discussion in Kuhlmann and Schenkel, *Ibj*, p. 83 n. 340. For a critique and corrections see E. B. Pusch, SAK 5 (1977): 211.

104 Pusch, LÄ 6 (1986): 607f.

105 Similar remarks are in Ranke, "Schlangenspiel," 12.

106 Earl of Carnarvon and H. Carter, *Five Years' Explorations at Thebes* (London, New York, Toronto, and Melbourne, 1912), 56–59, fig. 1, and pl. xlviii. See also E. Drioton, "Un ancient jeu copte," BSAC 6 (1940): 177–206; Vandier, *Manuel*, 4: 508f on the thirty-point game).

107 Drioton, "Ancient jeu," 186–206.

108 Ibid., 177–86.

109 Ibid., 177, 181f.

Chapter 7. Acrobatics

1 For the view of E. Brunner-Traut, see *Der Tanz im alten Ägypten nach bildlichen und inschriftlichen Zeugnissen*, AF 6, 2d ed. (Glückstadt, Hamburg, and New York, 1958); on the treatment of dance see Vandier, *Manuel* 4: 446–54.

2 On the dance see esp. Brunner-Traut, *Tanz*; Brunner-Traut, "Tanz," LÄ 6 (1986): 215–31; H. Wild, "Les danses sacrées de l'Egypte ancienne," *Sources orientales* 6 (Paris, 1963): 33–117; I. Lexová, *Ancient Egyptian Dances* (Prague, 1935); Vandier, *Manuel*, 4: 391–486.

3 Brunner-Traut, *Tanz*, 23f and fig. 8.

4 Ibid., 24.

5 Ibid., 25–27.

6 Ibid., 37.

7 Ibid., 39f.

8 Vandier, *Manuel*, vol. 4, fig. 231 [= Brunner-Traut, *Tanz*, fig. 15]; Vandier, *Manuel*, vol. 4, fig. 232.

9 Brunner-Traut, *Tanz*, 40f.

10 *Beni Hasan* II, pl. vii [= Brunner-Traut, *Tanz*, fig. 14], pl. xiii [= Touny and Wenig, *Sport*, fig. 44], and pl. xvii; *Beni Hasan* I, pl. xiii [= Vandier, *Manuel*, vol. 4, fig. 224b). Vandier, *Manuel*, vol. 4, fig. 225, brings together three of these scenes.

11 See Brunner-Traut, *Tanz*, 38. Vandier, *Manuel*, 4: 425f, also sees it as a pirouette.

12 See the excellent photograph in Touny and Wenig, *Sport*, pl. 64.

13 *Beni Hasan* II, pl. iv, xiii.

14 J. H. Breasted, Jr., *Egyptian Servant Statues* (Washington, 1948), 89f, pl. 84f.

15 H. Chevrier and P. Lacau, *Une chapelle d'Hatshepsout à Karnak*, 1 (Cairo, 1977): xx.

16 Ibid., 198, fig. 18; Keel, *Weisheit*, 39f and fig. 13.

17 Keel, *Weisheit*, fig. 14.

18 Ibid., fig. 11.

19 Brunner-Traut, *Tanz*, 49; Vandier, *Manuel*, 4: 431f; Keel, *Weisheit*, 39f; Chevrier and Lacau, *Chapelle*, 199f.

20 Keel, *Weisheit*, fig. 15.

21 Ibid., fig. 12; Vandier, *Manuel*, vol. 4, fig. 243.

22 *Beni Hasan* I, pl. xiii [= Vandier, *Manuel*, vol. 4, fig. 224c = Touny and Wenig, *Sport*, fig. 45].

23 *Beni Hasan* I, pl. xxix [= Vandier, *Manuel*, vol. 4, fig. 226].

24 There is a discussion of the scene in Brunner-Traut, *Tanz*, 37; see also Vandier, *Manuel*, 4: 426f.

25 Brunner, *Erziehung*, 47–49, figs. 3–4; see also H. G. Fischer, JEA 67 (1981): 167f.
26 *Beni Hasan II*, pl. iv, xii; Touny and Wenig, *Sport*, fig. 38 and following. See also Vandier, *Manuel* 4: 515f, where "jeu de bascule" is preferred.
27 See also p. 69–70.
28 *Beni Hasan II*, pl. xvi; Touny and Wenig, *Sport*, fig. 23.
29 The scenes are discussed as a group in H. Gauthier, *Les fêtes du dieu Min*, RAPH 2 (Cairo, 1931), 142–50; see also P. Lacau, "L'érection du mât devant Amon-Min," CdE xxviii (1953): 13–22; I. Munro, *Das Zelt-Heiligtum des Min*, MÄS 41 (Munich and Berlin, 1983), 51–53.
30 W. M. Müller, "The Ceremony of Pole-Climbing by Nubians," *Egyptological Researches* (Washington, 1904), 34–36.
31 A. Baday, "Min, the Cosmic Fertility God of Egypt," MIO 7 (1959): 163–79; this view was adopted by Touny and Wenig, *Sport*, 92f, and V. Olivová, *Sport and Spiel im Altertum* (Munich, 1985), 60.
32 Munro, *Zelt-Heiligtum*, 41; see also Helck, LÄ 5 (1984): 276f.
33 Munro, *Zelt-Heiligtum*, 38f.
34 QT, document 43.
35 W. van Rengen, "Les jeux de Panopolis," CdE xlvi (1971): 136–41.

Chapter 8. Hunting

1 On the delicious flavor of hippopotamus meat see DeVries, "Attitudes," 111 n. 2.
2 On neighboring cultures see W. Heimpel and L. Trumpelmann, "Jagd," *Reallexikon der Assyriologie*, vol. 5 (1977), ed. E. Ebeling, B. Meissner, and D. O. Edzard, pp. 234–38.
3 Decker, *Leistung*, 145ff.
4 See esp. T. Säve-Söderbergh, *On Egyptian Representations of Hippopotamus Hunting as a Religious Motive*, Horae Soederblomianae 3 (Uppsala, 1953).
5 M. Stracmans, CdE xxxvi (1961): 24, fig. 3.
6 See pSallier I, 6, 2–3; see also pAnastasi IV, 15, 7–16, 1.
7 Vandier, *Manuel*, 4: 773ff; H. Altenmüller, *Jagd im Alten Ägypten* (Hamburg and Berlin, 1967), 20–40.
8 Illustrated in the exhibition catalogue edited by J. Settgast, *Tutanchamun*, no. 32; see also W. Decker, KBSW 8–9 (1979–80): 99–103.
9 K. Lange and M. Hirmer, *Ägypten* (Munich, 1967), pl. 66; Altenmüller, *Jagd*, pl. 15.
10 Säve-Söderbergh, *Hippopotamus Hunting*, 5–12.
11 QT, document 14, p. 50.
12 QT, document 23.
13 H. Altenmüller, "Jagdmethoden," LÄ 3 (1980): 230f; H. Guksch, "Die Szenen der Wüstenjagd in den thebanischen Gräbern der 18. Dynastie" (M.A. thesis, Heidelberg, 1974), 9–15.
14 Vandier, *Manuel*, 4: 968f, discusses the scenes as a group.

15 J. Leclant, "Un parc de chasse de la Nubie pharaonique," *Le sol, la parole et l'écrit: 2000 ans d'histoire africaine: Mélanges en hommage à R. Manny*, Bibliothèque d'outre-mer, n.s., 5–6) (Paris, 1981), 727–34. In my view the area near the palace grounds of Qantir in the eastern delta could have been a hunting park, but J. Boessneck and A. von den Driesch believe it was to have been a royal zoo; see their *Studien zu subfossilen Tierknochen aus Ägypten*, MÄS 40 (Munich and Berlin, 1982), 136–43.

16 QT, document 35.

17 H. Ranke, *Alter und Herkunft der "Löwenjagdpalette,"* SHAW 1924–25, 9, 5 (Heidelberg, 1925).

18 QT, document 14, p. 40.

19 QT, document 24.

20 Wreszinski, *Löwenjagd*, 21.

21 QT, document 15.

22 QT, document 14.

23 QT, document 12.

24 QT, document 14. On the rhinoceros hunt of Tuthmosis III see esp. L. Störk, *Die Nashörner: Verbreitung und kulturgeschichtliche Materialien unter besondere Berücksichtigung der afrikanischen Arten und des ägyptischen Kulturbereiches* (Hamburg, 1977), 241–96.

25 Decker, *Leistung*, 54; Störk, *Die Nashörner*, 286–96, esp. photographs and sketch on pp. 287f.

26 Swamp hunting is attested in predynastic times as well; see Schäfer, *Kunst*, fig. 256. On the swamp hunt in general see also P. Kaplony, *Studien zum Grab des Methethi*, Monographien der Abegg-Stiftung Bern, 9 (Bern, 1976): 9–20.

27 For example, A. Piankoff, "Les peintures dans la tombe du roi Ai," MDAIK 16 (1958): 247–52, esp. 248 with pl. xxi, 2.

28 The ambiguity of the swamp hunt has been treated by Hermann, *Liebesdichtung*, 17f, 63f, 163; W. Westendorf, "Bemerkungen zur 'Kammer der Wiedergeburt' im Tutanchamungrab," ZÄS 94 (1967): 139–50. For a contrary view see H. Buchberger, "Sexualität und Harfenspiel: Notizen zur 'sexuellen' Konnotation der altägyptischen Ikonographie," GM 66 (1983): 11–43. See also the response from P. Derchain in GM 73 (1984): 85–87.

29 W. Helck insists on a meaning connected exclusively with sport in "Rituale," LÄ 5 (1984): 280.

30 Caminos, *Literary Fragments*; QT, documents 8–9.

31 W. Gugliemi, "Die Feldgöttin Sḫ.t," WdO 7 (1974): 206–27.

32 QT, document 8, pp. 34f.

33 For a general discussion of the scenes of bird catching with a net see Vandier, *Manuel*, 5: 307–97.

34 For example, *Beni Hasan I*, pl. xxxiii.

35 QT, document 9.

36 QT, document 22.

37 See also R. A. Gillam, "An Instance of the Title imy-r šwt nšmt on a Statuette in a Private Collection," GM 36 (1979): 15–26.

38 W. Guglielmi uses this expression effectively in *Reden, Rufe und Lieder auf*

altägyptischen Darstellungen der Landwirtschaft, Viehzucht, des Fisch- und Vogelfanges vom Mittleren Reich bis zur Spätzeit, TÄB 1 (Bonn, 1973), 145.

39 The question is discussed in A. Brack and A. Brack, Das Grab des Haremhab. Theben Nr. 78, AV 35 (Mainz, 1980): 59f.

40 F. Hess, "Boomerangs, Aerodynamics and Motion" (Ph.D. diss., Groningen, 1975), 69–73. For this reference I am indebted to W. V. Davies.

41 B. George, "Drei altägyptische Wurfhölzer," Medelhavsmuseet Bulletin 15 (1980): 7–15; H. Carter, Tut-ench-Amun III (Leipzig, 1934), pl. 74 C, 75 A–B.

42 M. Alliot, "Les auxiliaires de chasse du tueur d'oiseaux au baton de jet," BSFF 6 (April 1951): 17–24.

43 H. Balcz, "Zu den Szenen der Jadgfahrten im Papyrusdickicht," ZÄS 75 (1939): 32–38; Vandier, Manuel, 4: 738–46; see also Y. M. Harpur, "Zšš w3ḏ: Scenes of the Old Kingdom," GM 38 (1980): 53–61.

44 B. George, Medelhavsmuseet Bulletin 15 (1980): 13.

45 Vandier, Manuel, 4:726–33, 764–68; Schäfer, Kunst, 245ff.

46 Settgast, Tutanchamun, no. 35; see also W. Decker, KBSW 8–9 (1979–80): 98f.

47 Settgast, Tutanchamun, no. 28 and the illustration on the inside front of the jacket. See also W. Decker, KBSW 8–9 (1979–80): 94–98. On both scenes see the comprehensive documentation in M. Eaton-Krauss and E. Graefe, The Small Golden Shrine from the Tomb of Tutʿankhamūn (Oxford, 1985), 15–17, 36–38, and pl. xiv and following.

Chapter 9. The History of Research

1 Krause, Gymnastik und Agonistik.

2 Klebs, Reliefs das alten Reiches; Klebs, Reliefs und Malereien des mittleren Reiches; Klebs, Reliefs und Malereien des neuen Reiches.

3 A. Erman and H. Ranke, Ägypten und ägyptisches Leben im Altertum (Tübingen, 1923).

4 H. Schäfer, "König Amenophis II als Meisterschütz," OLZ 32 (1929): 233–44; Schäfer, "Weiteres zum Bogenschieß-enim Alten Ägypten," OLZ 34 (1931): 89–96; Schäfer, "Die kupferne Zielscheibe in der Sphinxinschrift Thutmosis des IV," ZÄS 67 (1931): 92–95.

5 J. A. Wilson, "Ceremonial Games in the New Kingdom," JEA 27 (1931): 211–20.

6 S. Hassan, "The Great Limestone Stela of Amenhotep II," ASAE 37 (1937): 129–34. The standard publication for the important stela is Zivie, Giza, 64–89.

7 B. van de Walle, "Les rois sportifs de l'ancienne Egypte," CdE xiii (1938): 234–57.

8 Z. Saad, "Khazza lawizza," ASAE 37 (1937): 212–18.

9 Brunner-Traut, Tanz; Lexová, Dances.

10 H. Wild, La danse dans l'Egypte ancienne; a synopsis is in Bulletins des Musées de France 10 (1938): 127f. See also Wild, Danses sacrées.

11 Wilsdorf, Ringkampf; for subsequently discovered materials, see W. Decker,

"Neue Dokumente zum Ringkampf im alten Ägypten," KBSW 5 (1976): 7–24.

12 J. Vandier d'Abbadie, "Deux nouveaux ostraca figurés," ASAE 40 (1940): 467–88.

13 Brunner, Erziehung.

14 E. Hornung, "Zur geschichtlichen Rolle des Königs in der 18. Dynastie," MDAIK 15 (1957): 120–33; see also the works cited in n. 1 to chapter 3.

15 Decker, Leistung.

16 Caminos, Literary Fragments.

17 DeVries, "Attitudes."

18 Touny and Wenig, Sport.

19 Vandier, "Tanz," "Spiel," "Jagd," Manuel, 4: 291–486, 486–527, 717–833.

20 W. Decker, Quellentexte du Sport und Körperkultur im alten Ägypten (St. Augustin, 1975).

21 W. Decker, Annotierte Bibliographie zum Sport im alten Ägypten (St. Augustin, 1978).

22 W. Decker "Bibliographie zum Sport im Alten Ägypten für die Jahre 1978 und 1979," Stadion 5 (1979): 161–92; Decker, "Bibliographie . . . 1980 und 1981," Stadion 7 (1981): 153–72; Decker, "Bibliographie . . . 1982 und 1983," Stadion 8–9 (1982–83): 193–214; Decker, "Bibliographie . . . 1984 und 1985," Nikephoros 1 (1988): 245–68.

23 W. Helck, E. Otto, and W. Estendorf, eds., Lexikon der Ägyptologie, 5 vols. to date (Wiesbaden, 1975–).

24 W. Decker, "Tutanchamun und der Sport im Alten Ägypten," KBSW 8–9 (1979–80): 77–112.

25 McLeod, Composite Bows; McLeod, Self Bows.

26 Tait, Game-Boxes.

27 Littauer and Crouwel, Chariots.

28 Wiedemann, Lauf.

29 Pusch, Senet-Brettspiel.

30 Weiler, Sport.

31 H. Altenmüller and A. M. Moussa, "Die Inschriften auf der Taharkastele von der Dahschurstraße," SAK 9 (1984): 7–37.

Bibliography

I. Bibliographies and Dictionaries

Decker, W. *Annotierte Bibliographie zum Sport im alten Ägypten*. St. Augustin, 1978.

———. "Bibliographie zum Sport im alten Ägypten für die Jahre 1978 und 1979," *Stadion* 5 (1979): 161–92.

———. "Bibliographie . . . 1980 und 1981," *Stadion* 7 (1981): 153–72.

———. "Bibliographie . . . 1982 und 1983," *Stadion* 8–9 (1982–83): 193–214.

———. "Bibliographie . . . 1984 und 1985," *Nikephoros* 1 (1988): 245–68.

———. "Bibliographie . . . 1986 bis 1989," *Nikephoros* 2 (1989). In press.

Helck, W., Otto, E., and Westendorf, W., eds., *Lexikon der Ägyptologie*. Wiesbaden, 1975–.

II. Sources

Decker, W. *Quellentexte zu Sport und Körperkultur im alten Ägypten*. St. Augustin, 1975.

Wreszinksi, W. *Atlas zur altägyptischen Kulturgeschichte*. 3 vols. Leipzig, 1923–42.

III. Surveys

DeVries, C. E. "Attitudes of the Ancient Egyptians toward Physical-Recreative Activities." Ph.D. diss., University of Chicago, 1960.

Touny, A. D., and Wenig, S. *Der Sport im Alten Ägypten*. Leipzig, 1969.

Vermaak, P. S. "Sport en Spel in Ou Egipte." M.A. thesis, University of Stellenbosch, 1984.

Weiler, I. "Ägypten," *Der Sport bei den Völkern der Alten Welt*. Darmstadt, 1981.

Bruyère, B. "Le Sphinx de Guizeh et les épreuves du sacre," CdE xix (1944): 194–206.

Davies, N. de G. "The King as Sportsman," BMMA 30, no. 2 (November 1935): 49–53.

Decker, W. Die physische Leistung Pharaos: Untersuchungen zu Heldentum, Jagd und Leibesübungen der ägyptischen Könige. Cologne, 1971.

———. "Sportliche Elemente im altägyptischen Krönungsritual," SAK 5 (1977): 1–20.

———. "Tutanchamun und der Sport im alten Ägypten," KBSW 8–9 (1979–80): 77–112.

Der Manuelian, P. Studies in the Reign of Amenophis II. HÄB 26. Hildesheim, 1987. Pp. 171–213.

Walle, B. van de. "Les rois sportifs de l'ancienne Égypte," CdE xiii (1938): 234–57.

Zivie, C. M. "La stèle d'Aménophis II à Giza," SAK 8 (1980): 269–84.

V. Individual Disciplines

Running

Altenmüller, H., and Moussa, A. M. "Die Inschriften auf der Taharkastele von der Dahschurstraße," SAK 9 (1981); 57–84.

Decker, W. "Die Lauf-Stele des Königs Taharka," KBWS 13 (1984): 7–37.

Wiedemann, D. "Der Sinn des Laufes im alten Ägypten." Ph.D. diss., Vienna, 1975.

Archery

Burkert, W. "Von Amenophis II zur Bogenprobe des Odysseus," Grazer Beiträge 1 (1973): 69–78.

Decker, W., and Klauck, J. "Königliche Bogenschießleistungen in der 18. ägyptischen Dynastie: Historische Dokumente und Aspekte für eine experimentelle Überprüfung," KBSW 3 (1974): 23–55.

Edel, E. "Bemerkungen zu den Schießsporttexten der Könige der 18. Dynastie," SAK 7 (1979): 23–39.

McLeod, W. Composite Bows from the Tomb of Tut'ankhamūn. TTS 3. Oxford, 1970.

———. Self Bows and Other Archery Tackle from the Tomb of Tut'ankhamūn. TTS IV. Oxford, 1982.

Schäfer, H. "König Amenophis II als Meisterschütz," OLZ 32 (1929): 233–44.

———. "Weiteres zum Bogenschießen im alten Ägypten," OLZ 34 (1931): 89–96.

———. "Die kupferne Zielscheibe in der Sphinxinschrift Thutmosis des IV," ZÄS 67 (1931): 92–95.

Decker, W. "Der Wagen im Alten Ägypten," *Achse, Rad und Wagen*, ed. W. Treue. 2d ed. Göttingen, 1986. Pp. 35–59.

Deines, H. von. "Die Nachrichten über das Pferd und den Wagen in den ägyptischen Texten," MIO 1 (1953): 3–15.

Hofmann, U. *Fuhrwesen und Pferdehaltung im Alten Ägypten*. Diss., Bonn, 1989.

Littauer, M. A., and Crouwel, H. *Chariots and Related Equipment from the Tomb of Tut'ankhamūn*. TTS 8. Oxford, 1985.

Wiesner, J. *Fahren und Reiten*. Archaeologia Homerica F. Göttingen, 1968.

Combat Sports

Decker, W. "Neue Dokumente zum Ringkampf im alten Ägypten," KBSW 5 (1976): 7–24.

Vandier-d'Abbadie, J. "Deux nouveaux ostraca figurés," ASAE 40 (1940): 467–88. On stick-fighting see pp. 467–81.

Wilson, J. A. "Ceremonial Games in the New Kingdom," JEA 17 (1931); 211–20.

Wilsdorf, H. *Ringkampf im alten Ägypten*. Körperliche Erziehung und Sport. Beiträge zur Sportwissenschaft 3. Würzburg, 1939.

Aquatic Sports

Jarrett-Bell, C. D. "Rowing in the XVIIIth Dynasty," *Ancient Egypt* 15 (1930): 11–19.

Keimer, L. "Remarques sur les 'cuillers à fard' du type dit à la nageuse," ASAE 52 (1954): 59–72.

Mehl, E. *Antike Schwimmkunst*. Munich, 1927.

Wallert, I. *Der verzierte Löffel: Seine Formgeschichte und Verwendung im alten Ägypten*. ÄA 16. Wiesbaden, 1967.

Weber, L. "Rekonstruktionsversuch der ägyptischen Rudertechnik in der 18. Dynastie." Diploma essay, Deutsche Sporthochschule, Cologne, 1978.

VI. Games

Borghouts, J. F. "The Evil Eye of Apopis," JEA 59 (1973): 114–50.

DeVries, C. E. "A Ritual Ball Game? *Studies in Honor of J. A. Wilson*. SAOC 35. Chicago, 1969. Pp. 25–35.

Kendall, T. *Passing through the Netherworld: The Meaning and Play of Senet, an Ancient Egyptian Funerary Game*. Belmont, Mass., 1978.

Needler, W. "A Thirty-Square Draught-Board in the Royal Ontario Museum," JEA 39 (1953): 60–75.

Pusch, E. B. *Das Senet-Brettspiel im Alten Ägypten*. Vol. 1. *Das inschriftliche und archäologische Material*. MÄS 38. Munich and Berlin, 1979.

———. "Eine unbeachtete Brettspielart," SAK 5 (1977): 199–212.

Saad, Z. "Khazza lawizza," ASAE 37 (1937): 212–18.

Tait, W. J. *Box-Games and Accessories from the Tomb of Tut'anchamūn*. TTS 7. Oxford, 1982.

Vandier, J. *Manuel d'archéologie égyptienne*. Vol. 4. Paris, 1964. Pp. 486–527.

VII. Acrobatics

Brunner-Traut, E. *Der Tanz im alten Ägypten nach bildlichen und inschriftlichen Zeugnissen*. AF 6. 2d ed. Glückstadt, Hamburg, and New York, 1958.

Keel, O. *Die Weisheit spielt vor Gott*. Freiburg and Göttingen, 1974.

Vandier, J. *Manual d'archéologie égyptienne*. Vol. 4. Paris, 1964. Pp. 486–527.

VIII. Hunting

Altenmüller, H. *Darstellungen der Jagd im alten Ägypten (Die Jagd in der Kunst)*. Hamburg and Berlin, 1967.

Buchholz, H.-G., Jöhrens, G., and Maull, I. *Jagd und Fischfang*. Archaeologica Homerica J. Göttingen, 1973.

Caminos, R. A. *Literary Fragments in the Hieratic Script*. Oxford, 1956.

George, B. "Drei altägyptische Wurfhölzer," *Medelhavsmuseet Bulletin, Stockholm* 15 (1980): 7–15.

Guksch, H. "Die Szenen der Wüstenjagd in den thebanischen Gräbern der 18. Dynastie." M.A. thesis, Heidelberg, 1974.

Leclant, J. "Un parc de chasse de la Nubie pharaonique," *Le sol, la parole et l'écrit: 2000 ans d'histoire africaine: Mélanges en hommage à Raymond Manny*, Bibliothèque d'outre-mer, n.s., 5–6. Paris, 1981. Pp. 727–34.

Säve-Söderbergh, T. *On Egyptian Representations of Hippopotamus Hunting as a Religious Motive*. Horae Soderblomianae 3. Uppsala, 1953.

Staehelin, E. "Zur Bedeutung der Jagd im alten Ägypten," *Spiel und Sport im alten Agypten: Beiträge und Notizen zur Ausstellung im schweizerischen Sportmuseum Basel. 1.9.–30. 10. 1978*. Ed. M. Triet. Basel, 1978. Pp. 23–35.

Vandier, J. *Manuel d'archéologie égyptienne*. Vol. 4. Paris, 1964. Pp. 717–833.

Wreszinksi, W. *Löwenjagd im alten Ägypten (Morgenland 23)*. Leipzig, 1932.

Illustration Credits

1. MKNAW 33 (1970): 243, fig. 2
2. Photo W. Decker
3. Photo W. Decker
4. Photo W. Decker
5. MKNAW 33 (1970): 242, fig. 1
6. Photo W. Decker
7. Photo J.-P. Lauer
8. Emery, *Ägypten*, fig. 37
9. Photo D. Johannes
10. Kees, NGWG (1938), 21, fig. 1
11. Emery, *Ägypten*, fig. 5
12. Goedicke, *Blocks Lisht*, no. 84
13. McLeod, *Composite Bows*, pl. 14
14. McLeod, *Composite Bows*, pl. 11
15. Brunner, *Erziehung*, p. 26, fig. 2
16. Drawing M. Decker
17. Photo W. Decker
18. CdE xiii (1938): 250, fig. 3
19. Rowe, *Scarabs*, pl. 28, p. 61
20. Davies, *Rekh-mi-Re'*, pl. 23
21. Bass, "Cape Gelidonya," p. 54, fig. 56
22. Littauer and Crouwel, *Wheeled Vehicles* (HdO), fig. 42
23. Photo W. Decker
24. Quibell and Hayter, *Teti Pyramid*, pl. 12 (above)
25. Leclant, *Ägypten*, vol. 2, fig. 226
26. Courtesy Metropolitan Museum of Art, gift of J. Pierpont Morgan, 1917 (17.194.2297)
27. Wreszinski, *Atlas*, vol. 1, pl. 69
28. Photo W. Decker
29. Littauer and Crouwel, *Wheeled Vehicles* (HdO), fig. 47
30. Photo Egyptian Museum, Cairo
31. Photo S. Wenig
32. Schäfer, *Kunst*, fig. 135
33. Photo S. Schott
34. Lexová, *Dances*, fig. 31
35. Photo S. Wenig
36. Photo S. Wenig
37. Photo W. Decker
38. *Beni Hasan I*, pl. 15
39. Photo W. Decker
40. Photo W. Decker
41. *Beni Hasan II*, pl. 5
42. Photo W. Decker
43. *Beni Hasan II*, pl. 19
44. Photo W. Decker
45. BIFAO 69 (1971): 80, fig. 6
46. Drawing M. Decker, from photo by L. Riefenstahl
47. Photo W. Decker
48. Hölscher, *Medinet Habu*, pl. 19
49. Keel, *Weisheit*, fig. 6

50. Photo S. Wenig
51. Keel, *Weisheit*, fig. 7
52. Photo S. Schott
53. Photo W. Decker
54. Photo S. Wenig
55. Photo Musée du Louvre
56. Keel, *Weisheit*, fig. 9a
57. Keel, *Weisheit*, fig. 8
58. Photo S. Wenig
59. Emery, *Ägypten*, fig. 114
60. Photo Musée du Louvre
61. Photo Musée du Louvre
62. Yoyotte, *Kunstschätze*, 182
63. Capart, *Documents*, vol. 1, pl. 73A
64. Photo Ägyptisches Museum, Berlin
65. Photo S. Schott
66. Vandier, *Mo'alla*, fig. 74
67. Photo A. Hermann
68. Photo S. Schott
69. Photo L. Weber
70. Photo L. Weber
71. Photo S. Schott
72. Photo D. Johannes
73. Photo D. Johannes
74. Photo W. Decker
75. Photo Egyptian Museum, Cairo
76. Kestner-Museum, Hannover
77. Keel, *Weisheit*, fig. 1
78. Keel, *Weisheit*, fig. 2
79. Photo S. Schott
80. Wreszinski, *Atlas*, vol. 3, pl. 22
81. Wreszinski, *Atlas*, vol. 3, pl. 16
82. Photo S. Wenig
83. *Beni Hasan II*, pl. 16
84. Kendall, *Senet*, jacket illustration
85. Photo W. Decker
86. Courtesy Metropolitan Museum of Art, gift of the Egyptian Exploration Fund, 1901 (01.4.1A–P)
87. Tait, *Game-Boxes*, fig. 1
88. Courtesy Metropolitan Museum of Art, Rogers Fund, 1912 (12.182.72)
89. Tait, *Game-Boxes*, pl. 16 (upper left)
90. R. Hachmann, *Frühe Phöniker*, no. 24 (photo M. Zorn)
91. Pusch, *Senet-Brettspiel*, 1–2, pl. 30
92. Photo W. Decker
93. Photo Ägyptisches Museum, Berlin
94. Photo Rijksmuseum van oudheden, Leiden
95. Emery, *Ägypten*, fig. 150
96. Carnarvon and Carter, *Thebes*, pl. L
97. BSAC 6 (1940): 183, figs. 2–3
98. Wreszinski, *Atlas*, vol. 3, pl. 31
99. Lexová, *Dances*, fig. 35
100. Lexová, *Dances*, fig. 27
101. Photo Museo della antichitá egizie, Turin
102. Courtesy Brooklyn Museum
103. Photo W. Decker
104. Photo S. Schott
105. Photo S. Schott
106. Keel, *Weisheit*, fig. 11
107. Photo S. Schott
108. Photo S. Schott
109. Touny and Wenig, *Sport*, fig. 45
110. Touny and Wenig, *Sport*, fig. 39
111. Touny and Wenig, *Sport*, pl. 68
112. Scamuzzi, *Museum Turin*, iii
113. Leclant, *Ägypten*, vol. 2, fig. 165
114. Wreszinski, *Atlas*, vol. 1, pl. 271
115. Blankenberg-van Delden, *Scarabs*
116. Wreszinski, *Atlas*, vol. 1, pl. 26
117. Photo W. Decker
118. Touny and Wenig, *Sport*, pl. 61
119. Courtesy Metropolitan Museum of Art, Carnarvon Collection, gift of Edward S. Harkness, 1926 (26.7.1453)
120. Blankenberg-van Delden, *Scarabs*, pl. 11, C2
121. Photo W. Decker
122. Wreszinski, *Atlas*, vol. 2, pl. 114a

123. Wreszinski, *Atlas*, vol. 1, pl. 294
124. Courtesy Metropolitan
     Museum of Art, Museum
     Excavation 1920 (20.3.6)
125. Photo W. Decker
126. Wreszinski, *Atlas*, vol. 1, pl. 174
127. *Beni Hasan I*, pl. 32
128. *Beni Hasan I*, pl. 34
129. Photo W. Decker
130. Photo W. Decker
131. Edwards, *Tutankhamun*, no. 48
132. Eaton-Krauss and Graefe,
     Shrine, pl. 15

207

_____

Illustration
Credits

Index